Democracy and Civil Society

On the Predicaments of European Socialism, the
Prospects for Democracy, and the Problem of
Controlling Social and Political Power

JOHN KEANE

VERSO

London · New York

First published by Verso 1988

Verso
UK: 6 Meard Street, London W1V 3HR
USA: 29 West 35th Street, New York, NY 10001 2291

Verso is the imprint of New Left Books

British Library Cataloguing in Publication Data
Keane, John, *1949-*
    Democracy and civil society : on the
    predicaments of European socialism, the
    prospects for democracy and the problem of
    controlling social and political power.
    1. Western Europe. Democracy
    I. Title
    321.8′094
ISBN 0-86091-201-9
ISBN 0-86091-917-X Pbk

Library of Congress Cataloging-in-Publication Data
Keane, John, 1949-
    Democracy and civil society.

    Includes index.
    1. Socialism—Europe.   2. Europe—Politics and
government—1945-   .   3. Social control.
4. Democracy.   I. Title.
HX239.K424   1988   320.5′31′094   87-37121
ISBN 0-86091-201-9
ISBN 0-86091-917-X (pbk.)

Typeset by Leaper & Gard Ltd, Bristol, England
Printed in Great Britain by Biddles Ltd, Guildford

To C.B. Macpherson
1911–1987

Contents

CONTENTS

Preface

These essays reconsider some central themes in democratic thought since the eighteenth century. They soberly examine the dangers facing democratic institutions in present-day Europe. And they propose wholly new terms for thinking about how to guarantee the survival and future growth of democracy.

Some readers may consider this undertaking futile. After all, the twentieth century is unlike any other, in that nearly all governments, parties and movements claim to stand for genuine democracy. In semantic terms, this global preference for democracy represents something of a victory for popular pressure. For until the middle of the nineteenth century, the demand for democracy was the radical weapon of the powerless. It unnerved European statesmen as well as the dominant social classes, often frightening them into brutal measures of self-defence. When Burke remarked in 1790 (in *Reflections on the Revolution in France*) that a perfect democracy was the most shameless thing in the world, he was summarizing two thousand years of resistance by the powerful to its legitimacy. Since Burke's time, the word democracy has experienced a steady, if always contested, revaluation. The troubling paradox is that the growing respectability of democracy has turned out to be a disappointing affair – certainly if democracy means (as it does for me) a pluralistic system of power wherein decisions of concern to collectivities of various sizes within civil society and the state are made directly or indirectly by all their members. In Europe, democracy in this sense is today everywhere threatened by a variety of anti-democratic forces and trends. Among the most invisible and alarming – of these dangers is a failure of the democratic imagination itself. Large parts of the European democratic tradition have become diffident. Many democrats have lost the habit of asking questions about established beliefs and procedures. They seem unable to think in unfamiliar ways about familiar situations – let alone comprehend the new developments that endanger the democratic achievements and potential of our times.

These essays take issue with this stagnant orthodoxy. They strive to think unconventionally and constructively about how the European democratic tradition can best survive and flourish. They propose an open-minded, uncompromisingly pluralist, cosmopolitan and historically informed conception of democracy. The method underpinning this conception has several distinctive features. Since this method is often implicit – and sometimes deliberately hidden – it should be spelled out, if only to clarify and explain the overall direction of my arguments.

To begin with, the scope of my arguments for more and better democracy is deliberately wide-ranging. I reject the narrow complacency of those who consider democracy as simply government by means of party competition, majority rule and the rule of law. The subject encompasses much more than this. It extends from topics such as sovereignty, revolution, ideology and the threats to civil and political liberties posed by 'invisible' state power, neo-conservatism and regimes of the Soviet type, to a cluster of new issues, including the restructuring of the global economy, the gradual poisoning of the ecosystem, the decline of party politics and the emergence of social movements.

Secondly, the interpretation of democracy proposed here is genuinely *pluralist*, philosophically and politically speaking. It is opposed to the arrogant search for ultimate truth and ultimate solutions. It denies the possibility of a democratic 'meta-discourse'. It instead sketches the outlines of a more democratic system containing an authentic plurality of forms of life – temporary and permanent, formal and informal, local and central. This commitment to pluralism is evident in my resort to literary dialogue and the essay form, which are among the most democratic modes of writing, and is reflected in the substance of my political arguments and social observations. It is also apparent in my attempt to address an unusually wide spectrum of readers, including those who consider themselves liberals, conservatives, socialists or anarchists (nineteenth-century categories whose exact meanings are becoming ever harder to specify), or mainly as (part-time or full-time) participants within the new social movements of black people, pacifists, women, gays and lesbians, ecologists and others.

A further distinctive feature of these essays is their European orientation. European developments are central to my analysis because the fate of particular west European democracies is now tied together as never before, and because Anglo-Saxon discussions of democracy, which remain inward-looking, have much to learn from the experiences of their continental European neighbours. Consonant with this perspective, I summarize for western readers – for the first time as far as I am aware – key aspects of the exciting revival of the democratic spirit in the central-eastern half of Europe, which virtually disappeared from the map of western political thinking during the past four decades. In concentrating on European developments, I do *not* assume secretly that they hold the key to understanding the whole world. That haughty presumption has blinded European democratic thinking since the late eighteenth century – with often disastrous consequences for both Europe and its (former) *imperium*. The democratic theory presented here discards this old European arrogance. It does not take European democratic traditions for granted – if anything it experiences them as threatened and in danger of being overpowered – and recognizes as well the responsibility of Europe for the fate of democracy everywhere. It acknowledges that the destruction of democracy in one country represents a blow against democratic liberties of citizens everywhere. It therefore supposes that the creation (or strengthening) of democracy in countries such as Britain, Poland, Yugoslavia and the Bundesrepublik would sensitize more European citizens and governments to the need for radically different policies towards Africa, Asia and Latin America, where corrupt and blood-stained despotisms are today the grim rule, and not the unlucky exception.

Fourthly, this book prepares a case for a forward-looking democratic politics with eyes in the back of its head. In matters concerning democracy, the past is crucial for the present. Tradition is not the private property of conservatives. I show that the viability of contemporary democratic theory must be judged *not* by its capacity to forget the past and embrace 'the new', but at least in part by its ability to retrieve, build on, and imaginatively transform the subversive themes of old bodies of social and political thinking, particularly those of the Enlightenment. My repeated references to the social and political thought of the age of the democratic revolution – the period in Europe after 1760, when old loyalties snapped and many people experienced obedience to existing authority as a form of humiliation – is symptomatic of this. My elaboration of the distinction between civil society and the state also highlights this belief in the importance of the early modern past for the present. So too does my particular concern to develop this period's remarkable insights into the perennial problem of how to apportion and control the exercise of power.

Finally the conception of democracy developed here is informed by my own radical criticisms of the socialist tradition. Contemporary socialism is no longer describable as a dynamic social movement for radical change, as it was in Europe a century ago. Socialism has lost both its self-confidence and its revolutionary fervour. Today the idea of standing on a soap-box and speaking on behalf of socialism – as tens of thousands did in the past, and as I myself did recently – seems ridiculous. Socialist ideas and politics are in deep trouble – shaken by doubts, riven by failures, embarrassed by calamities of their own making. They may even have outlived their historical moment of relevance, and thus stand condemned to stumble exhausted into the future, as dying traditions always do.

Socialists must face up honestly to their critics' questions: In which country have socialist movements and governments actualized the old socialist ideals of equality with liberty and solidarity? In western Europe, where 'socialism' means for most people either the blind pragmatism of social democracy, or poorly defined utopias, or the dismal reality of state-dominated regimes of the Soviet type? In central-eastern Europe, where key socialist ideas and symbols have been appropriated by oppressive totalitarian regimes bent on stamping out civil society? Or on the margins of Europe – in socialist regimes such as Ethiopia's, which spends millions on military hardware and lavish anniversary celebrations to hide away the landless peasants and ragged crowds of skeletons who wander its lands in search of justice?

Such questions should activate profound doubts about whether democratic theory and politics can learn anything from the socialist tradition. Why have I bothered with a phenomenon with a discoloured past and present and a shaky future? Isn't the socialist idea, even if revised and made more sophisticated, no longer a significant option at the end of the twentieth century? Doesn't that imply that efforts such as mine to recast the terms of democracy by engaging the socialist tradition are bound to be self-crippling as foolish as the attempt of Baron von Munchhausen to free himself from a swamp by tugging at his own pigtails?

My response to these vital questions is neither sanguine nor pessimistic. I acknowledge my profound doubts about whether socialism in Europe can be revived as a living discourse – as something distinct from the mere survival of ailing late socialist regimes of the Soviet type and social democratic parties, pressure groups and governments of the western type. I argue that an honest examination of the theoretical and institutional roots of the deepening crisis of European socialism is required urgently. I even admit that there are many circumstances within the new social movements, or in the central-eastern half of Europe, for example – in which the socialist label creates more misunderstandings and difficulties than it is worth. But these essays offer no requiem for socialism. They maintain that the reasons for its contemporary paralysis and decline are fundamentally important, not merely for socialists, but for democrats of *all* persuasions. And they try to show, on that basis, how the meaning of socialism can and must be altered radically – into a synonym for the democratization of civil society and the state.

In this respect, this book builds upon my *Public Life and Late Capitalism*, which introduced the concept of democratic public spheres and defended the distinction between civil society and the state. The work emphasized that democratization could not be synonymous with the extension of total state power into the non-state sphere of civil society; and, conversely, that neither could it be defined as the abolition of the state and the building of spontaneous agreement among citizens within civil society. The 'democratic road to socialism', I argued, must steer a course between these two unworkable extremes, and that it is best envisaged as a difficult and extended process of apportioning power to a multiplicity of public spheres within and between the institutionally distinct realms of civil society and the state.

This new volume develops this general argument in new and more precise ways. The idea of a plurality of democratic public spheres and the distinction between civil society and the state remain central. But much greater emphasis is given to the social and political problem of how to institutionalize public spheres within and between the state and civil society. The resulting proposals are intended as a more concrete and politically engaged companion of *Civil Society and the State: New European Perspectives*, which is published simultaneously. I hope that both books will encourage attempts to refine and elaborate their perspectives. I intend to develop several additional themes, to do with the early modern theory of despotic power, the techniques of contemporary dictatorships, and the prospects for civilian rule, in a forthcoming book, *Despotisms of the Late Twentieth Century*.

I should like to express my thanks to Anna del Nevo, Charlotte Greig, Malcolm Imrie, Annette Kuhn, Neil Belton and Colin Robinson of Verso for their competent and cheerful editorial support. I am also indebted to a number of friends, colleagues and political acquaintances, to whose suggestions and criticisms of earlier drafts of these essays I tried hard to respond: Zygmunt Bauman, A.G. Brain, Penelope Connell, Bernard Crick, Graeme Duncan, Ferenc Fehér, Václav Havel, Brian Head, David Held, Agnes Heller, Peter Uwe Hohendahl, Jan Kavan, Jürgen Kocka, Arthur Lipow, Adam Michnik, Claus Offe, Christopher Pierson, Darka Podmenik, Edward Thompson, Mihály Vajda, Stuart Weir, David Wolfe and Nancy Wood. For their support and constant encouragement, I should especially like to thank Tomaž Mastnak, Paul Mier and Wendy Stokes.

London
November 1987

1

The Limits of State Action

What we have now to secure is the liberty and power of self-development of *Societies* other than the State. It is in regard to such societies ... that for the next two generations or more the issue is going to be joined. The battle will be inevitable and terrific between those who believe and those who do not believe that 'there are no rights but the rights of the State, there can be no authority but the authority of the republic'.

J.N. Figgis (1905)

During the past decade, there has been a vigorous upsurge of public debate in western Europe about the future of socialism. Among the most pressing issues of controversy (evident in the lively debates sparked by the string of electoral defeats for socialist governments in Britain, France and the Bundesrepublik[1]) is the reduced popularity of socialism because of its identification with the centralized bureaucratic state. This controversy is timely and of great political and theoretical significance. None the less, it is hampered by four major deficiencies – which help to explain why it has so far worked largely against the socialist tradition.

First, the debate about the future of socialism is marked by excessively vague and imprecise reflections on the theoretical principles and corresponding institutional requirements of a more democratic socialism. There is an emerging consensus about the need for a long-term socialist 'public philosophy' which

1

emphasizes less bureaucracy, more decentralization and more democracy. Yet there seems to be an inability to go beyond these general slogans, and this vagueness produces a deep impasse within the contemporary socialist tradition. Today, 'socialism' means either the dismal reality of state-dominated Soviet-type regimes or a vaguely defined future condition that bears little or no resemblance to present-day 'capitalist' realities.

Second, the controversy about the bureaucratic image of socialism often reflects a striking insularity. The important discussions and new democratic policy initiatives already underway in other west European countries are barely acknowledged, if at all. Worse still, the harsh reality of late socialist regimes in the central-eastern half of Europe is ignored, explained away, passed over in embarrassed silence or dismissed as a topic for right-wingers.

Third, and not unrelated to this problem of insularity, is the continuing *dogmatism* of the socialist idea. West European socialist groups, unions and parties frequently sense the democratic potential of such social initiatives as compaigns against ethnic and sexual discrimination, nuclear power and the erosion of civil liberties. Yet these initiatives are usually thought of as either marginal or 'non-socialist' (or even labelled as 'anti-socialist'), on the grounds that they do not conform to the fixed essence of the socialist idea – the abolition of capitalist production and exchange, and the institution of a collectively owned and regulated property system. In this way, the socialist tradition loses the trust and support of its potential allies. Socialist ideas and politics become defensive and frozen. Cloistered from much that is novel and complex in the world, they become incapable of learning from, and forging new alliances with other (potentially) democratic institutions, groups and movements.

Finally – and most controversially – socialists who call for less bureaucracy have failed, with few exceptions, to recognize that some things can be learned by engaging neo-conservatism, which has taken the lead in popularizing the demand for less state action – and in branding the socialist tradition as the guardian of bureaucratic state power. Neo-conservatism has produced several provocative and telling criticisms of the Keynesian welfare state (with which west European socialism has been identified strongly in recent decades). Accordingly, its criticisms deserve a careful and extensive evaluation, particularly as they bear on the weaknesses and complacencies of the socialist tradition.

In these essays I want to address these four weaknesses. I

presuppose that thinking *differently* about socialism is vital and urgent if it is to regain its position as a theoretically credible and practical political and social alternative. I argue that the counterproductive identification of socialism with centralized state power can be shattered only if the term 'socialism' is redefined in a radical way, so that it becomes a synonym for greater democracy – for a differentiated and pluralistic system of power, wherein decisions of interest to collectivities of various sizes are made autonomously by all their members. More precisely, my argument is that questions about democracy and socialism can be posed fruitfully only by rethinking the relationship between the state and civil society; that is, between the complex network of political institutions (including the military, legal, administrative, productive and cultural organs of the state) and the realm of social (privately owned, market-directed, voluntarily run or friendship-based) activities which are legally recognized and guaranteed by the state. This relationship between the state and civil society must be rethought in a way that affirms the necessity and desirability of drawing stricter limits upon the scope of state action, while expanding the sphere of autonomous social life. In my view, a socialism that is theoretically viable and worthy of respect in practice must be synonymous with the democratization of society and the state, as well as those bodies (such as political parties) which act as their intermediaries. From this revised perspective, socialism involves maintaining – not abolishing – the division between the political and social spheres by making state policy more accountable to civil society and by democratically expanding and reordering non-state activities within civil society itself.

State-administered Socialism

The analytic distinction between civil society and the state, upon which my case for the radical redefinition of socialism rests heavily, also happens to be very useful in highlighting the reasons for the dwindling popularity of the Keynesian welfare state, or what I call 'state-administered socialism'. Despite its considerable achievements during the post-war years, the programme of state-administered socialism has lost much of its radical appeal in western Europe because it has failed to recognize the desirable form and limits of state action in relation to civil society. This is true in at least three related respects.

To begin with, the model of state-administered socialism – which includes nationalized industry, public intervention into scientific research and development, state-provided health services, households regulated on the model of the patriarchal family through social policies – assumed that state power could become the caretaker and modernizer of social existence. Intervening in civil society to secure the private investment of capital, to reduce unemployment and to expand welfare opportunities, the state tended to assume an omniscience over definitions of citizens' social needs and wants. Crudely speaking, the motto of state-administered socialism was: 'Rely on the present government and its welfare state bureaucracies. They know what's best. They'll take care of things for you.'

The practical effect of this motto was to encourage the passive consumption of state provision and seriously to undermine citizens' confidence in their ability to direct their own lives. The passivity of the policytakers was assumed to be a necessary condition of the achievement of socialism by gradually extending networks of administrative state power into civil society. In retrospect, it is hardly surprising that among its unforeseen effects were a profound loss of trust in the apparatus of government, a deeper scepticism about expertise and a general decline in the legitimacy of 'socialism'.[2] The fact that the struggle for socialism originated in social movements which invented new forms of local participation within the interstices of civil society – the co-operative, the trade union branch, the friendly society and the publishing collective – is today virtually forgotten. In the rhetoric of the political opponents of socialism, and in the actual experience of many citizens in daily contact with welfare state institutions, it has become widely assumed that socialism means bureaucracy, surveillance, red tape and state control.

Secondly, the shortcomings of state-administered socialism are compounded when successive governments progressively fail to 'deliver the goods', as they inevitably do within the present circumstances of the international capitalist economy. The severe economic restructuring presently taking place in western Europe and elsewhere reminds us that the growth of the capitalist economy has never been steady, but riddled with fits of contraction and expansion. These perturbations are strongly evident in the present period. Two decades ago, the massive post-war wave of capitalist growth began to give way to deep stagflationary trends – price inflation, mounting levels of unemployment and sluggish economic output. This stagflationary downturn had numerous economic causes. Among the most important were changes in the international trading and monetary systems; the saturation of markets for automobiles and other types of durable consumer goods; private firms' attempts to raise prices and to make workers redundant as a means of reversing the post-war gains made by trade unions; and the dramatic growth of trans-national production.[3] More recently, these trends have intensified pressure on firms everywhere to 'modernize', to reduce their labour costs by substituting capital for workers – a factor which is presently contributing to major breakthroughs in the field of microelectronics. The commerical application of information-intensive technologies within key sectors of the economy is also undermining the old technological paradigm modelled on the assembly line and mass production.[4] It is generating a great number and variety of process innovations (relative to product innovations), enhanced savings on materials, more flexible output, and dramatic increases in both productivity and unemployment – the combined result of which is a form of 'jobless growth' which has shaken the strategy of state-administered socialism to its foundations. Jobless growth highlights the deep tensions between the organizing principles of state policy and capitalist markets. It undermines the assumption (of state-administered socialism) that gradual state intervention can secure economic growth, reduce unemployment and expand social welfare. Jobless growth brings sharply into focus the state's incapacity to realize the ideals of welfare socialism, as it drama-tizes the bureaucratic, inequitable and often repressive character of many state policies.

The reliance upon bureaucratic power and the circumstances of economic restructuring are not the only stumbling blocks for state-administered socialism. These two factors have been reinforced by a third: the dramatic expansion of state agencies at national, regional and local level. There are grains of truth in the claim that the state has been victimized by 'overload', that by attempting too much, it has often failed, thereby sabotaging the coherence of its policies and undermining its own authority.[5] Several examples are worth citing. The accelerating growth of the state has proved to be progressively more costly, creating shortages in public finances and leading to pressures for selective (and arbitrary) reductions in particular policy areas, such as health, education and environmental protection. Moreover, in order to implement their stated objectives, pro-welfare state governments expanded and diversified their bureaucratic structures. This increased the chances of severe conflicts between different departments of their bureaucracies. Consequently there have been growing *internal* pressures upon governments to 'rationalize' policies by favouring some (defence, for example) and downgrading others considered less strategically important.

Finally, state effectiveness was further weakened by attempts to broaden the regulation and control of social life through corporatist forms of intervention. Various state organs came increasingly to mediate the interaction of civil society's best organized interests, transforming them from social power groups into 'private interest governments'.[6] Under the influence of strategies of state-administered socialism, the state ceased to resemble a competitive marketplace, wherein social interests are brokered by political power. It became more like an organized battleground, in which the most privileged social groups (financial and banking interests, industrial corporations, professional associations and certain trade unions) more easily gained access to state channels, which in response favoured those social demands at the expense of others. Contrary to expectations, this steady shift from parliamentary (or territorial) to corporatist (or functional) forms of representation did not secure social and political stability. Instead, corporatist bargaining (which is conditional upon the *active* compliance of both state and non-state partners) made the state more dependent upon and vulnerable to the veto powers and resistance of powerful social groups. For all these reasons, the hand of the state became more visible during the era of state-administered socialism while becoming no more capable of effective democratic reforms.

The Rise of Neo-conservatism

It is a sadly ironic fact that these three broad difficulties of state-administered socialism have been popularized most successfully by neo-conservatism.[7] While the regressive consequences of neo-conservatism are not of prime concern here, it is important to stress that these difficulties have both played into the hands of neo-conservatives and highlighted the political and theoretical vulnerability of state-administered socialism. This is true in two decisive respects.

First, neo-conservatism is preoccupied with the need to redraw the boundaries between the state and civil society. It aims to redifferentiate the highly interdependent spheres of social and political life, and to popularize a distorted interpretation of the virtues appropriate to civil society – self-interest, hard work, flexibility, self-reliance, freedom of choice, private property, the patriarchal family and distrust of state bureaucracy. It calls rhetorically for a 'neo-Copernican revolution' which privileges civil society over the state.[8] This so-called libertarian ideology is evident in the quest for privatization of state industries, greater flexibility in the labour market, and the expansion of 'popular' share-owning, private house ownership and pension schemes. These proposals allege that comprehensive state regulation saps both individual initiative and the social resources that make self-organization, social responsibility and mutual aid possible. State-administered socialism 'does not require any commitment or initiative, nor can any moral energy be invested into it. In fact, nobody bears any responsibility, nobody is accountable, nobody needs to show loyalty ... to this abstract system.'[9] It also destroys market transactions, thereby increasing inefficiency in economic life. Consumers and workers become feckless and indolent; liberal morals become slack and corrupt. Above all, private property in the means of production – the most important barrier against state despotism – is threatened. Kolakowski's warning is characteristic of this anxiety about the decline of privately controlled markets: 'if the motives of private profit in production are eradicated, the organizational body of production – i.e. the state – becomes the only possible subject of economic activity and the only remaining source of economic initiatives. This must, not by bureaucratic ambition but by necessity, lead to a tremendous growth in the tasks of the state and its bureaucracy.'[10]

Such claims about the negative consequences of state-administered socialism have enjoyed a considerable measure of success in recent years precisely because they mobilize that considerable (if unevenly distributed) body of cynicism, distrust and dissatisfaction with which citizens have come to regard the interventionist welfare state. Certainly, there is little evidence that state-administered socialism produced popular demands for *lowering* public expenditure on, say, health, education and social welfare.[11] Rather, the interventionist welfare state has heightened public concern about the *form* of state provision and about the limited degree of 'choice' presently available to its consumers, clients and producers. In other words, the political success of neo-conservative lobby groups, parties and governments has been parasitic upon the profound difficulties produced by the socialist advocacy of state intervention and control of civil society. State-administered socialism has prepared the ground for public suspicion of bureaucratic administration. It has thereby fuelled neo-conservative calls to disembarrass the world of socialism and its statist prejudices.

Secondly, neo-conservatism tries to capitalize upon the failure of welfare state governments to keep many of their promises. It seeks to distance itself from such promises – and discredit their considerable achievements in practice. The political strategy of neo-conservatism is driven by a declared aversion to generalized state control over civil society. But it is also founded on the potentially self-contradictory belief that the power and authority of the state must be *increased*. Neo-conservatives love to dwell on the present crisis of political authority. Governing institutions, it is said, are losing their legitimacy. The confidence of political elites is being sapped by excessive voluntarism; and political stability and liberal democratic traditions are threatened by the reduction of the state to a marketplace of conflicting demands.

What is to be done to counteract these threats? The state must be unburdened of certain functions (through privatization and 'cutbacks' of social policy provision, for example) as a means of saving on costs, raising state revenues, and increasing the coherence and legitimacy of state power. The authority of the state must be strengthened by reducing the scope of corporatist bargaining mechanisms; concentrating power in the executive branch of government; curbing the powers of public sector trade unions and uncompliant local or regional governments; and by increasing the visibility and scope of state-organized means of repression. The sinews of a 'free' polity, it is claimed, are provided by coherent administrative power, the bold and decisive action of statesmanlike politicians and governments' willingness to enforce national traditions and the rule of law – against the disorders and confusions of civil society. In these ways, neo-conservatism attempts (in the words of one of its defenders, Jean-Marie Benoist) to replace *l'état gérant* (the managerial state championed by state-administered socialism) with *l'état garant* (a sovereign state which secures the civil order against its internal and external enemies).[12] It attempts, in other words, to increase the effectiveness of state policies by downgrading the instrumental dimensions of the state (as a provider of goods and services to civil society) in favour of its role as a powerful, prestigious and enduring guardian of the Nation against its external enemies, and as a guarantor of domestic law and order, social stability and a 'flexible' and competitive economy. This is neo-conservatism's recipe for simultaneously restricting the scope of the state *and* increasing its power.

There are many reasons why this attempt to redraw the boundaries between the state and civil society cannot succeed. Only those who live sheltered, obtuse or selfish lives will fail to recognize the negative social consequences of this strategy. The abolition of welfare state policies based on universal benefits and increasing standards of provision, and their replacement by disciplinary state policies based on minimalist, means-tested and discretionary benefits subject to cash limits, rationing and queueing, is resulting in a hideous increase in levels of pauperization. (In Britain, for example, after a decade of neo-conservative government, more than a third of the population lives at or below the poverty line and/or in badly degenerating environmental conditions.) It is also marginalizing formerly thriving social communities, and transforming inner urban areas into wastelands of grim looks, shabby clothes, boarded-up shops, rubbish piles and alleys and stairways soaked in urine.

The economic policies of neo-conservatism, with their harshly Darwinian attempt to promote efficiency, growth and employment by extinguishing the unfit, are also unlikely to succeed. Aside from worsening ecological conditions, the strategy of resuscitating market forces and encouraging business at any price is based on a false premise. It *assumes* that private capitalist firms will rush to occupy the newly available market territory by making new investments and hiring new workers, thereby restoring economic growth, 'full employment' and price stability. This strategy underestimates the ways in which market competition typically generates uncertainty and 'holding back' among capitalist investors. Free-market capitalism is self-crippling because it tends to increase many investors' reticence to invest in growth- and employment-oriented business strategies. Far from creating boom conditions and full-time jobs for all, the strategy of privatization is likely to promote further disinvestment, or investment in job-saving technologies, thus deepening jobless growth trends in manufacturing industry and encouraging firms to relocate part or all of their investments to the Third World.[13]

Neo-conservatism also underestimates the patterns of (future) opposition to its unjust policies and authoritarian directives. No doubt, the uncanny ability of neo-conservatism to avoid general domestic confrontations, and to pick off its opponents one at a time – a form of divide and rule from above practised successfully from below by early socialists against their opponents[14] – has helped to diffuse social resistance and to modify serious political backlashes, neo-conservatism's penchant for resorting to state coercion, its knack of emphasizing commitment to 'abstract' entities (such as 'the Nation') and its encouragement of trampling and elbowing have made more difficult the task of preserving or creating public spheres based on reciprocity and solidarity. The dangers of arrogant nationalism, rampant egoism and a spirit of mistrust are high, and increasing. Yet it is doubtful whether all these trends can succeed in strengthening state power, and in fully atomizing civil society into an apolitical market, thus destroying the social bases and breaking the will of the oponents of neo-conservatism. Some traditional patterns of (regional, class and ethnic) loyalty cannot be broken so easily. Meanwhile, new patterns of solidarity and resistance – especially evident in the new social movements – are already emerging.

Considered in terms of its moral appeals, neo-conservatism is also vulnerable. It is incapable of realizing the 'libertarian' values it affirms – above all, those of freedom of choice, mutual aid and self-reliance. Male-dominated households, a capitalist-directed economy and the strong state, which are the trump cards in the hand of neo-conservatism, directly contradict its professed anti-bureaucratic principles. This suggests that only the democratic tradition, and *not* neo-conservatism, can genuinely defend the libertarian ideals of mutual aid, democratic accountability and the taming and restriction of state power. It further suggests, and this point is fundamental when considering the future of social-ism, that the capacity of democrats to rework and publicly articulate the issues of state and civil society, which neo-conser-vatism has helped to make a public problem, is a crucial factor in determining whether its present grip on the public agenda can be loosened. Neo-conservative ideologues and policymakers have promoted a discussion about the limits of state-administered socialism with which democrats of all persuasions have no choice but to engage. 'Their morals versus ours' is a self-defeating position for democrats to adopt in the struggle against neo-conservatism. It concedes too much. The rich, if historic, vocabu-lary of neo-conservatism (freedom of choice, individual rights, freedom from state bureaucracy) can be neither confidently neglected nor left unquestioned. Nor should this vocabulary be dismissed as simply a rootless nostalgia for roots. The pseudo-libertarian appeals of neo-conservatism are a central plank in its strategy of attempting to control both the present and the future by redefining and mastering the dominant, collectively shared sense of the historical past. Its struggle to rewrite history serves as an important reminder that social and political traditions are not inherited 'naturally', but are constantly made and unmade. Its attempts to transform the popular sense of history also provide the reminder that the debate over who shall inherit the old European vocabulary of freedom, equality and solidarity is long overdue, and that gaining the upper hand in these controversies is imperative for the future survival of socialism.

Complex Equality and Liberty

The weaknesses of state-administered socialism and the sources of success of neo-conservatism listed above necessarily raise normative questions. If these two options are to be rejected, is there a third, more viable option? What alternative form might state action and civil society take, and how should their relationship be defined from a more fully democratic perspective?

An adequate response to these questions requires socialists to reconsider some basic issues of democratic theory. There are signs that this effort is already underway. There appears to be a growing awareness among west European socialists that if opposition to neo-conservatism is to become publicly credible and viable it must re-emphasize the old goals of equality *and* liberty. This conclusion can be expressed schematically: Neo-conservatism counterposes a statist conception of equality (which it assesses from a wholly negative point of view) against negative liberty (which it sees as wholly a good thing). In this way, it concerns itself, in its rhetoric anyway, with reduced state interference in citizens' existence and the application of 'free-market' principles to more and more aspects of social life. It wants the kind of freedom that will maintain existing inequalities and, if political action and social conditions allow, to restore inequalities removed by a century of social reform. State-administered socialisms, by contrast, emphasized the state's capacity to create equality of opportunity by flinging many citizens on to a Procrustean bed. It downplayed questions of liberty and, hence, usually contented itself with the notion of a 'big state' commissioned to impose equality on civil society. Viewed in this way, the important question posed by the growing awareness among socialists in favour of equality and liberty is how the state and civil society can be combined to promote and maximize equality *with* liberty.

In my view, these goals cannot be realized through changes of rhetoric alone. They require socialists to recognize the need for adopting more complex notions of equality and liberty. Simple, undifferentiated conceptions of equality – those which suppose that every citizen could and should simultaneously enjoy identical possessions and the same social and political institutions – are based on the mistaken premise that one or two distributive principles (e.g., the market; the centralized state) should prevail. Since these distributive principles aim to simplify and homogenize the complex reality to which they are applied, they are abstract and oppressive, and (as the case of state-administered socialism indicates) normally unworkable. For these reasons, they need to be abandoned in favour of a pluralist conception of equality. This would aim to destroy large and permanent monopolies of privilege by developing a less hierarchical and more complex relationship among citizens, mediated by the goods they produce and distribute among themselves according to multiple criteria of distributive justice. These criteria could extend from the friendship, voluntary association, organized social conflict and market exchanges of civil society to party conflict, legislative decisions, legal judgements and other forms of state policymaking. In this way, the democratic idea of complex equality recognizes that the gap between 'the haves' and 'the have nots' can be closed only by developing institutional mechanisms which distribute different goods to different people in different ways, and for different reasons.[15]

Undifferentiated conceptions of liberty also need to be abandoned, for they too have an overly simplified view of social and political life. They suppose that there are one or two procedural rules for enabling all citizens to determine how they wish to live. An influential example is the abstract and unworkable principle that all citizens must 'make the decisions which affect their lives'. This principle correctly understands that citizens are free to the extent that they are bound by the decisions they themselves take. It rightly acknowledges that liberty is the capacity of continuous initiative in social and political affairs. But it overlooks some elementary points about life as it is (and would be) in complex democratic systems. It forgets that not all citizens can be in the same place at the same time to make such decisions (and that, even if they could be, genuinely free time would become a thing of the past, as Oscar Wilde and others have observed). It also overlooks the vital point that there is a great *diversity* of liberties, whose pertinence for different categories of citizens is therefore inescapably variable and subject to continuous modification. In a fully democratic regime, citizens will likely choose (as they presently do) to concentrate their energies in different ways and in various spheres of life. From time to time, they will also want to change their loci of freedom. For all these reasons, simple conceptions of liberty need to be abandoned in favour of a more complex and differentiated notion. The homogeneous political community of the Greek *polis*, where citizens rule and are ruled in turn, cannot be recreated in the modern world, except sometimes in the momentary ecstasy of revolutionary situations. Heroic attempts to institute an undifferentiated system of self-government on a large scale normally end in confusion, disappointment and sometimes in a bloody fiasco, as Hegel observed of Jacobinism.[16] The secret of liberty, whose maximization requires the maximization of complex equality among citizens, is the division of decisionmaking powers into a variety of institutions within and between civil society and the state. The maximization of citizens' liberty entails the enlargement of their choices – particularly among those presently worse off. Choice enlargement requires, in turn, an increase in the variety of social and political spheres in which different groups of citizens *could* participate, if and when they so wished.*

If simple, undifferentiated notions of equality and liberty need to be jettisoned in favour of a more complex understanding of their mutual interdependence, how can this ideal be institutionalized? In my view, such a goal can be realized only by recognizing the need for reforming and restricting state power and

---

* The stipulation that citizens *could* participate within particular spheres of civil society and the state *if* they so wished is important. The interpretation of democracy being sketched here does not require individuals to be full-time political animals. Some critics have overlooked this. In a letter dated 27 March 1987, Roger Scruton writes: 'In the end, you will always be attracted by the image of politics as an activity of "opposition" and a form of "solidarity". I think that politics should be neither an activity, nor oppositional, but a process of conciliation, which occupies the smallest part of a decent human life ... founded on obedience to the sovereign.' I am aware of the importance of 'conciliation' as a positive force in social and political life. The tolerance necessary for complex equality and liberty within a democratic civil society and state would certainly require a large measure of conciliation – or civility – among its citizens. There is truth in the old English maxim: civility doesn't cost a penny. And yet civility has two faces. The powerful like to disguise themselves within its codes, which is why activities of solidarity and opposition among the less powerful are necessary for maintaining a *genuine* or *democratic* civility. Without these activities, civility always degenerates into pomposity, which is what Scruton seems to intend. As for the necessity of obedience to the sovereign, Scruton's remark closely resembled Carl Schmitt's view, whose despotic implications are examined in essay 5.

expanding and radically transforming civil society. What is meant here by the old-fashioned term civil society? In the most abstract sense, civil society can be conceived as an aggregate of institutions whose members are engaged primarily in a complex of non-state activities – economic and cultural production, household life and voluntary associations – and who in this way preserve and transform their identity by exercising all sorts of pressures or controls upon state institutions. In more concrete terms, I certainly don't wish to restrict the definition of civil society to the stiff-necked terms of neo-conservatism, as if civil society could only ever be synonymous with a non-state, legally guaranteed sphere dominated by capitalist corporations and patriarchal families. Civil society in this limited sense is real enough today in western Europe. But contrary to neo-conservative thinking, civil society has no natural innocence; it has no single or eternally fixed form. It has a vital additional meaning. It has the potential to become a non-state sphere comprising a plurality of public spheres – productive units, households, voluntary organizations and community-based services – which are legally guaranteed and self-organizing.

Understood in these terms, democratization – the 'road to socialism' – would mean attempting to maintain and to redefine the boundaries between civil society and the state through two interdependent and simultaneous processes: the expansion of social equality and liberty, and the restructuring and democratizing of state institutions. Two conditions would be necessary for the successful enactment of these processes. First, the power not only of private capital and the state, but also of white, heterosexual, male citizens over (what remains of) civil society would need to be curtailed through social struggles and public policy initiatives that enabled citizens, acting together in 'sociable' public spheres, to strive for equal power, and so maximize their capacity to play an active part in civil society.

Secondly, state institutions would have to become more accountable to civil society by having their functions as protectors, co-ordinators and regulators of citizens' lives recast. Democratization would consequently avoid the well-known pitfalls of both classical anarcho-syndicalism – of attempts by civil society to pull itself up into emancipation by its own bootstraps – and the excessive bureaucratic regulation of state-administered socialism. It would reject the assumption that the state could ever legitimately replace civil society or vice versa. It would thereby defend and enrich the principle, broached in early modern

Europe by Paine, Tocqueville, J.S. Mill and others,[17] that the separation of the state and civil society must be a permanent feature of a fully democratic social and political order, in which productive property, status and the power to make decisions – and therefore historicity itself – would no longer be appropriated privately.

Civil society and the state, thus, must become the condition of each other's democratization. State institutions ought not to be understood as embodiments of the universal – an originally Hegelian position which is today defended by an unholy global alliance of dictatorships and totalitarian regimes trained, funded and backed militarily by the superpowers. Rather, state institutions must be understood as devices for enacting legislation, promulgating new policies, containing inevitable conflicts between particular interests within well-defined legal limits, and for preventing civil society from falling victim to new forms of inequality and tyranny. In this scheme of things, on the other hand, a multiplicity of social organizations, ranging from self-governed trade unions and enterprises or housing co-operatives to refuges for battered women, independent communications media, and neighbourhood police monitoring associations, must increase their powers in order to keep their political 'representatives' under control. Civil society should become a permanent thorn in the side of political power. In short, I am arguing that without a secure and independent civil society of autonomous public spheres, goals such as freedom and equality, participatory planning and community decisionmaking will be nothing but empty slogans. But without the protective, redistributive and conflict-mediating functions of the state, struggles to transform civil society will become ghettoized, divided and stagnant, or will spawn their own, new forms of inequality and unfreedom.

Redrawing State Boundaries: West European Proposals

To speak in this novel way of socialism as democratization is more than simply a plea for clarifying some key terms in the west European debate about the meaning and future of socialism. The relationship between civil society and the state is also becoming a prominent theme in west European discussions of *practical* socialist policies. I should like to illustrate this trend briefly by examining new democratic initiatives in four policy areas: investment, employment, trade unions and childcare arrangements.

To begin with the question of investment: Since 1975, extensive discussions have occurred within the Swedish left about the ways in which a gradual extension of social ownership of productive property can be achieved. One proposal to emerge from these discussions was the Meidner Plan.[18] Its details are complex, but the thrust of its programme, as interpreted by Korpi and others,[19] is to create the means for counteracting the concentration of private capital by increasing the level of *socially* controlled investment. This would be done by recognizing the important role still to be played by trade unions in handling wages policy and safeguarding the interests of employees in the workplace. It also involves formulating an egalitarian ('solidaristic') wages policy (equalizing unjust differentials and keeping wages within limits tolerable to an open, internationally competitive economy). And, most importantly, it would attempt to use increased taxes on the profits of large companies to create investment (or 'wage earner') funds (*löntagarfonder*) on a local and regional basis which is citizen-controlled. This proposal seeks to avoid the problem whereby wage restraint leads traditionally to higher rates of private profit without increasing investment, let alone greater social control over productive resources. The Meidner Plan seeks to underwrite the process of capital investment by ensuring that profits are ploughed back into projects within civil society, rather than being saved, transferred overseas or used to increase private shareholders' wealth. In this way, the proposal recognizes, correctly, that clashes of interest between private capital and wage-earners and other citizens are presently a fundamental source of conflict within capitalist civil societies. The Plan recognizes, again correctly, that there can be no full democratization in a capitalist civil society, and that the claims of those who contribute their labour and consume or use its products must take precedence over those who presently supply and manage capital. But these insights do not produce the conclusion that only state intervention in the economy can eliminate class conflict by nationalizing the vast concentrations of unaccountable economic power which are at the root of these conflicts. In the long run, the Plan aims to break with the conventional view (of state-administered socialism) that state planning and fixing of markets plus selective nationalization plus spending money equals socialism. It recognizes the importance of property as a weapon against overextended state power. But it rejects the neo-conservative view that private profit in production is a necessary condition of civil liberty. Instead, it foresees 'social enterprise without owners'

(Wigforss) as an alternative to both private capitalist and state nationalized property relations (see essays 3, 4).

The emphasis on social self-determination within a political framework is also evident in the West German Greens' proposals for dealing with the present unemployment problem, and particularly with the growing cleavage between the holders of secure full-time jobs and marginalized groups of the partly employed, the unemployed and the unwaged.[20] This cleavage, the Greens argue, cannot be overcome through a 'return' to full employment, an ideal which is rejected as both unworkable and undesirable (since, for instance, it does not address the 'overworking' of women both within the labour market and the household). The core idea of Green proposals on unemployment is to redistribute and reduce waged and salaried labour by weakening the monopoly grip of the labour market on citizens' lives, and by encouraging the growth of non-market forms of co-operative production within civil society. The Greens support proposals to gradually reduce the standard length of the paid working week (initially to thirty-five hours), with full pay and no intensification of work. But they are asking more than this. The Greens propose that individuals should be legally guaranteed the right to be employed less (according to their personal time- or income-needs) or to withdraw periodically or permanently from the labour market. It is argued that the extent to which individual citizens exercise this option – and therefore the volume of new spaces made available for those presently unemployed – cannot be left to market forces alone. It would depend upon such factors as the range of uses to which citizens could put their extra free time; the status and benefits derived from work performed outside of employment; and the availability of childcare arrangements. It is further argued that these conditions could be satisfied by the state's support and subsidization of a 'parallel economy' of self-governing and ecologically supportive productive units and service facilities (known as 'alternative projects'[21]). Citizens' willingness to invest their skills and energies in this sector could be maximized by guaranteeing them a citizen's wage, financed through general taxation and sufficient to satisfy their basic needs without resorting to paid employment in the labour market.[22] It is also recognized that citizens' equal participation in the parallel economy could be guaranteed only when men assume equal responsibility for housework and childcare, and when adequate childcare facilities are widely available, without charge for people on lower incomes.

The immediate aim of the Greens' proposals is to create and enlarge democratic public spheres which enable individuals within civil society to escape the compulsions of both the private household and the labour market. These proposals can be seen as a renewal of the old socialist struggle to create 'islands' of co-operative production,[23] with the important difference that they also call into question the conventional patriarchal division between household and labour market. The novelty of Green 'de-employment' proposals is also evident in their abandonment of the blind technological optimism and pro-industrialism of the earlier twentieth-century socialist tradition. The Greens' search for new frameworks for protecting the right to socially useful and co-operative work forms part of their larger strategy of opposition to a political economy in which private corporations and state bureaucracies decide on work processes, products and the social and ecological conditions of life of most citizens. The Greens' strategy of 'social defence' emphasizes the quality of life and work rather than profit, efficiency and growth. It is sympathetic to all groups, social movements and political initiatives which promote decentralized and ecologically conscious production, the demo-cratic application of new technologies, and the empowerment of citizens against both the power of private capital and the bureaucratic state.

Such proposals have radical implications for trade unions, some of which have been explored since the late 1970s in France by the Confédération Démocratique du Travail (CFDT).[24] The CFDT has attempted – in the face of employer resistance, government intransigence, trade union division and signs of worker apathy – to create a new and non-sectarian form of solid-arity within civil society. This strategy not only implies struggling for new and more advantageous compromises with employers (for example, legally obliging them to concede new rights for trade unions, and encouraging them to participate in tripartite employment committees at the local and regional levels). It also addresses the problem of the 'break up of the working class' (Gorz) by agitating for the recognition of the needs of workers who experience racism, as well as those who have low wages, precarious jobs and no trade union representation. The CFDT's priorities have been increases in the real minimum wage, remun-eration for low wage groups, an overall reduction of the working week, more just and flexible working hours, the retooling of industries, the creation of new publicly-funded 'social enter-prises', and greater self-government in both private and state-sector firms. The CFDT has also emphasized the need to consider *what* and *how* to produce. It thereby challenges the blind faith in scientific-technological development and growth-centred strategies characteristic of the post-war boom. In general, the CFDT is concerned to stimulate the independent formulation of broad social demands upon both employers and the state. It pursues a strategy not for enhanced trade union powers for their own sake – it is opposed to self-interested corporatist arrangements – but for trade union solidarity with the less powerful in civil society. And while recognizing the importance of the state as a potential agent of reform, the CFDT strategy, significantly, is opposed to the blind reliance upon state power (e.g. in the form of demands for state intervention, nationalization of private firms, and protectionism). It seeks a course between *étatisme* and *syndicalisme*. It emphasizes the state's responsibility for establishing broad national economic priorities and pushing through new rights and reforms for all workers, and its own role as an independent trade union capable of stimulating a social dynamic which leads to the restructuring of the capitalist economy to the advantage of all workers, whether unionized or non-unionized, full-time or part-time.

A final example of new socialist attempts to democratically expand civil society through state support is feminist and local government initiatives in the field of childcare in Britain.[25] These policy initiatives are broad-ranging, including not only increased funding of existing voluntary childcare organizations, but also the establishment of free, year-round creches linked with job training schemes, the development of co-operative laundries, as well as proposals for better provision for childminders, drop-in centres for mothers who choose not to enter the labour market, and small children's centres providing such additional services as meals, bulk-buying and laundering. These initiatives question, and attempt to reduce, the social inequalities of power crystallized in present forms of housework and childcare. They are also a belated response to the rapid growth in the number of employed mothers, and to the fact that housework and childcare facilities (or the lack thereof) decide what kind of jobs women can perform.

At the same time, these policy initiatives attempt to counter the socially regressive consequences of the neo-conservative strategy of privatizing social policy and underwriting the model of the patriarchal family. As threats to state-provided welfare and local community services increased in recent years, feminists and other local activists recognized the need to go beyond a reactive 'Stop the Cuts' campaign – which implied support for institutions unworthy of full support – and to develop links between grassroots projects and campaigns, on the one hand, and local government facilities on the other. This recognition coincided with the election of a number of Labour councils. These councils realized that state-administered socialism is based on the dogmatic assumption that since socialism means opposition to private ownership of the means of production it must be opposed also to private (i.e. non-state) ownership of the means of social policy production and consumption. They perceived that this assumption encourages support for policies (such as bans on council house sales) which conflict with citizens' desire for greater autonomy and, thus, plays into the hands of neo-conservatism and its 'libertarian' rhetoric. These local authorities have abandoned this dogmatic premise of state-administered socialism. They instead view their power (now heavily under siege) not as an end in itself, but as a resource to be shared and used in alliance with social groups and movements so as to effect changes in the distribution of social power. The policy initiatives in the field of childcare illustrate this new socialist strategy. These initiatives are reminiscent of the activities of the Co-op Women's Guilds (who, at the end of World War I, argued for co-operative kitchens and washhouses, kindergartens and communal electric power and central heating), and they suggest that state institutions of social policy can be turned into something more positive and democratic if control of them is reclaimed or 'leased back' to the citizens who use and service them. Although remaining publicly funded, social policies would be regulated neither by capitalist markets nor by state bureaucracy. They would instead be guided by a third, more complex criterion: voluntary co-operation and social need generated by producers' and consumers' decisions, which are legally underwritten and politically protected. From this perspective, the state would guarantee the resources and facilities for childcare, health clinics or schools, while leaving the government of these organizations to self-determining local constituencies.*

---

* 'Leased-back' institutions under social control imply new legal arrangements, especially in countries whose law is mainly bipolar, that is, centred on the rights and duties of either the individual or the state. Self-governing, publicly funded associations within civil society would need to be recognized as special legal subjects endowed with definite legal privileges independent of the state. Their

Political Democracy

These policy examples are evidently rooted in their specific social and political conditions of birth, and therefore cannot be transferred directly from one country to another. (The Meidner Plan, for example, presupposes the existence of an actively reformist socialist party that cannot be durably excluded from office, and will therefore stand firm in the face of threats by private capital and its supporters. Also, it presupposes the existence of a 'solidaristic wage policy' capable of effectively managing distributive conflicts among trade unions and their rank-and-file members.) Their regional specificity does not reduce their general pertinence for the democratic tradition, however. They are important because they explicitly recognize the urgent need to deal with the undesirable elements of bureaucratic regulation, state surveillance and invisible government, which have grown enormously since 1945. These policies are important for a second reason: they indicate ways in which new forms of social solidarity, especially among the less powerful citizenry, can be developed against the atomizing effects of the current restructuring of state bureaucracies and private capitalist markets. These policies acknowledge the contemporary dangers of 'uprootedness', and the felt need of many citizens to put down roots within civil society through forms of association which preserve particular memories of the past, a measure of stability in the present, and particular expectations for the future.[26] Finally, the policy examples sketched here suggest the strategic importance of local initiatives for empowering less powerful citizens. They renew the old insight that the decentralization of power is sometimes the most effective cure for an undue parochialism; that through participation in local organization citizens overcome their localism (see essay 2). And these examples stimulate awareness of an important new insight about

---

hybrid status as property might be formulated in terms similar to the characteristic medieval notion of 'seisin'. This right ensured that ownership was neither exclusive nor perpetual. The right of seisin was situated between the Latin civil law notion of absolute and unconditional private 'property' and the weaker notion of 'possession'. Seisin guaranteed a protected ownership against casual appropriations and conflicting claims, while retaining the feudal principle of multiple ties to the same object. On the right of seisin, see P. Vinogradoff, *Roman Law in Mediaeval Europe*. London 1909, especially pp. 74-7, 86, 95-6. Some of the broad legal implications of leased-back institutions are suggested in the theory of social law pioneered by Duguit and Hauriou, and developed by Georges Gurvitch in his *L'idée du droit social*, Paris 1932. More recently, see Pierre Rosanvallon, 'The Decline of Social Visibility', in John Keane, ed., *Civil Society and the State*.

power. They recognize that large-scale organizations, such as state bureaucracies and capitalist corporations, rest upon complex, molecular networks of everyday power relations – among friends, neighbours, parents, children and others – and that the transformation of these molecular powers necessarily induces effects upon these large-scale organizations.

Of course, these policies entail a range of practical difficulties and likely unforeseen consequences. It is especially important to understand that such moves towards reviving and democratizing civil society do not automatically secure more decentralized, horizontally structured and egalitarian patterns of social life. They will surely be resented and resisted by the more powerful social classes, groups and organizations of existing civil society. Even assuming that such opposition could be neutralized by other groups within civil society, these redistributive policies will never produce self-stabilizing outcomes. A democratic civil society which maximizes complex liberty and equality will never resemble a happy and contented family. It would always tend to be self-paralysing. Precisely because of its pluralism, and its lack of a guiding centre, a fully democratic civil society would be endangered permanently by poor co-ordination, disagreement, niggardliness and open conflict among its constituents. No doubt, 'conflict is a form of socialisation' (Simmel). But civil society can also degenerate into a battlefield, in which the stronger – thanks to the existence of certain civil liberties – enjoy the freedom to twist the arms of the weaker. Under extreme conditions, civil society could even haemorrhage to death.[27]

That is why vigorous *political* initiatives, funding and legal recognition are necessary for the survival and expansion of civil society. For several reasons, sovereign state power is an indispensable condition of the democratization of civil society. Pluralism, the multiplication of decisionmaking centres and space for individual and group autonomy, tends constantly to generate 'anarchy'. Thus it necessitates centralized planning and co-ordination, which could be done efficiently and effectively only by means of political institutions, created especially for this purpose. Similarly, the competing claims and conflicts of interest generated by civil society could be settled peacefully only by means of laws which are applied universally. Since universal laws cannot emerge spontaneously from civil society, their formulation, application and enforcement would require a legislature, a judiciary and a police force, which are vital components of a state apparatus.

Furthermore, present-day attempts to democratize civil society within a particular country operate within a global system of nation states and empires. To some extent, this system could be weakened and co-ordinated in future by the development of a genuinely international civil society.[28] But so long as the present system of nation states and empires remains a dangerous state of nature, in which heavily armed friends and enemies come and go, standing military institutions for defending each particular civil society would be a disagreeable necessity – unless of course civil society were to become fully militarized, which would also be undesirable because incompatible with democratization.

These considerations point to the conclusion that a democratic civil society could never go it alone, and that it requires state power actively to defend its independence. Democratization is neither the outright enemy nor the unconditional friend of state power. It requires the state to govern civil society neither too much nor too little; while a more democratic order cannot be built *through* state power, it cannot be built *without* state power. As Lammenais observed in the early nineteenth century, democratic liberty is incompatible with a monistic, over-centralized state, which produces apoplexy at its centres and anaemia at its margins. Thus, a second and equally important condition of a new strategy for socialism becomes crucial: the reform of state policymaking and administration, its transformation from an *état protecteur* to a publicly accountable *état catalisateur*.[29]

So far, within the west European socialist tradition at least, recognition of the need to democratize political institutions has been limited. It has been confined mostly to calls for the creation of new governmental ministries, the reform of party leadership, and poorly defined demands for more 'open' administration. This parochial focus neglects a whole variety of other issues which socialists must address if they are to play a prominent role in the battle for extending citizens' political rights. Certain long-standing issues in the democratic tradition must be given renewed prominence. Among these are reform of the electoral system and (where it is still absent) the introduction of proportional representation. Other reforms of this type might include the expansion of local government power against rigid, centralized state bureaucracies; the repeal of 'official secrets' legislation and the many other informal rules and regulations used by governments to shield themselves from public opinion; and the subjection of ministerial power and administrative rule-making to effective judicial scrutiny and the rule of law.

In addition, consideration must be given to a number of relatively new (and worsening) blindspots within conventional parliamentary democratic theory and politics (see essays 4, 5). Foremost among these is the massive growth of unaccountable and invisible government – quasi-governmental authorities, state-owned and state-subsidized industries and services, nuclear regulatory and processing bodies, secret police and 'national security' organs conducting covert intelligence and military operations. Furthermore, the implications for political democracy of supranational policymaking and administration, which has grown considerably during the past half-century, must be examined more closely. The relative proportion, as well as the authoritarian effects and democratic potential, of the various mass communications media controlled by bodies within the state and civil society should be made a key theme of democratic politics. Also urgent are radical reforms of the legal and prison systems – the strengthening of laws against sexual, ethnic and other forms of discrimination, the improvement of police procedure, increased prison accountability, and changes in the training and selection of lawyers – in order to remove fully their biases in favour of male, white, middle-class citizens. The undemocratic features and democratic potential of political parties and other 'messenger' institutions – those responsible for sending, receiving and recoding demands between civil society and the state – must also be moved to the centre of democratic politics.

Finally, it should be recognized that none of these strategies for making the political system more democratic will enjoy full success unless an old and difficult problem, publicized once more in recent west European controversies about nuclear rearmament, is confronted. This problem concerns how the requirements of democratic political life (openness, controversy, pluralism, universal participation) can be reconciled with those branches of the state responsible for maintaining order by means of their monopoly of the means of violence. Institutions such as the police and the military thrive on practices deeply antithetical to political democracy. These undemocratic practices include secrecy, cunning, enforced unanimity, and the constant growth of the means of physical violence. Consequently, their 'taming' by means of active unionization within the armed forces, increased parliamentary control of the state, enhanced local community control of the police, and dealignment and demilitarization,[30] must occupy a key place in a programme of political democratization.

Democracy and Socialism

To summarize, I have argued that west European socialism today must break with its defensive and statist character, and become synonymous with the vitalization of civil society and the democratic reform of state power. In my view, policies informed by this general theoretical sketch could play a decisive part in current public debates prompted by the failures of state-administered socialism and the unjust and authoritarian initiatives of neo-conservatism. To speak of socialism in this unfamiliar way – as synonymous with the democratization of social and political power – is certainly not beyond controversy. The acceptance of this radically revised, genuinely pluralist, definition of socialism is bound to be resisted by certain democrats, whose indifference or outright hostility to 'socialism' blinds them to the compatibility of their views with those sketched in this and subsequent essays.

The acceptance of this revised definition of socialism is likely to prove equally painful for many traditional socialists.[31] It requires them to see that they can learn something from the content of neo-conservative propaganda and – a not unrelated point – that the severe crisis affecting comtemporary socialist groups, parties and governments is not merely conjunctural, but also traceable in part to ambiguities, confusions and contradictions within the original socialist interpretation of the modern state and civil society (a point explained in essay 2).

The revised definition of socialism presented here also requires socialists to abandon their deep misgivings about the extension and deepening of democratic public life. Many socialists still continue to view democracy (in my sense) in purely instrumental terms. It is good only to the extent that it delivers, or promises to deliver, 'socialism', itself defined narrowly in terms of economic equality or, less fashionably, state control of civil society. This traditional socialist reticence about greater democracy stems partly from the *correct* recognition that empowerment of previously disadvantaged constituencies within civil society does not necessarily work in favour of traditional definitions of socialism, based as they are on white, male, heterosexual, working-class, state-centred and ecologically destructive views of the world. One important implication of the proposals outlined in this book (and in *Civil Society and the State*) is that democratization will prove to be a pandora's box for conventionally minded socialists. The development of new democratic mechanisms within and between the state and civil society does not guarantee approval for traditional socialist ideas, particularly those centred on the collective ownership and state control of the means of production. On the contrary, democratic mechanisms invariably produce surprising outcomes (whereas stable despotisms usually bore their subjects rigid). Unexpected outcomes are one of the more fascinating features of democracy, whose extension and deepening is likely to increase the frequency of surprises for all groups, movements, parties and governments, socialists included. Genuinely democratic socialism must acknowledge the probability and legitimacy of surprising and sometimes awkward outcomes. It must also resist the temptation to prevent such outcomes by resorting to underhanded lobbying, bribery, conspiracy, educative dictatorships, terrorism and other forms of revolutionary alchemy. And it must recognize that democratic procedures are superior to all other types of decisionmaking *not* because they guarantee better results, but because they offer citizens the right to judge (and to reconsider their judgements about) the quality of these results.

Finally, to speak of socialism as equivalent to the separation and democratization of civil society and the state requires socialists to abandon the habit of postulating – for the purpose of practically abolishing – such dualisms as centralism/decentralism, state planning/private markets, statutory/voluntary, professional/lay and public property/private property. Such dualisms are manifestly unhelpful, and in practice paralysing, especially when they are used to reinforce arguments for either a state-centred or 'self-managing' conception of socialism. The perspective defended in this book transcends this choice. It suggests that the traditional twentieth-century choice between statist models of socialism (such as social democracy and communist revolution to strengthen the state in the name of abolishing it) and syndicalism and other forms of 'libertarianism' is now exhausted. Proposals for democratizing the state and civil society require socialists to distance themselves from post-war social democracy and its unworkable model of state-administered socialism. Equally, they require socialists to abandon whatever unsuspecting trust they might still have in the 'socialist' potential of the one-party regimes of central-eastern Europe, whose totalitarian governments refuse to acknowledge the legitimacy of an independent and pluralist civil society (see essays 4, 6, 7). Conversely, proposals for democratizing the state and civil society require socialists to abandon the nineteenth-century question of whether a complex social system without any political/legal restraints is possible or even desirable

– for certainly it is not, as I have explained above.* The arguments presented here for reforming the state and radically transforming civil society, for creating a *socialist* civil society, defy and transcend all these old alternatives. They suggest, instead, that the decisive question facing all democrats at the end of the twentieth century is how to enact the complex strategy of creative reform and planning guided by state action, and innovation from below through radical social initiatives which expand and equalize civil liberties.

---

* See also my *Public Life and Late Capitalism*, introduction and chapters 5, 7. On this point of complexity and the impossibility of abolishing state institutions, the strong parallels between my argument and early twentieth-century pluralist and Guild Socialist theories break down. Both types of theory understated the *permanent* likelihood of conflicts among *parties belligérantes* within a post-capitalist order; underestimated therefore the dangers of social stagnation and political decay; and thus failed to specify the political/legal mechanisms for reducing and pre-empting that possibility. Thus, pluralist doctrines continually emphasized 'the vast complex of gathered nations' (John N. Figgis, *Churches in the Modern State*, London 1914, p. 70) to which citizens are drawn, and to which they are entitled to give their allegiance. This multitude of social groups is not obligated to the state. In the event of conflict among them, the victory of society over the state is wholly justified – here pluralism falls back on romantic assumptions about harmony through complexity – since it is in accordance with the principle of the free and peaceful reign of voluntary groups. Similar assumptions about a 'natural' tendency to social equilibrium are strongly evident in Guild Socialist Theories. Their line of reasoning is different, however. Guild socialism typically underestimated the *multiple* sources of (potential) social conflict by viewing civil society through the eyes of male, industrial working-class producers and consumers. See, for example, Harold Laski's explanation of the basic importance of *industrial* democracy in *The Foundations of Sovereignty, and Other Essays*, London 1921, pp. 76-7. Guided by this narrow productivist interpretation of the dynamics of civil society, many Guild Socialist thinkers supposed, in opposition to Fabian socialism, that the abolition of the wage-labour/capital antagonism would lead to the withering away of fundamental conflicts. This would facilitate self-government by guilds, their simple and peaceful co-ordination by an administrative entity (e.g. parliament) which resembles the medieval 'community of communities'. In this way, the abolition of the centralized state as we know it would become possible. This conclusion was resisted by A. Orage and S.G. Hobson, but it is drawn explicitly in G.D.H. Cole's *Social Theory*, London 1920, chapter 8, and summarized in Ernest Barker, *Political Thought in England 1848 to 1914*, London 1932, p. 228: 'And if we ask, "What is to happen if guild quarrels with guild, each trying to get the best conditions for its own members? What is to happen if the Conference of the Guilds, with its own policy and its own feeling, quarrels with the parliament of the State?" we must content ourselves, as Montesquieu sought to content himself when he thought of the possibility of struggles arising from the separation of powers, by the thought that "since by the natural movement of things they are forced to move, they will move together."'

Notes

1. See Stanley Hoffman and George Ross (eds), *The Mitterrand Experiment. Continuty and Change in Modern France*, Cambridge 1987; Alain Touraine, *L'Après-socialisme*, Paris 1980; Pierre Rosanvallon, 'The Decline of Social Visibility', in John Keane, ed., *Civil Society and the State: New European Perspectives*, London and New York 1988; Oskar Negt, 'The SPD: A Party of Enlightened Crisis Management', *Thesis Eleven*, 7, 1983, pp. 54-66; Claus Offe, *Contradictions of the Welfare State*, edited John Keane, London 1984; Gavin Kitching, *Rethinking Socialism*, London 1983; Ernesto Laclau and Chantal Mouffe, *Hegemony and Socialist Strategy. Towards a Radical Democratic Politics*, London 1985; Paul Q. Hirst, *Law, Socialism and Democracy*, London 1986.

2. This self-paralysing tendency of post-war social democracy is treated at greater length in my *Public Life and Late Capitalism. Toward a Socialist Theory of Democracy*, Cambridge and New York 1984, especially the introduction and chapters 1, 3 and 7.

3. These trends are analysed in John Keane and John Owens, *After Full Employment*, London 1986.

4. This development suggests the inadequacy of Keynesian frameworks of analysis (which emphasize the management of demand), and the pertinence of neo-Schumpeterian interpretations of the present economic restructuring. These interpretations emphasize technical innovation, the rise of new industries based on new technological paradigms, and structural changes and disequilibria as chronic features of capitalist economic growth. See J.A. Schumpeter, *Business Cycles: A Theoretical, Historical and Statistical Analysis of the Capitalist Process*, two vols, New York 1939. More recently, see Christopher Freeman et al., *Unemployment and Technical Innovation: a study of long waves and economic development*, London 1982; Carlota Perez, 'Structural Change and Assimilation of New Technologies in the Economic and Social System', in Christopher Freeman, ed., *Design, Innovation and Long Cycles in Economic Development*, London 1984, pp. 51-82; and David A. Wolfe, 'Socio-political Contexts of Technological Change: Some Conceptual Models', in Brian Elliott, ed., *Technology and Social Process*, Edinburgh 1988.

5. See Wilhelm Hennis, ed., *Regierbarkeit: Studien zu ihrer Problematisierung*, Stuttgart 1977; S. Brittan, *The Economic Consequences of Democracy*, London 1977; and Samuel P. Huntington, 'The United States', in Michel Crozier et al., eds, *The Crisis of Democracy*, New York 1975.

6. Wolfgang Streeck and Philippe C. Schmitter, eds, *Private Interest Government. Beyond Market and State*, London, Beverly Hills, New Delhi 1985.

7. The main outlines of neo-conservative politics are discussed in Peter Steinfels, *The Neoconservatives. The Men Who Are Changing America's Politics*, New York 1979; Helmut Dubiel, *Was ist Neokonservatismus?*, Frankfurt am Main 1985; Stuart Hall and Martin Jacques, eds, *The Politics of Thatcherism*, London 1983. To argue that neo-conservatism (or the New Right) has most successfully popularized the weaknesses of state-administered socialism is not to deny that other forces – especially the new social movements – have also played a decisive role in this same process. See essay 4, and Alberto Melucci, *Challenging Codes: Social Movements in Complex Societies*, edited John Keane and Paul Mier, London 1989.

8. Jean-Marie Benoist, *Les outils de la liberté*, Paris 1985.

9. Anton Zijderveld, 'The Ethos of the Welfare State', *International Sociology*, vol. 1, 4, December 1986, pp. 452-3.

10. Leszek Kolakowski, 'The Myth of Human Self-Identity: Unity of Civil and Political Society in Socialist Thought', in Leszek Kolakowski and Stuart Hampshire, eds, *The Socialist Idea. A Reappraisal*, London 1977, p. 31; the same

claim is defended by Robert Nozick, *Anarchy, State and Utopia*, Oxford 1974, pp. 177f, and by Jean-François Revel, *How Democracies Perish*, Brighton 1985, p. 342.

11. Peter Taylor-Gooby and Hugh M. Bochel, *Politicians' Attitudes, Public Opinion and the Welfare State*, unpublished essay, Canterbury 1987.

12. Jean-Marie Benoist, *Les outils de la liberté*, pp. 162-65, 229-44. According to other neo-conservatives, the state and civil society should not be viewed ideally as separate or antagonistic entities. The state should be viewed as the highest spiritual 'expression' of civil society, and not merely its physical guardian and defender. See Roger Scruton, *The Meaning of Conservatism*, Harmondsworth 1980, pp. 47-8, and his *Thinkers of the New Left*, London 1986, pp. 201-3. The pre-eighteenth-century and Hegelian roots of this undemocratic view are examined in essay 2, and in my 'Despotism and Democracy. The Origins and Development of the Distinction Between Civil Society and the State, 1750-1850', in John Keane, ed., *Civil Society and the State*.

13. This argument is elaborated in the context of British and American case studies in *After Full Employment*, chapters 5-7.

14. An example was the tactic of *Einzelabschlachtung* (picking off employers one by one) used by German trade unions at the end of the nineteenth century; see Carl E. Schorske, *German Social Democracy, 1905-1917. The Development of the Great Schism*, Cambridge, Mass., and London 1983, chapter 2.

15. See the pathbreaking work by Michael Walzer, *Spheres of Justice. A Defense of Pluralism and Equality*, New York 1983.

16. See G.W.F. Hegel, 'Absolute Freedom and Terror', in *Phenomenology of Mind* (1807), New York 1967, pp. 599-610. His treatment of the Jacobin republic is well discussed in Judith N. Shklar, *Freedom and Independence: A Study of the Political Ideas of Hegel's 'Phenomenology of Mind'*, Cambridge 1976: and Charles Taylor, *Hegel*, Cambridge 1975, chapter 15 and *Hegel and Modern Society*, Cambridge 1979, chapter 2, section 5.

17. See essay 2, and *Civil Society and the State*, part one.

18. Named after Rudolf Meidner, the economist who headed the Swedish Confederation of Labour (*Landsorganisationen i Sverige*, or LO), the Meidner Plan was adopted by the 1976 LO Congress. The bourgeois parties and organized business (e.g. the October 4th Committee) mounted a sustained offensive against the Plan. The Social Democratic Party's reaction has been cautious and disappointing. The Party leadership initially avoided taking a position on the Plan. In 1981, LO and Party committees eventually agreed on a compromise formulation, and in 1983 a highly watered-down version of the original Plan was brought into legislation. For the main text, see Rudolf Meidner, *Employer Investment Funds: An Approach to Collective Capital Formation*, London 1978. More recently, see the interview with Meidner, 'Ein unbequemer Vater', *Die Zeit*, 2, 2 January 1987, p. 19. Further details are discussed in Andrew Martin, 'Wages, Profits, and Investment in Sweden', in Leon N. Lindberg and Charles S. Maier, eds, *The Politics of Inflation and Economic Stagnation*, Washington DC 1985, pp. 403-66.

19. W. Korpi, *The Working Class in Welfare Capitalism*, London, Boston, Melbourne and Henley 1978, and his *The Democratic Class Struggle*, London, Boston, Melbourne and Henley 1983, chapter 10.

20. An excellent introduction to these proposals is Karl Hinrichs, Claus Offe and Helmut Wiesenthal, 'Time, Money and Welfare State Capitalism', in John Keane, ed., *Civil Society and the State*.

21. See Joseph Huber, *Wer soll das alles ändern. Die Alternativen der Alternativebewegung*, Berlin 1981, and Angelo Bolaffi and Otto Kallscheuer, 'Die Grünen: Farben-Lehre eines politischen Paradoxes. Zwischen neuen Bewegungen und Veränderung

der Politik', *Prokla*, 51, 1983, pp. 75-9.

22. The complex debates about the financing, administration and scope of the citizen's wage are examined in Michael Opielka and Georg Vobruba, eds, *Das garantierte Grundeinkommen. Entwicklung und Perspektiven einer Forderung*, Frankfurt am Main 1986, and Thomas Schmid, ed., *Befreiung von falscher Arbeit. Thesen zum garantierten Mindesteinkommen*, Berlin 1984. The importance for women of *individual* (rather than household) entitlement to such a wage is emphasized in Ute Gerhard, 'Den Sozialstaat neu denken? Voraussetzungen und Preis des Sozialstaatskompromisses', *Vorgänge*, 87, May 1987, pp. 14-32.

23. On the earlier twentieth century German tradition of strategies of expanding workers' self-government, the socialization of key sectors of the private economy and the development of 'sozialistischer Inseln', see Klaus Novy, *Strategien der Sozialisierung. Die Diskussion der Wirtschaftsreform in der Weimarer Republik*, Frankfurt am Main 1978.

24. See Hevré Hamon and Patrick Rotman, *La Deuxième gauche: Histoire intellectuelle et politique de la CFDT*, Paris 1982; and George Ross, 'French Unions Face the 1980s', *Political Power and Social Theory*, vol. 3, 1982, pp. 53-75.

25. The background to these local initiatives – which encompass broader experiments, ranging from decentralized service delivery and municipal enterprise, to popular planning, workers' co-operatives and anti-racist initiatives – is examined in Martin Boddy and Colin Fudge, eds, *Local Socialism? Labour Councils and New Left Alternatives*, Basingstoke and London 1985; John Gyford, *The Politics of Local Socialism*, London 1985, especially chapter 3; and Robin Murray, 'New Directions in Municipal Socialism', in Ben Pimlott, ed., *Fabian Essays in Socialist Thought*, London 1984, pp. 206-29.

26. Simone Weil, *The Need for Roots. Prelude to a Declaration of Duties Towards Mankind*, London 1952.

27. Norbert Elias, 'Violence and Civilization', in John Keane, ed., *Civil Society and the State*.

28. I have examined this point in depth in 'Civil Society and the Peace Movement in Britain', *Thesis Eleven*, 8, 1984, pp. 5-22.

29. This distinction is discussed in B. Cazès, 'L'Etat protecteur contraint à une double manoeuvre', *Futuribles*, 40, January 1981. This proposal does not amount to a battle-cry of 'civil society against the state', as has been claimed by Boris Frankel, *The Post-Industrial Utopians*, Cambridge 1987, p. 204.

30. 'Civil Society and the Peace Movement in Britain'; cf. the arguments for a new global consensus based on respect for pluralism and tolerance of a variety of political and social systems in Mary Kaldor and Richard Falk, eds, *Dealignment*, Oxford 1987. Dealignment proposals of this kind recognize an important rule of modern times: that the degree of civil and political liberty within a country is inversely proportional to the military pressures exerted on its borders.

31. An example of this likely reaction is foreshadowed in the (muddled) remarks of Jean-Pierre Chevènement, 'Winning Ways', *New Socialist*, December 1986, p. 23: 'The state has to be modernized. And the state is not something external to what we might call civil society: it isn't a case of the good individuals on the one side, and the big bad state with its dastardly functionaries on the other. Civil society and the state belong in reality to a single unified society.... Indeed, I don't think any socialist – at least any socialist worthy of the name – can work on the basis of an ideological vision of a civil society placed in an opposing camp to the state. The state is amongst other things the instrument of a particular will and of a social class or stratum. Or at least it is a site where a balance is struck, a site of struggle. In itself, the state is neither good nor bad.... We can and must therefore use the state in a progressive manner, while remaining aware that the problem of bureaucracy is a real one. We must democratize the state.'

2

Remembering the Dead

Civil Society and the State from Hobbes to Marx and Beyond

> Wie nah sind uns manche Tote und wie tot sind so viele die leben.
> (*How close to us are some of the dead, and how dead are so many who live.*)
>
> Wolf Biermann

A 'Socialist' Civil Society?

The novel idea of a democratic or 'socialist' civil society – whose outlines were first broached by central European writers – generates unease among most conservatives and liberals.[1] Its reception within socialist circles is usually no warmer. Especially within the Marxian tradition, the phrase 'socialist civil society' is viewed as self-contradictory, even a nonsense. According to Poulantazas, for example, the concept of a civil society separated from the state is an invention of eighteenth-century political theory. Developed by Hegel and the young Marx, it refers to the 'world of needs', to the bourgeois economy of producing and consuming 'individuals', who are in reality divided into social classes which function as the foundation of the modern state.[2] This view is commonplace within the socialist tradition. It presumes that the meaning of civil society, as well as its separation from the modern state, is relative to a particular historical period. Originating in the seventeenth and eighteenth centuries, the term 'civil society' signifies the

31

historically established domination of the bourgeoisie over the proletariat, expressed in the 'extra-political' relationship of private capital and wage labour. Not merely the content, but also the form of civil society is bourgeois. Civil society is the state-guaranteed realm of commodity production and exchange – of private property, greedy market competition and private rights. How then, it is asked, could one possibly speak of a *socialist* civil society?

Many things can be said in response to this type of (Marxian-inspired) question. It is best to begin with two preliminary points, which help to define the problem explored in this essay. The first concerns the restricted sociological horizons of the Marxian understanding of modern civil societies.[3] The Marxian theory evidently devalues the distinction between the state and civil society because of its tendency to reduce the state to the form of political organization of the bourgeoisie. On that basis, it further conflates the complex patterns of stratification, group organization as well as the conflicts and movements of civil society to the logic and contradictions of a mode of production – the capitalist economy. The importance of *other* institutions of civil society – such as households, churches, scientific and literary associations, prisons and hospitals – is devalued. Their fate is assumed to be tied unequivocally to the overwhelming power of 'capitalism'. Reductionist explanations of this kind are embedded deeply in Marx's own writings. I cite only one example, from *The Poverty of Philosophy*, where Marx quotes approvingly from John Francis Bray's remarkable work, *Labour's Wrongs, and Labour's Remedy* (1839): 'The only way to arrive at truth is to go at once to First Principles ... Let us ... go at once to the source from whence governments themselves have arisen ... By thus going to the origin of the thing, we shall find that every form of government, and every social and governmental wrong, owes its rise to the existing social system – to *the institution of property as it at present exists* – and that, therefore, if we would end our wrongs and our miseries at once and for ever, *the present arrangements of society must be totally subverted.*'[4]

A second preliminary point supplements this remark concerning the problem of reductionism. The conventional Marxian understanding of the distinction between civil society and the state forgets that the term civil society *pre-dated* the emergence of the bourgeoisie, being well-developed, for instance, in classical and medieval political thought;[5] and, most importantly, that the distinction has a *variety* of early modern meanings, all of which are concerned however with the *political* problem of how, and under which circumstances, state power can be controlled and rendered legitimate.

To continue to speak of the state–civil society distinction as equivalent to capitalism is to do violence to whole traditions of rich and suggestive political discourse. It involves destroying a cornucopia of political insights which are superior to those of contemporary political thinking – at least in respect of their deep sensitivity to some 'perennial' questions concerning how to limit and apportion power – and which therefore should not be allowed to pass into the musty oblivion of libraries and archives. To propose that socialism be redefined as a synonym for the democratic maintenance and transformation of the division between civil society and the state is to propose a renewal and development of the early modern concern with civil society and 'the limits of state action' (to recall the title of an influential essay by Wilhelm von Humboldt in the early 1790s[6]). It is to engage in a type of future-oriented memory, a remembering of the dismembered, a rescuing or 'redemption' of the lost treasure of authors, texts and contexts which have been pushed aside by the socialist tradition as 'outdated' or as 'bourgeois'.[7] This type of future-oriented memory – a political theory with eyes in the back of its head – can be of considerable importance in stimulating the contemporary democratic imagination. It can be a subversive weapon in the hands of those who support (often in the name of future generations) the present-day extension of democracy. An active democratic memory recognizes that the development of fresh and stimulating perspectives on the present depends upon criticisms that break up habitual ways of thinking, in part through types of criticism which remember what is in danger of being forgotten. Hence, the democratic remembrance of things past is neither nostalgic nor atavistic. It turns to the past not for the sake of the past – as if the secrets of present miseries were hidden there – but for the purpose of securing more democracy in the present and future. An active democratic memory knows that past traditions of political discourse can furnish us with more than a few surprises and provoke us into enlightening disagreements. They can remind us of some of the 'perennial' problems of political and social life. And, thereby, they can help us understand who we are, where we stand, and what we might hope for.

Admittedly, a democratic theory which seeks to develop an active memory confounds the conventional distinction between left and right. Traditionally, the right was recognizable by its nostalgia and backward-looking orientation, whereas the left, building upon the present, usually looked towards the future with optimism. The approach adopted in this essay cuts across this unhelpful distinction. It refuses to believe that tradition is the exclusive property of conservatives. It knows that a short memory limits future expectations. It suggests that the viability of democratic theory is to be judged not according to its capacity for forgetting the past and embracing 'the new', but instead by the degree to which it builds on, and imaginatively transforms, the subversive themes of old bodies of political thinking.

Consider the early modern tradition of 'liberal' discourse from the time of the English Civil War until the abortive 1848 revolutions. This tradition did not merely seek to make the world safe for capitalism, as has been argued by writers as different as Laski and Horkheimer and Adorno,[8] and as is often still assumed among many socialists. Early liberal political philosophy was concerned not only with the growth of modern capitalism. It was also preoccupied with the fundamental problem of reconciling the freedom of different individuals, groups and classes with political order and coercion. Typically, the state was seen as a product of reason, as an institution which collectively restrains private interests and passions, and thereby secures a controlled and ordered liberty in the face of possible exercises of pure strength and/or disorder and chaos. Political reason is *raison d'état*: it serves to justify an entirely new apparatus of anonymous power – the modern bureaucratic state – whose monopoly of the weapons of violence is reinforced by means of collecting taxes, conducting foreign policy, articulating and administering law, and 'policing' its subjects. Most early modern liberal thinkers understood that the unconditional recognition of the sovereign power of this state could – and frequently did – result in the deprivation of the powers of its subjects. Consequently, while early liberal thinkers sought to justify the centralized state as necessary, they attempted at the same time to justify limits upon its potentially coercive powers. The history of liberal political thought from the mid-seventeenth century until the time of Marx is thus the history of attempts to justify might *and* right, political power *and* law, the duties of subjects *and* the rights of citizens.

A central element of the liberal concern with limiting state power is its attempt to differentiate the apparatus of the state from a pre-state or non-state condition. It is possible to discern five different versions (or models) of this theoretical attempt to distinguish between the non-state and state spheres and, hence, to draw limits upon the scope of legitimate state action.

(a) A first version (represented by Bodin, Hobbes, Spinoza and others) considers the state as the radical negation of the natural condition. This pre-state condition is sometimes understood as relatively peaceful, but most often it is seen as highly unstable and anti-social, as a condition of perpetual war. The state receives its legitimacy or mandate to overthrow this natural condition of war through a process of contractual agreement among its fearful inhabitants. The resulting civil society is seen as equivalent to the state and its laws.

(b) According to a second version (Pufendorf, Locke, Kant, the Physiocrats, Adam Ferguson and other Scottish Enlightenment thinkers), society is natural. It must be conserved and regulated by the state, whose function is not to *replace* the natural condition (as in model (a)). Rather, the state is an instrument of society, actualizing or completing its (potential) freedom and equality. As Kant says, there can very well be a society in the state of nature, but not a civil (*bürgerliche*) society, that is, a political arrangement which secures and guarantees mine and thine through public laws. Because of its emphasis on conserving and completing the natural condition, this second version characteristically blurs the distinction between civil society and the state (Locke, for example, draws on the Latin meaning of *societas civilis* to refer not to a pre-state condition of existence, but to political society and, thereby, the state).

(c) A third version, which pushes the Pufendorf–Locke model almost to its limits, is evident in Tom Paine's reply to Burke's *Reflections on the Revolution in France*. Here the theme of civil society against the state becomes central for the first time. The state is deemed a necessary evil and natural society an unqualified good. The state is nothing more than a delegation of social power for the common benefit of society. There is, we are told, a natural propensity to society, which existed prior to the state, and whose networks of reciprocal interest and solidarity promote universal security and peace. Thus, the more perfect civil society is, the more it regulates its own affairs, the less occasion it has for government. There is an inverse relationship between *société libre, gouvernement simple* and *société contrainte, gouvernement compliqué* (Bastiat).

(d) According to a fourth version (Hegel), the task of the state is to conserve and transcend civil society, which is conceived not as a natural condition of freedom (as it is for model (c)), but as a historically constructed arrangement of ethical life that includes the economy, social interest groups, and institutions responsible for administering civil law and 'welfare'. The state is neither a radical negation of a society in perpetual war (Hobbes, Spinoza) nor an instrument which perfects society (Pufendorf, Locke), but a new moment which contains and preserves the independence of civil society in order to transform it from a 'formal universality' into an 'organic reality'. Civil society both requires and provides the prerequisites for an institutionally separate sovereign state, which holds together the elements of civil society in a self-determined whole, and thereby brings ethical life to an all-encompassing, higher unity. Only by acknowledging and keeping civil society in a subordinate position can the state preserve its freedom.

(e) A fifth version conducts something of a rearguard action against its predecessor. It fears that civil society is being suffocated by new forms of state intervention. It urges the importance of protecting and renewing civil society, understood as a self-organizing, legally guaranteed sphere which is not directly dependent upon the state. This view is evident in the writings of John Stuart Mill, and in Tocqueville's concern with a new modern type of popularly elected despotism. Here, the decisive political problem of modern times concerns how the equalizing tendencies triggered by democratization can be preserved by preventing the state from abusing its powers, swallowing up civil society, and robbing its citizens of their freedoms.

A selective reconsideration of these models of state power can help dispel the historical ignorance and lack of clarity and outright confusion in recent discussions of the state–civil society distinction.[9] Also, it can help specify the limits of the Marxian understanding of the modern state and civil society – thereby preparing the ground for a more precise and convincing conception of a democratic civil society.

The Security State

The first model of state power considered here – the *security state* defended in Thomas Hobbes's *Leviathan* (1651)[10] – is striking, if only because, compared with its successors, it restricts the theme of the limits of state action to virtual insignificance. Hobbes emphasizes that there cannot be peace and material comfort on earth unless individuals, who have no 'natural' respect for others, are subjected to a highly visible and well-armed sovereign state, whose function is permanently to order and pacify these individuals. This peaceful order enforced by the security state is called Civill Society. It is considered the radical negation of a natural condition of violent competition among contentious, acquisitive individuals. Hobbes's justification of the security state thus rests upon a dramatic contrast between war and Civill Society. The modern world is offered a choice: either the violence and confusion of the natural condition or 'peaceable, sociable, and comfortable living' (216) through the near-total subjection of individuals to unlimited state power.

Hobbes argues that war may be prevented, and the security state formed, in two ways: through *acquisition* (the subjection of one state by another through foreign invasion) or *institution*, in which case a majority of individuals, again pressured by fear, 'consent' to be governed by a few others. In each case, the security state is deemed by Hobbes to be legitimate, because it is formed 'voluntarily': its rulers receive their mandate to permanently overthrow the natural condition of war through the *inferred* (and, thus, hypothetical!) process of contractual agreement among its terror-stricken inhabitants.[11] Once established, the security state is absolute. Individuals relinquish forever a quantity of their rights and powers of self-direction to a body which monopolizes the means of violence, taxation, public opinion formation, policymaking and administration. The price of peace is high: individual subjects surround themselves with a web of state powers from which they can never again escape.

Hobbes emphasizes that the legitimate scope of these powers is unlimited in principle: 'he that is not superiour is not supreme; that is to say not Soveraign' (246). From the point of view of this first model, civil society and the state are synonymous. All that facilitates the state's capacity to rule is good and just, all that facilitates subjects' capacities to question and resist its power is bad and unjust. The subjects possess no rights of altering the form of the security state, nor even of choosing those who occupy the office of sovereign – Hobbes denies the parliamentarian doctrine of limited or revocable contractual sovereignty. They cannot appeal to God to justify their acts (or intentions) of disobedience, for the sovereign is God's interpreter on earth – Hobbes denies the royalist doctrine of divine right. Minorities *qua* minorities have no rights of dissent. Not even majorities can accuse the sovereign power of unjust or injurious acts, for they possess no legitimate powers of punishing or putting to death sovereigns for their wrongdoings.

Hobbes does point out that subjects *as individuals* can legitimately exercise a right of resistance against state attempts to deprive them of certain natural rights to life (such as access to food, water or medicine) or to manipulate them into ending their own lives (through, for example, a forced confession which results in the subject's execution). But this right of individual resistance is a pure formality. All *collective* resistance to acts of arbitrary state power – even rebellion designed to *preserve* forms of life governed by the precepts of natural law – is strictly forbidden, because potentially contrary to the peace and safety of the body politic (286-7). Only where sovereign rulers lose their capacity to protect their subjects can the latter exercise their collective rights of self-preservation against the state (2760, 272). Otherwise, the security state (or Civill Society) is unchallengeable. Illegitimate sovereign power is a contradiction in terms. By definition, sovereigns cannot engage in unjust or injurious acts: 'The Soveraign ... is the absolute Representative of all the subjects' (275); 'No Law can be Unjust. The Law is made by the Soveraign Power, and all that is done by such Power, is warranted ...' (388). Concerned to watch, order and civilize its subjects, the sovereign is sole legislator and holds exclusive rights to make appointments, to determine his or her successor, and to hear and decide controversies arising among subjects. The essential feature of the security state is its monopoly on deciding what is necessary for preserving (or restoring) peace at home and abroad. This monopoly is neither divisible nor transferable to its subjects, Hobbes insists, because any Civill Society whose state power is divided or dispersed cannot long survive the multitude of natural passions and clamours which lead inevitably to violent civil war.

It should be clear from this brief summary that in the model of the security state the early modern liberal discussion of the limits of state action begins rather poorly. It is committed to civil peace by whatever means necessary, and it is opposed explicitly to what Hobbes calls Tyrannophobia – the fear of being governed strongly (370, 722). Certainly, Hobbes is not a friend of the *arbitrary* exercise of power. In his view, sovereign power should always be exercised in accordance with general 'laws of nature' which forbid the destruction of life or its means of preservation.[12] And it is true that Hobbes specifies the existence of a private realm within Civill Society, in which individual subjects can exercise certain negative liberties. These consist of activities which the sovereign has not (yet) prohibited, for example, individuals' freedom 'to buy, and sell, and otherwise contract with one another; to choose their own aboad, their own diet, their own trade of life, and institute their children as they themselves think fit' (264). Considered together, these activities are supposed to constitute a realm of private freedom (or what Hobbes calls 'Private Systemes' (274-5)) which is independent of the sovereign's reach. This sphere of freedom from state action is meant to preserve something of the substance – minus the overt violence – of the natural condition. Thanks to 'the silence of the Law' (271), individual subjects can shift for themselves within private transactions and associations (or what Hobbes calls 'Leagues', 'Private Bodies', 'Corporations' or 'Societies' (274-88)).

This concession to the principle of limiting the scope of absolute political power is more apparent than real. For not only is the regulation of family life within this private realm in the hands of fathers, who are licensed to govern their wives and children absolutely (285). The *whole* of the private sphere is subject constantly to the prerogatives, invasions and 'civilizing' initiatives of sovereign power. In all realms of life, subjects are watched over and administered by this power, before which (to repeat the Hobbesian simile) they can only ever at best resemble small stars in the presence of an overpowering sun (238).

The Constitutional State

That unlimited state sovereignty might be excessive and dangerous, because it is incompatible with private freedoms guaranteed by the rule of law, is a problem which becomes better focussed in a second model, that of the *constitutional state* (represented here by John Locke's *An Essay Concerning the True Original, Extent, and End of Civil Government* (1689?)[13] Certainly, there are strong affinities between the security state and constitutional state models. In both, for instance, the state is designed to restrain the (often violent) conflicts generated among individuals living together on earth. Both models refer to this condition of politically enforced tranquillity as civil or political society. As a condition of 'comfortable, safe and peaceable living' (375), civil society consists of a complex of stable interactions among 'free, equal and independent' male individuals, whose properties (in the broadest sense) are secured politically, that is, through their subjection to a state which monopolizes the process of formulating, administering and enforcing laws. Despite such similarities, there are two important respects in which the image of the constitutional state defended by Locke differs from the security state. Both differences contribute decisively to the formulation of the problem of how, and to what degree, the power of the modern state should be limited in favour of civil society.

In the first place, the theory of the constitutional state weakens considerably the strong contrast (drawn by Hobbes) between the war of the natural condition and the peace of civil society. The possibility of 'natural' social solidarity is admitted. The natural condition, though an unstable condition of anti-social sociability (as Kant later was to say), tends also to be a condition of reciprocity, in which (adult, male, property- owning) 'individuals', who are each others' equals, enjoy freedom to dispose of their powers and possessions as they choose.[14] There are several sources of this propensity for society, which is pre-political and therefore predates the formation of modern civil society. Locke argues that the patriarchal household is the original, and most basic form of natural solidarity (361-2; 380-2). Furthermore, men are prone naturally to form themselves into larger collectivities in order to defend themselves against their common enemies in neighbouring lands (383-6). Finally, the possibility of a natural 'class solidarity' is envisaged. The natural condition is not a situation of licence and violence, Locke emphasizes, for most (adult, male, property-owning) 'individuals' are inclined to act in accordance with definite laws of nature – which forbid acts of violence and destruction and, in general, encourage them to respect each other's property and keep the peace.

This argument about natural social solidarity explains why the state is not seen as the absolute negation of the natural condition but, rather, as the remedy for its imperfect sociality. The state is viewed as an instrument which is charged with the double function of conserving and rectifying, and therefore 'completing' natural society. In this way the theory of the constitutional state challenges the idea of absolute, self-perpetuating sovereign power. This is the second decisive respect in which the constitutional state model differs from its predecessor. Locke's constitutional state model objects strongly to the (Hobbesian) requirement that sovereigns, whether an assembly or monarch, have a free hand in naming their successors and an absolute right to govern – without at the same time being subject to the civil laws which they themselves formulate and administer. Subjects should not be the playthings of absolute rulers.[15] After all, rulers are only human – like all other 'individuals' they make mistakes, are subject to various passions and, consequently, tend to develop distinct and separate interests from those whom they rule. Therefore they cannot be left to be exclusive judges of their own cases (316; 399). In civil society no individual should be exempted from the rule of law. Locke emphasizes that there should not be 'one Rule for Rich and Poor, for the Favourite at Court, and the Country Man at Plough' (409)

This point is clarified through the insistence that political power is only ever held on trust. Those who govern civil society through the constitutional state are trustees of the governed.[16] This means, to take some examples, that they must govern through promulgated or known standing laws, which are consonant with the laws of nature and which are applied universally. Legislators, who are the supreme power, may be subject to periodic elections, which must not be rigged or cancelled. Property in life, liberty and estate (including taxation) cannot be taken without the consent of a majority of the enfranchised, or their representatives (even if the exercise of these property rights leads to a highly unequal distribution of wealth and power in civil society). Finally, since political and paternal power are distinct (Locke here turns against Filmer and Grotius), sovereigns cannot trespass into the patriarchal household, wherein men 'naturally' exercise absolute power over 'their' women, children and servants (357; 366).

For these reasons, state decisionmakers who act contrary to the trust granted them are deemed to have declared war against their male, property-owning subjects. In the event of war in this sense being declared, the enfranchised are absolved from obligations to the existing state authorities, and are at liberty to establish new political authorities, even through forceful rebellion: 'And thus the Community perpetually retains a Supream Power of saving themselves from the attempts and designs of any Body, even of their Legislators, whenever they shall be so foolish, or so wicked, as to lay and carry on designs against the Liberties and Properties of the Subject' (413). This doctrine of the right of rebellion of the enfranchised ('the Community') against unconstitutional government by no means sanctions disorder and violent confusion. This is because the theory of the constitutional state – here it breaks decisively with its security-minded predecessor – relies on the crucial distinction between society and the state.[17] The dissolution of unconstitutional government through lawful resistance is seen as equivalent to a return to a pre-political condition of natural solidarity among 'free, equal and independent' individuals capable of living within the bounds of natural law. In contrast to the security state model, the constitutional state model thus distinguishes between the dissolution of state institutions and the dissolution of 'fellowship and societie' (430). Certainly, whenever society is dissolved (for example, through sovereign conquest or invasion), its corresponding state institutions cannot last long. But the reverse does not hold necessarily: society can legitimately oppose the unconstitutional state, without 'individuals' being drawn into violent conflict with others.

The Minimum State

The suggestion that natural society should sometimes be defended against the state may be interpreted, contrary to Sheldon Wolin and others, as a first, but decisive step in the early modern concern with limiting state power in favour of civil society.* This step is taken explicitly in a third model, that of the *minimum state*. The anarchistic liberalism of Thomas Paine's *Rights of Man* (1791-2)[18] well illustrates this development, in which the theme of restricting state action is pushed almost to its limits. In the model of the minimum state, the state is deemed a necessary evil and natural society an unqualified good. The legitimate state is nothing more than a delegation of power for the common benefit of society. The more perfect civil society is, the more it regulates its

---

* According to Wolin's well-known thesis, the 'rediscovery of society' in post-Hobbesian political thought left little scope or prestige for the 'distinctively political'. The growth of interest in the social was synonymous with the destruction of concern for the political – understood by Wolin mainly in its classical sense. See Sheldon S. Wolin, *Politics and Vision. Continuity and Innovation in Western Political Thought*, Boston 1960. Wolin's interpretation of the 'rediscovery of society' is insufficiently analytic; it fails to distinguish the different meanings of the 'social' sketched in this essay (and its treatment of the social as synonymous with production, exchange and consumption shares much in common with the reductionism of the Marxian account of civil society). It also neglects the democratizing consequences of the defence of society against despotic states (see my 'Despotism and Democracy. The Origins and Development of the Distinction Between Civil Society and the State, 1750-1850' in *Civil Society and the State*, London and New York 1988). Finally, the premises of Wolin's defence of the political are thoroughly anti-modern. They tacitly suppose the possibility of recreating the homogeneous political community of the Greek *polis* under post-modern conditions. These same weaknesses are evident in Hannah Arendt's criticism of the social in *The Human Condition*, Chicago 1958, especially pp. 23-9, 38-49, 110, 159, 257.

own affairs, and the less occasion it has for government.

This possibility of a naturally self-regulating society administered by a minimum state is contrasted by Paine with the present
age of despotism. Everywhere, with the notable exception of
America, states crush and barbarize their populations. The global
condition of despotism, Paine complains, has made individuals
fearful of thinking; reason is considered as treasonable; and individuals' natural rights to freedom are hunted to every corner of the
earth. The modern world is 'uncivilized' (105) because it is over-
governed. Individuals become caught in an endless labyrinth of
political institutions which prevent them from scrutinizing the
principles, good or bad, upon which existing laws are founded. This
makes them wretched, for the overwhelming force of states and their
laws denatures individuals by tearing them away from themselves,
and from each other. Individuals are degraded and victimized by a
global system of *political* alienation: in this world turned upside
down by despotic governments, (potentially) self-determining and
sociable individuals become lost, causes and effects appear reversed,
and states represent themselves as the real and proper source of
property, power and prestige.

These inversions have highly dangerous consequences. Paine
emphasizes that despotic states are responsible for maintaining
the patriarchal form of power within households; despotic states
rest upon, and presuppose for their functioning, despotic households, in which the arbitrary exercise of power by fathers
(bequeathing property to their first-born sons, for instance)
reinforces 'family tyranny and injustice' (105). Despotic states
also institute class divisions within society by loading their
subjects with exorbitant rates of taxation. This in turn throws
parts of society into poverty and discontent. The propertyless are
impoverished and oppressed, the rich become ever more privileged, and violent struggles between classes ensue. Self-aggran-
dizing, despotic governments also seek to extract power and
revenue from their societies by cultivating bellicose national prejudices and preparing for armed conflict with other states. It is no
accident that the age of despotism is also an age of war. Wars
between states increase their power over their populations and
this, in turn, further undermines the possibility of social
harmony. Contrary to the theories of Hobbes and Locke, individuals become each other's enemies *because* of a surplus of state
power.

Paine is convinced that this global subsumption of societies by
despotic states is only termporary. The dissolution of arbitrary

political power is merely a matter of time; despotic states are weak and unpopular because they are 'unnatural'. Pointing to the example of the American Revolution, Paine stresses repeatedly the need for citizens to resist state power which encroaches upon their liberties. This conviction is nourished by two related, but quite different types of argument, which lead to social and political conclusions very different from those of the security state and constitutional state models.

In the first place, the legitimate state is that which is guided by the principles of active consent of the governed and natural rights (to free speech, public assembly, freedom of worship, and so on). Here the model of the minimum state radicalizes and universalizes the contractualist arguments employed in the models of the security state and the constitutional state. It is stressed that the power of states is only ever delegated, on trust, by actively consenting male and female individuals, who can legitimately retrieve this power at any time by withdrawing their consent. This follows from the principle that 'man [sic] has no property in man' (64). All individuals are born equal, and with equal natural rights. (The textual evidence on this point suggests that Paine universalizes the Lockean theory of consent, to include not only minorities, but also women and the underclasses.) These natural rights predispose individuals to respect each other according to the (Christian) principle 'do as you would be done by'. They enable individuals to act freely and reasonably and for their comfort and happiness, without injuring or trespassing upon the natural rights of others. These God-given rights are by definition neither annihilable nor transferable nor devisable and, contrary to Burke and others, no generation is empowered to intercept or cut off these rights from their heirs. States can be considered as legitimate or 'civilized', therefore, only when they have been formed through the explicit consent of individuals themselves, and when this active consent is formulated constitutionally and articulated continuously through parliamentary, representative mechanisms. Civilized governments are constitutional governments empowered by the active consent of naturally free and equal individuals. These governments have no rights, but only duties before their citizens, who are permanently sovereign. In cases of disputes between citizens and their governments, therefore, the following maxim applies: *In favorem vitae, libertatis et innocentiae omnia praesumuntur* (everything is assumed in favour of life, liberty, and innocence).

Paine proceeds from this conclusion to a second thesis. This decisively extends the horizons of early modern theories of the limits of state action by distinguishing explicitly between civil society and the state. Paine seeks to explain why, contrary to the security and constitutional state models, free and equal individuals living together on earth actively desire peaceful and co-operative forms of social life which are self-reliant and independent of state institutions. According to Paine, there are two respects in which individuals are naturally disposed to co-operative forms of social life.

First, individuals' natural wants exceed their individual powers, and this means that they are incapable of realizing their powers and satisfying their diverse wants without the labours and assistance of others. Consequently, they are driven ('as naturally as gravitation acts to a centre' (185)) to establish and develop forms of commercial exchange based on reciprocal interest. This market dependence of individuals upon others for the satisfaction of their diverse wants is reinforced, or so Paine argues, by 'a system of social affectations' (185). This deep yearning for solidarity with others is a natural affection and, paradoxically, it is replenished constantly by the motivating force of individuals' market interests. This felicitous coincidence of instrumental market interest and the love of others, Paine concludes, predisposes individuals to live together harmoniously by exercising their natural rights to freedom and happiness within a civil society which is unhindered by state institutions and recognizes only the rules of mutual respect, the satisfaction of interest and the safety and freedom of all individuals.

Certainly, Paine is aware that social life can be corrupted and deformed, and that this has degrading political effects (99; 126). Once individuals' desire for society is aroused, however, despotic states quickly begin to crumble into ruins. Indeed, the more civil society develops a confidence in its capacity to govern itself, the less need there is for state institutions and laws. A confident, self-governing society requires only a minimum of political mechanisms – what Paine calls 'government' – to ensure the natural interaction of the various parts of civil society upon each other. Paine is certain that minimum states guided by societies bonded together by reciprocal interest and mutual affection would make for a condition of (international) order and harmony. Freely interacting individuals thrive on the aid they receive from each other, and from other societies. Common interest and stability is the 'law' of civil society. This 'law' far exceeds the importance and steadying influence of positive laws enacted and administered by state institutions. 'The instant formal government is abolished, society begins to act. A general association takes place, and common interest produces common security' (186). Common security without state interference is conceived by Paine as a consequence of natural forces (and not, say, as a *historical* achievement). Individuals tend to interact with others spontaneously, and this leads them to form interlocking and self-sufficient social networks emancipated from conflict. If states were everywhere constructed upon this natural social foundation they would become limited in scope, peace-loving, and cheap and simple in their operations. Social divisions and (domestic and international) political unrest would wither away. Politics would be replaced by the 'cordial unison' (189) of civil society.

The Universal State

The model of the *universal state*, expressed clearly in G.W.F. Hegel's *Grundlinien der Philosophie des Rechts* (1821)[19] makes two important and indispensable contributions to modern theories of civil society and the state. First, in contrast to the model of the minimum state defended by Paine, civil society (*bürgerliche Gesellschaft*) is conceived not as a natural condition of freedom, but as a *historically produced* sphere of ethical life which is 'positioned' between the patriarchal household and the state. It includes the economy, social classes, corporations and institutions concerned with the administration of 'welfare' (*Polizei*) and civil law. Civil society is a mosaic of private individuals, classes, groups and institutions whose transactions are regulated by civil law and, as such, are not directly dependent upon the political state itself. Hegel emphasizes that civil society in this sense is not a pre-given and invariable substratum of life existing outside of space and time. Civil society is rather the outcome of a long and complex process of historical transformation: 'The creation of civil society is the achievement of the modern world' (339). Moreover, the 'system of needs' it develops represents a decisive and evident break with the natural environment (346-60). The modern bourgeois-directed economy, for instance, is a system of commodity production by means of commodities. It transforms nature into an instrument for the satisfaction of needs, which multiply and diversify, and therefore can no longer be understood as 'natural' (341-3; 346-51).

Hegel's second novel (and equally compelling) contribution to early modern theories of civil society and the state follows from this critique of naturalism. According to him, there is no necessary identity or harmony among the various elements of civil society. Harmony nourished by unadulterated love is an essential characteristic of the patriarchal family, but things are otherwise in civil society. Its multiple forms of interaction and collective solidarity are often incommensurable, fragile, and subject to serious conflict. Modern civil society is a restless battlefield where private (male) interest meets private (male) interest. It unfolds and develops in a blind, arbitrary, quasi-spontaneous manner. This means not only that it cannot overcome its own particularities, but also that it tends to paralyse and undermine its own pluralism; the exuberant development of one part of civil society may, and often does, impede or oppress its other parts.

This self-crippling tendency of civil society greatly troubles Hegel. It indicates why he emphasizes that modern civil society is incapable of overcoming its own fragmentation and resolving its inherent conflicts by itself. Civil society cannot remain 'civil' unless it is ordered politically. Only a supreme public authority – a constitutional state managed by the monarchy, the civil service and the Estates – can effectively remedy its injustices and synthesize its particular interests into a universal political community. From this perspective, the ideal state is neither a radical negation of a natural condition in perpetual war (Hobbes), nor an instrument for conserving and completing natural society (Locke), nor a simple mechanism for administering a naturally given and automatically self-governing civil society (Paine). Rather, the political state is conceived by Hegel as a new moment which re-presents society in its unity. Thanks to the supreme public authority, civil society is *aufgehoben*: it is at the same time preserved and overcome as a necessary, but subordinate aspect of a wider, more complex and higher community which is organized politically. According to Hegel, if the state demands from civil society only what is necessary for itself, and if it limits itself to guaranteeing this necessary minimum, then beyond this limit the state can and should permit considerable scope for the freedom of male individuals and groups living within civil society.

While Hegel consequently recommends against dissolving the separation of civil society from the state, it is clear that the degree to which civil society enjoys freedom from the state cannot be fixed through hard and fast general rules. Ultimately, from his perspective, the relationship of state and society can be determined only by weighing up, *from the standpoint of political reason*, the advantages and disadvantages of restricting the independence, abstract freedom and competitive pluralism of civil society in favour of universal state prerogatives. Hegel supposes two conditions under which state intervention (in his words, the state's 'purging of privileges and wrongs') is legitimate. First, the state may intervene in order to remedy injustices or inequalities within civil society – such as the domination of one or more classes by another, the pauperization of whole groups or the establishment of local oligarchies (within a region or municipality, for instance). Secondly, the supreme public power is justified in intervening directly in the affairs of civil society to protect and further the universal interests of the population – which the state itself defines!

Considered together, these two conditions constitute a very broad licence for state regulation and dominance of social life. In contrast to the model of the minimum state, moreover, the problem of how, and under which conditions, male citizens can question, reconsider and resist state power falsely claiming to be universal – the problem of political democracy and active citizenship – falls into obscurity. Simply stated, if the requirements of the public good set limits upon the autonomy of civil society, and if the state itself – a monarchic one at that – is ultimately responsible for determining these requirements, how can its interventions be identified and prevented as illegitimate? Hegel's failure to deal adequately with this quintessentially modern problem of (democratic) checks and balances on the universal state – his assumption that the monarchic state in the last instance is sovereign vis-à-vis all relationships within the family and civil society – weakens, even contradicts, his claims on behalf of an independent civil society which guarantees the 'living freedom' of individuals and groups. From the perspective of Hegel's metaphysics, indeed, the ideal of the universal state is understood as 'absolutely rational' (11-28; 399). It is the highest and concluding moment of a process of historical development in which reason actively works itself into the existing world. The universal state is the embodiment of the ethical idea, of mind (*Geist*) consciously realizing itself on earth. Given that the process of human history in this sense is 'the movement of God in the world' (403), the universal state conceived by Hegel must be regarded as a secular deity, whose claims upon its male citizens and female subjects are always for their benefit and, ultimately, unquestionable and unchallengeable.

The Democratic State

The final model with which I shall deal, the model of the *democratic state*, is defended in Alexis de Tocqueville's *De la démocratie en Amérique* (1835-40).[20] This work provides one of the earliest and most stimulating attempts to draw attention to the political dangers implicit in the model of the universal state. For Tocqueville, arguments in defence of a state which governs civil society in the name of the universal interest are implicated in a dangerous development little examined by his contemporaries: the growth of a new type of state despotism which is popularly elected. Drawing upon his study of American government and society (as well as his re-examination of the French Revolution in *L'Ancien Régime et la Révolution*), Tocqueville argues that it is not conflict and disorder generated by particular interests, but rather this new form of elected state despotism which is the principal danger confronting modern nations. More and more, social life is overpowered by political institutions which claim to represent and protect society in its unity. Paradoxically, an age which is committed strongly to democratic mechanisms for resisting inequalities of power and checking privilege also favours, in the name of equality and uniform provision, the gradual concentration of power and privilege in the hands of a centralized, administrative state. The power invested by civil society in this political apparatus is turned back on civil society itself. In the name of democracy, society falls under the sway of a 'benevolent', inquisitive and meddlesome state power which secures its well-being and robs it of its freedoms. The state becomes a regulator, inspector, adviser, educator and punisher of social life. It functions as a tutelary power without which civil society cannot cope: 'Centralized administration succeeds without difficulty in imparting a regularity to the daily routine of business; skilfully directs the details of the policing of society; represses small disorders and petty offences; maintains the status quo, such that society neither declines nor improves; and perpetuates in the social body a type of administrative drowsiness which the heads of the administration are inclined to call good order and public tranquillity' (158, vol. 1).

Tocqueville is appalled by this development. In his view, it threatens to sabotage the decisive victories of the democratic revolution and its goals of equality and freedom for all citizens. Consequently, he reasons that the decisive political problem of modern times concerns how the equalizing tendencies triggered by this democratic revolution can be preserved without allowing the state to abuse its powers and rob its citizens of their freedom. Tocqueville insists that equality with freedom *cannot* be secured by abolishing state institutions or reducing them to a minimum. Active and strong political institutions (here Tocqueville repeats an argument hinted at by Locke) are both necessary and desirable conditions of democratic freedom and equality. Just as all speakers of a language must have recourse to definite grammatical forms in order to express themselves, so citizens living together in a democracy are obliged to submit themselves to a political authority, without which they would fall into confusion and disorder. This is especially so within large and complex democratic countries, whose common interests, such as the formulation and administration of positive law and the conduct of foreign policy, cannot be taken care of effectively without a powerful and centralized governmental apparatus. However, in order to prevent the yoke of state despotism from descending on to the modern world, Tocqueville argues that mechanisms for preventing monopolies of power must be strengthened within the spheres of the state and civil society.

Within the realm of *political* institutions – here some key themes of the *Rights of Man* resurface – the self-paralysis of democracy can be minimized by ensuring that political power is distributed into many and various hands. A legislative power subject to periodic elections, combined with a separate executive authority, and an independent judiciary, for instance, minimize the risk of despotism by ensuring that the political power which governs civil society frequently changes hands and adopts different courses of action, and is therefore prevented from becoming excessively centralized and all-encompsassing. Tocqueville also stresses the very rich democratic consequences of citizens' action *within* state institutions. The American jury system is seen as exemplary of this principle of supplementing representative democratic mechanisms (e.g., citizens' election of representatives to the legislature) with *direct* citizen participation. The jury system, in his view, facilitates citizens' self-government as well as teaching them how to govern others prudently and fairly; they learn how to judge fellow citizens as they would wish to be judged themselves (376, vol. 1).

Tocqueville is certain that these kinds of political checks upon despotism must be reinforced by the growth and development of civil associations which lie beyond the immediate control of state institutions. Tocqueville no doubt underestimated the democratic potential of workers' resistance to the grip of capitalist manufacturing industry. He failed to consider the possibility of a *socialist* civil society – a type of ultra-modern civil society no longer dominated by capitalist enterprises, patriarchal households and other undemocratic forms of association. Tocqueville nonetheless saw correctly that forms of civil association such as scientific and literary circles, schools, publishers, inns, manufacturing enterprises, religious organizations, municipal associations and independent households are crucial barriers against state despotism. He never tires of repeating that the 'independent eye of society' (236, vol. 1) – comprising a plurality of interacting, self-organized and constantly vigilant civil associations – is necessary for consolidating the democratic revolution. In contrast to political forms of involvement (such as participation in elections and jury service) which focus upon wider, more general interests of the community, civil associations consist of combinations of citizens preoccupied with 'small affairs' (150, vol. 2). Civil associations no doubt enable citizens to negotiate wider undertakings of concern to the whole polity. But they do more than this: they also nurture and powerfully deepen the local and particular freedoms so necessary for maintaining democratic equality and preventing the tyranny of minorities by majorities. Tocqueville probably underestimated the likelihood of conflicts among different civil associations and with the state itself (a consequence of his tendency to exaggerate the extent of democratization in modern societies). He nonetheless saw correctly that civil associations are arenas in which individuals can direct their attention beyond their own selfish, conflictual, narrowly private goals; through their activities in civil associations, they come to perceive that they are not self-propelling monads, and that in order to obtain their fellow citizens' support they must often lend them their co-operation.

Tocqueville acknowledges that civil associations always depend for their survival and co-ordination upon centralized state institutions. Yet freedom and equality among individuals and groups depend also upon preserving types of organizations which nurture local freedoms and provide for the active expression of particular interests. A pluralist and self-organizing civil society independent of the state is an indispensable condition of democracy. Whoever promotes the unification of state and civil society endangers the democratic revolution. State power without social obstacles is always hazardous and undesirable, a licence for despotism.

The Myth of Collective Harmony

By the time of Tocqueville, the early modern discussion of the relationship between civil society and the state reaches a climax. It then enters a period of decline, appearing only sporadically. (It is evident, for example, in the late nineteenth-century liberal protest against growing state intervention; in Durkheim's theory of the importance of intermediate social organizations – small 'safety nets' between the individual and the state – for administering property, guaranteeing mutual aid and preventing anomie and other pathologies resulting from the decline of the family, church and territorial units; and in the theory of functional democracy developed by the Guild Socialists and the Austro-Marxists.)[21] From the second half of the nineteenth century, European political and social thought begins increasingly to embrace the mythical assumption that complex social systems can be brought to order, pacified and emancipated from conflict by annulling the division between social and political power. Guided by this myth of collective harmony, political and society theory sets itself the task of undoing and reversing an important achievement of European modernity: the differentiation between social life and state institutions.

This yearning for organic unity is most strongly evident in nineteenth-century utopian thought. Many self-proclaimed utopians believed that the material causes of social and political events could be studied by methods analogous to those of the natural sciences, and that the knowledge so gleaned could unearth a principle of human perfectibility and universal harmony operating in society with the efficiency and comprehensiveness of Newtonian laws of motion.[22]

The anticipation of organic unity is not restricted to utopianism. Its influence is much wider, and generally comprises two forms. One type of organicism is evident in the writings of Comte and St-Simon, Marx and Engels, the anarchists and, as Gouldner observed, many contributors to the nineteenth-century sociological tradition.[23] Their version of the myth of collective harmony extends the horizons of the model of the minimum state by defending the thesis of the (inevitable or possible) withering away of the modern state. It is argued that future forms of social life can be emancipated from state force and other obsolete or parasitic forms of power, and that this would result in homeostasis: the interdependent elements of the future social order would tend towards a relatively stable, peaceful and self-ordering equilibrium. The second version of the myth of collective harmony is inspired by exactly the inverse assumption. It pursues the terms of the model of the universal state beyond Hegel, by supposing that the state can and should fully integrate or abolish society. Among the earliest and most influential examples is Lorenz von Stein's *Geschichter der sozialen Bewegung in Frankreich von 1789 bis auf unsere Tage* (1850). Within this tradition, existing civil society is conceived as a realm of disorder, domination or corruption which therefore must be regulated, dominated and annulled through the superior rationality and order guaranteed by state power.

These two variants of the myth of collective harmony have strongly influenced the socialist tradition. They are conventionally recognized, respectively, as self-managing socialism and state socialism. An early example of the former is Robert Owen's essay on *Home Colonies* (1841).[24] This sketches the transition to an ideal society comprising hundreds of interdependent small communities linked together not by state institutions, but by railways! These 'home colonies' would be guided by an elected governor and administered by non-political committees. The colonies would be based primarily on the principles of agricultural production, communal living, voluntary co-operation and a new morality based on rational knowledge, benevolence and happiness. They would be self-sufficient, and provide every member with the necessities and comforts of life. Distribution would be determined mainly by the principle of need, waged labour would be abolished, and monetary transactions would virtually disappear. Children would be compulsorily educated into the physical, moral, intellectual and technical ways of the colony. Scientific inventions would reduce the quantity of manual labour, and transform it into a 'healthy and agreeable exercise' (67). Expanded leisure time for both sexes would make possible 'mental improvement and rational enjoyment' (69); the abundance of wealth resulting from scientific invention would facilitate the building of baths, scientific observatories, gymnasia, libraries, pleasure parks and landscaped gardens. Within these self-governing communities, the social and political evils generated by modern capitalism – private property, poverty, sickness, false value standards, government authority and religion – would all disappear. The colonists would become rational, charitable and tolerant of others. Equality, happiness and peace would replace misery, greed and violence. Individuals would declare their solidarity with the co-operative principle, and the social obligations so formed would render conflicts unlikely, and unnecessary. In the new world of self-governing colonies, there would be 'no human slavery, servitude, or inequality of condition; except the natural inequality of age and experience; which will, for ever, preserve order and harmony in society' (2).

While Owen's *Home Colonies* is by no means a 'representative' text of the self-managing tradition of socialist thought, it does highlight several of its deepest and most pivotal assumptions. Self-managing socialism emphasizes the ultimate aim of abolishing political power through social initiatives and class struggles from 'outside' or 'underneath' the state. And on the basis of the reductionist assumption that all important power conflicts are ultimately traceable to property-based (i.e., class) antagonisms, it is supposed that under conditions of genuine socialism no serious conflicts of interest will arise among individuals or groups, and that therefore the production, management and distribution of goods and services will not depend upon political power and its mechanisms of conflict mediation and suppression; the state, like handicrafts, would become a historical curiosity, to be replaced by routinized bookkeeping and the mere administration of things. It is further supposed that all decisions in public affairs, no matter how small or insignificant, will be taken directly by the community as a whole, and without serious conflicts of interest. Separate political bodies for reaching agreement, encouraging compromises or reducing conflict will therefore be unnecessary. Exploitation would become a thing of the past. Social relations would become unified and transparent. Associated individuals would take complete charge of their lives.

Since the Bolshevik Revolution, the other socialist tradition, state socialism, has exerted a stronger influence upon left-wing politics. Advocates of state socialism emphasize the need to regulate and incorporate civil society from above through political means. They typically suppose that the state is (or is capable of becoming) the living embodiment or caretaker of the universal interest. The ethical superiority of the state over all particular interests is seen to be crystallized in the consciousness of functionaries and/or party-political leaders. Only they are capable of identifying and merging their particular interest with the universal interest (expressed in phrases such as 'the emancipation of the working class'; 'the struggle to build socialism'; 'freedom and equality of all citizens'). Their universal consciousness and action within the state make possible the synthesis of the general good with the aspirations and struggles of particular strata of the social and political order. The state is the guarantor of the universal interest; its function is to emancipate civil society from its self-inflicted calamities.

This position is exemplified in Ferdinand Lassalle's *Arbeiter-Programm* (1862).[25] Every ruling class, Lassalle observes, invariably secures its property by maintaining the state to oppress the underclasses. The bourgeoisie are no exception. It conceives the state's ethical function in terms of the protection of the personal freedom and property of individuals. The working class – whose interests are synonymous with those of the entire human species – are justified in demanding the transformation of this 'night-watchman state' (65) into a State that nurtures and perfects freedom, which is the destiny of the human species. According to Lassalle (here quoting August Boeth) it is necessary to enlarge the ethical duties and tasks of the State to the fullest extent: 'the State should be the organization, in which the whole virtue of humanity should realize itself' (65). The State must formally grant universal suffrage (thereby enfranchising the universal class). It should improve the financial conditions of the working classes (guaranteeing them employment and an ample wage). Above all, the State should be responsible for the creation of an 'ethically ordered community' (64).[26] This state-dominated community would be based not on conflict and selfishness (as in the present bourgeois epoch), but on the harmonizing principles of the dawning historical era: solidarity and reciprocity.

Activists, officials and observers within the contemporary socialist tradition customarily think of self-managing socialism and state socialism as diametrically opposed ideals and strategies. Their mutual hostility is taken as self-evident: state socialism understands the essence of socialism as the abolition of social classes through the nationalization of property and social life as a whole; self-managing socialism envisages socialism as the abolition of the state and social classes, and their substitution by the 'free association of the direct producers' (Engels). This assumption is often reinforced by specifying the history of disputes between the two variants of socialism: the Fourierist–Owenite emphasis on building local networks of genuinely social communities versus the St-Simonian strategy of capturing national states, and transforming them into great productive organizations guided by scientific expertise; the conflict between Bakunin and Marx during the First International; Sorel's attack upon the programme of party-directed politics (see essay 4); the polemic of Anton Pannekoek against Kautsky's social democracy in *Neue Zeit*; Rosa Luxemburg's critique of Lenin; the resistance of the

Russian anarcho-syndicalists to Trotsky's proposal to nationalize the trade unions; the bitter conflict between the anarcho-syndicalist *Confederacion Nacional del Trabajo/Federaccion Anarquista Iberica* and the Communists; and so on.

No doubt, the life or death gravity and consequences of this fault line of conflicts running through the whole history of the socialist tradition should not be forgotten or underestimated. I would argue, nevertheless, that these conflicts – between 'libertarianism' and 'dirigisme' – normally have been embedded within a deeper *agreement* about the ultimate aim of unifying the social and political domains. In other words, they have been bound together secretly by their mutual anticipation of an end to social division and political conflict. (This deep ideology of homeostasis, of the possibility of constructing a society in which all particular interests are integrated into the whole, so that the actual social organism that results accords with the common interest, is suggested by the apparently eclectic combination of libertarian and statist assumptions within certain models of the stage-like transition to socialism, for instance, in the Bakuninist programme of direct action inspired by a revolutionary avant-garde,[27] or in the Marxian theory of the dictatorship of the proletariat.)[28] Seen in this light, the vast majority of disputes within the socialist tradition of the past century and a half have been mainly about the *means* of achieving a post-capitalist future. What has been left unchallenged, and therefore agreed upon tacitly, is the assumption that, at some ultimate point, and despite numerous recognized and unanticipated obstacles, human emancipation is possible through the abolition of class divisions, the consequent abolition of the distinction between civil society and the state and, thereupon, the trouble-free co-ordination and unification of the personal and collective existence of each individual and group. Thus, from the time of its appearance in the first quarter of the nineteenth century, the word 'socialism' means: living in common, sociably and harmoniously, within a system marked by the collective ownership of property, and the collective planning and regulation of the social environment within which human beings rationally interact.[29]

...And Marx?

Precisely this assumption about the possibility of homeostasis is strongly evident in Marx's discussion of civil society and the state, to which I return in closing. The modern bourgeois era, Marx pointed out, is unique in so far as it effects a 'separation' of political and social forms of stratification. It subdivides the human species for the first time into social classes; divorces individuals' legal status from their socioeconomic role within civil society; and sunders each individual into both private egoist and pubic citizen. By contrast, feudal society had a directly political character. The main elements of civil life (property, the household, forms of labour) assumed the form of landlordism, estates and corporations. The individual members of feudal society enjoyed no 'private sphere'. Their fate was bound up inextricably with the organization to which they belonged, and which was intermeshed in turn with a mosaic of other 'public' organizations. The 'throwing off of the political yoke'[30] is a distinguishing mark of modern bourgeois orders. Civil society, the realm of private needs and interests, waged labour and private right, is emancipated from political control, and becomes the basis and presupposition of the state.

It should be clear that by acknowledging the significance of the distinction between civil society and the state, Marx aligns himself with the preoccupations of the early modern tradition of political thought. Yet Marx is also highly critical of each of the post-Hobbesian attempts to delimit state action by distinguishing between the state and the non-state or civil spheres. His objections are often compelling. Yet they produce new problems, three clusters of which must be addressed by a fully democratic theory of civil society and the state.

To begin with, problems arise from Marx's attempt to explain the origins and development of modern civil society. In contrast to the first three models discussed (those of Hobbes, Locke and Paine), civil society is represented by Marx – correctly – as a contingent historical phenomenon, and not as a naturally given state of affairs. Modern, state-guaranteed civil societies do not conform to eternal laws of nature, and they certainly do not emerge under pressure from some 'natural propensity to society' (Paine). They are historically determinate entities, characterized by particular forms and relations of production, class divisions and struggles, and protected by 'corresponding' political-legal mechanisms. And not only are bourgeois civil societies products of modern times. Their life expectancy is limited, inasmuch as they give birth to the proletariat, the class with radical chains, the class in civil society that is not of civil society, the potentially universal class that signals the dissolution of all classes.

Although Marx correctly emphasizes the historical specificity of modern civil societies, his analysis of their growth and development is one-dimensional. Marx seemed incapable of developing a critical theory of civil society oriented not only to its system of production, but also to the crucially important dynamics of *other* forms of civil life, including households, voluntary associations, professions, communications media and disciplinary institutions such as schools, prisons and hospitals. In contrast to the contributions of Hegel and Tocqueville, the power relations of civil society are explained by Marx mainly in terms of forces and relations of *production*. Civil society is viewed as the economic form in which the bourgeoisie creates a world after its own image. The institutional complexity of civil society is thereby concealed: modern life is analysed in terms of the simplifying dichotomy of economic or political (and ideological) structures, that is, infra- or superstructural elements.

This 'economism' has plagued and crippled the Marxian theory since its inception, explaining why Marx had little or nothing of lasting importance to say about a variety of social phenomena of great importance to democratic theory and politics. For example, the original Marxian approach is blind to the ways in which the emergence of the modern bourgeois mode of production was facilitated by the *prior* development of social organs of self-defence in the market towns and peasant villages of the decaying feudal order. The development of the economic powers of the bourgeoisie depended on their prior capacity to insulate themselves from older feudal authorities and to develop new ways of life through a variety of *non-economic* associations, such as communes, unions, tribunals, leagues and confederacies.[31] Furthermore, the Marxian interpretation fails to see that bourgeois civil societies, past or present, cannot be understood purely and simply as spheres of egoism, private property and class conflict. Marx observed that the 'natural bonds' of human association are dissolved for the first time ever in the acid of bourgeois competition and egoism of civil society: 'Only in the eighteenth century, in "civil society", do the various forms of social connectedness confront the individual as a mere means towards his private purposes, as external necessity.'[32] Eager to stress the bourgeois-dominated character of modern civil societies, Marx exaggerated their degree of atomization. He neglected the important (if deeply ambiguous) role played by patriarchal households in securing male control of civil society *and* in facilitating workers' periodic withdrawal or permanent escape from the dictates of the labour market. (See essay 3. Hegel's exclusion of family life from the idea of civil society no doubt contributed to this error.) Marx also ignored the growth, from the eighteenth century, of new types of institutions – such as organizations of professional engineers, doctors, lawyers, architects and psychiatrists – whose knowledge, power and authority within civil society cannot be explained by a *class* model of power.[33] Finally, Marx's 'economistic' account of civil society led him to ignore the democratic potential of the type of citizens' associations cherished by Paine and Tocqueville. His lack of respect or enthusiasm for mechanisms such as an independent press, freedom of assembly and rights to vote – which were interpreted as the 'form' through which only bourgeois power is consolidated, rather than as a necessary condition of post-bourgeois democracy – exposed the Marxian idea of socialism to political dictatorship. It encouraged its deliverance into the hands of revolutionaries contemptuous of 'bourgeois freedom' and obsessed with trampling the *civil* roots of political democracy in the name of eliminating 'capitalism'.*

A second cluster of problems is generated by Marx's attack upon universalist conceptions of the modern state. The modern state, Marx argues persuasively, is not a rationally agreed upon apparatus capable of harmonizing the discordant elements of civil society and binding them into a higher unity. Under exceptional circumstances – Marx discusses the examples of Bismarck's Germany and the Bonapartist state in France – the modern state appears to develop a relatively greater independence from civil society, due either to the persistence of feudal remnants which block the growth of the bourgeoisie, or to a

---

*Cf. 'On the Jewish Question', pp. 236-7: 'none of the so-called rights of man [equality, liberty, security, property] goes beyond the egoistic man, the man withdrawn into himself, his private interest and his private choices and separated from the community as a member of civil society.' Some difficulties of this view are discussed by Steven Lukes, *Marxism and Morality*, Oxford 1985. Marx's failure to see the democratic potential of an undemocratic civil society independent of the state is explained in an interesting way by Svetozar Stojanović in a letter dated 25 September 1985: 'The idea of the division between civil society and the state in capitalism should be interpreted not primarily as a limit upon state action, making it accountable to civil society, but in a quite *radical* way: the emergence of capitalism saw the creation, for the first time in history, of a structure in which *no* class could *monopolize* or *directly* control the state. It is this development that makes democratization under capitalism possible. And this is why I think it important to distinguish between a *non-ruling dominant class* (like the bourgeoisie) and a *ruling class* (such as the *nomenklatura*).'

stalemate among the classes (or class fractions) of civil society.[34] But these are exceptions. Marx rejects the models of the state defended by Hobbes, Locke and Hegel, each of whom supposes that the state can be a separate entity that embodies universal interests and rules impartially over its subjects. The modern state is an illusory universal community. It is in fact a coercive institution which both reflects and reinforces the particular, historically specific interests of civil society. 'Legal relations as well as forms of state are to be grasped neither from themselves nor from the so-called general development of the human mind, but rather have their roots in the material conditions of life, the sum total of which Hegel, following the example of the Englishmen and Frenchmen of the eighteenth century, combines under the name of "civil society".'[35] The modern state is normally a secondary or derivative phenomenon. It is a bourgeois state, an instrument for protecting and managing the affairs of the bourgeoisie and its allies; 'the power of the state', comments Marx in a well-known sentence of the first volume of *Das Kapital*, is 'the concentrated and organized force of society'.[36]

Within its historical context, this thesis undoubtedly represented a liberating provocation against the whole of the early modern tradition of liberal political thought. Its fascination with *raison d'état* was subverted. In addition, the liberal silence (or pompous noise) about the forms of social power and exploitation crystallized in the market system of commodity production and exchange was effectively shattered. Yet this important breakthrough produced a new theoretical silence about the power specific to *state* institutions. By helping to overthrow the state-centred approach of the old liberal preoccupation with limiting state power in favour of civil society and, thus, by instituting a society-centred perspective on state and para-state institutions – by concluding that the anatomy of civil society is to be found in political economy – the Marxian theory generally defended a conception of the state as little more than an arena within which societal conflicts are fought out, interests mediated, and the ensuing results authoritatively confirmed.

A contemporary democratic theory of civil society and the state – one which seeks to challenge the statist practices of post-war social democracy, the advances of neo-conservatism, and the alarming growth rate of military dictatorships and totalitarian regimes – must reject this society-centred approach and its one-sided assumption that 'political conditions are only the official expression of civil society'. Democratic theory must supplement analyses of social power with investigations of the capacities of state institutions to transform both their domestic and international contexts. This approach would need to avoid the twin dangers of glorifying state power and overestimating its efficacy. It would address the sources of growth and decay of military dictatorships and totalitarian regimes. Where applicable, it would concentrate upon the complex patterns of *interaction* between civil societies and states. This approach would represent something of an extension of the central concerns of early modern political thinking prior to Marx. It would consider the extent to which various types of contemporary state (and para-state) mechanisms function to initiate, stabilize or reduce inequalities of social power, property and status, that is, to support or undermine given patterns of social closure and social openness. Consideration also would be given to the ways in which state policies often successfully pursue courses of action at variance with dominant social classes, groups and movements, thereby strengthening – in a zero-sum fashion – the scope and power of state institutions to tax their subjects, produce wealth, and to maintain domestic order and control over their international environment.

A post-Marxian theory of the interaction of state and civil society would need to acknowledge other possibilities, however. The power of civil society and the capacity of state institutions can increase together, in a positive-sum interaction, or they may also decline together, in a negative-sum way, as when the state's policymaking and administrative capacities stagnate along with civil society's capacity for independent, self-determined activity.[37] It is evident that democratization – the pluralization of power within a civil society protected and encouraged by an accountable framework of state institutions – is only one possible form of state/civil society relationship. Questions about how it might be achieved must be asked, and in a way that is free from the Marxian prejudice against democracy in this revised sense. These questions would likely be indebted to thinkers such as Paine, Hegel and Tocqueville, and could include: Which types of state intervention in civil society tend to paralyse the democratization process? How can this paralysis be prevented? Which types of post-capitalist property arrangements within civil society best facilitate its resistance to overextended state power? How can state institutions and policies be transformed so as to maximize their democratic character *and* effectiveness? Might the strengthening of certain state institutions and the weakening of others be a necessary condition of the democratization process? And which types of institutions can best operate as 'messengers' between civil society and the state?

A third set of problems derives from Marx's anticipation of the abolition of the state and the withering away of conflict in future communist society. In contrast to the minimum, universal and democratic models of state power discussed earlier in this essay, Marx perceives the modern separation of the state and civil society as a transitory and undesirable phenomenon. The modern state is alienated social power, and for this reason struggles to abolish alienation within civil society signal the obsolescence of the state. Modern civil society produces a universal class, the proletariat, whose growing resistance to the capitalist mode of production increasingly defines the pre-state or non-state condition not as a war of each against all (as in the models of the security state and the constitutional state), but as a site of struggle between social classes. Marx is convinced that the probable victories of the proletariat make possible the reabsorption of state institutions into an active social order freed from bourgeois domination. The exploiting social classes would be expropriated, and the means of production placed under the control of associations of producers. Only through this prior transformation of civil society by class struggle and the abolition of the division between civil society and its coercive state could the proletariat complete its emancipation. It would be able self-consciously to organize its powers of self-determination into a stable and harmonious social order – a communist society in which no one would rule over anyone else, and in which power would be exercised by all or, more accurately, by nobody. Power would simply disappear from communist society.

Marx believed that 'freedom consists in converting the state from an organ superimposed upon society into one completely subordinate to it.'[38] He assumed that the successful struggle of the working class for control over civil society would permit the abolition of the state. In turn, this would release a flood of creative activity. Freedom consists not in maximizing the independence of self-defining subjects acting within a framework of political-legal institutions. It rather consists in breaking down the barriers between different spheres of life, and thereby maximizing unity, harmony and fulfilment among self-determining and fully conscious social individuals. Marx supposed that state apparatuses could be abolished and replaced by simple administrative facilities. He believed that struggles between administrators and other communists, or conflicts over the distribution of the surplus product, would simply not arise. All communist beings would make decisions on all public matters, no matter how insignificance, and without resorting to separate political institutions for securing agreements or reconciling conflicts. Even the notion of being a citizen – acting in concert with others to resist or defend certain policy goals – would disappear.

In so defending a species of the collective harmony myth, Marx's formulation *presupposed* the central role of the working class in the struggle for socialism. It failed to recognize that the democratic potential of workers within any particular country depends upon such factors as historical traditions, the structure of industrial relations, state strategies, and their ability to form bonds of solidarity with other groups within civil society, and *not* upon their ascribed role as a 'universal class' or privileged subject of history. Marx's formulation also failed to consider whether the social victories of the proletariat might have led, along the lines of a radicalized, more property-sensitive version of Tocqueville's model of the democratic state, to the democratization of the state and to the preservation and radical democratic reform of civil society. The possibility of a state-guaranteed *socialist* civil society, one no longer dominated by commodity production and exchange, never occurred to Marx. Additionally, Marx's vision of a conflict- and power-free communist society failed to acknowledge that state institutions would always be required to some degree in complex, post-capitalist systems.[39] Consequently, he failed to see that these systems would necessitate safeguards against the abuse of state power so as to make it practically impossible for it to grow to suffocating proportions. By anticipating a 'true democracy' in which 'the functions of government become simple administrative functions',[40] the Marxian theory consigned a whole tradition of theoretical reflection on the scope and limits of state power to the museums of bourgeois prehistory.

There can be no doubt that the Marxian understanding of the state/civil society relationship has exercised an extraordinary influence upon the socialist tradition since the nineteenth century. Not all of this influence has been fruitless or unwarranted. It reminds us that political emancipation, as Marx argued against Bruno Bauer and others, is not equivalent to social emancipation. It emphasizes that the group structures and institutions of modern civil societies are not naturally given systems of life, subject only to spontaneous adaptations and modifiable only at considerable risks. The Marxian perspective thereby helped sensitize us to those unjust and undemocratic forms of class power in modern civil societies which early liberal discourse justified or took for granted. I am nevertheless convinced that the economism of the Marxian approach, its presumption of a 'universal class', and its explicit commitment to the myth of collective harmony must be rejected outright. If the 'road to socialism' is from here on to be considered as a process of democratically maintaining and transforming (and not, as Marx supposed, abolishing) the division between civil society and the state, then a central task of contemporary democratic theory is to stimulate awareness of the deficiencies of the Marxian theory discussed in this essay. I am not altogether certain where this type of discussion might lead – all genuinely democratic theory is adventurous, after all. But I am certain that the retrieval and reformulation of the old 'bourgeois' reflections on civil society and the limits of state power is a necessary condition of stimulating the contemporary democratic imagination. In turn, that attempt to retrieve what is important from the past while living fully in the present might imply the need for thoroughly rewritten, fully democratic versions of texts such as the *Rights of Man*, the *Grundlinien der Philosophie des Rechts* and *De la démocratie en Amérique*.

Notes

1. See Jan Tesař, 'Totalitarian Dictatorships as a Phenomenon of the Twentieth Century and the Possibilities of Overcoming Them', *International Journal of Politics*, vol. xi, 1, Spring 1981, pp. 85-100; Ladislav Hejdánek, 'Prospects for democracy and socialism in eastern Europe', in Václav Havel et al., *The Power of the Powerless*, edited John Keane, London 1985, pp. 141-51; Leszek Kolakowski, 'Marxist roots of Stanlinism', in Robert C. Tucker, ed. *Stalinism: Essays in Historical Interpretation*, New York 1977; Agnes Heller, 'Opposition in Eastern Europe: Dilemmas and Prospects', in Rudolf L. Tökés, ed., *Opposition in Eastern Europe*, London and Basingstoke 1979, pp. 187-208.

2. Nicos Poulantzas, *Political Power and Social Classes*, London 1973, pp. 124-5. Poulantzas here criticizes the state–civil society distinction for unnecessarily introducing 'subjectivism and historicism' into socialist theoretical debates. The distinction is seen to frustrate the 'scientific examination' of the relatively autonomous relationship between class struggle and the capitalist state, since it supposes that the agents of production are autonomous individual subjects, rather than (as they are in reality) agents of struggling social classes. In his last writings, Poulantzas's harsh criticism of the state–civil society distinction is moderated in favour of an understanding of democracy parallel to the one defended here. See, for example, *State, Power, Socialism*, London 1978, p. 256, where he insists that the essential political question facing contemporary socialists is 'how is it possible radically to transform the state in such a manner that the extension and deepening

of political freedoms and the institutions of representative democracy ... are combined with the unfurling of forms of direct democracy and the mushrooming of self-management bodies?'

3. See *Civil Society and the State*, introduction and part 2; and the seminal essay by Alvin Gouldner, 'Civil Society in Capitalism and Socialism', in *The Two Marxisms. Contradictions and Anomalies in the Development of Theory*, London and Basingstoke 1980, pp. 355-73. Similar themes are explored in Jean Cohen's *Class and Civil Society: The Limits of Marxian Critical Theory*, Amherst 1982, although its criticisms of the Marxian tradition rest upon an ahistorical (and therefore idealized) concept of civil society. Modern civil society is seen as equivalent to '*legality* (private law; civil, political, social equality and rights), *plurality* (autonomous, self-constituted voluntary associations), and *publicity* (spaces of communication, public participation, the genesis, conflict, reflection on, and articulation of political will and social norms)' (p. 255).

4. Karl Marx, *The Poverty of Philosophy*, Moscow 1973, pp. 60-61 (emphasis original). On Marx's indebtedness to early socialist theories of civil society and the state, see Richard Adamiak, 'State and Society in Early Socialist Thought', *Survey*, vol. 26, 1, Winter 1982, pp. 1-28.

5. See Thomas Eschmann, 'Studies on the Notion of Society in St Thomas Aquinas', *Mediaeval Studies*, vol. 8, 1944, pp. 1-42; Manfred Riedel, 'Gesellschaft, bürgerliche', in O. Brunner et al., eds, *Geschichtliche Grundbegriffe. Historisches Lexikon zur politisch-sozialen Sprache in Deutschland*, Stuttgart 1975, vol. 2, pp. 719-800; and my 'Despotism and Democracy. The Origins and Development of the Distinction Between Civil Society and the State, 1750-1850', in *Civil Society and the State*.

6. Wilhelm von Humboldt, *Ideen zu einem Versuch die Grenzen der Wirksamkeit des Staats zu bestimmen*, (1792), Stuttgart 1982.

7. These brief methodological remarks are elaborated in 'More Theses on the Philosophy of History', in James Tully, ed., *Meaning and Context. Quentin Skinner and His Critics*, Cambridge 1988.

8. Harold J. Laski, *The Rise of European Liberalism*, London 1962; Max Horkheimer and Theodor W. Adorno, *Dialektik der Aufklärung*, Frankfurt am Main 1969, p. 164: 'Every bourgeois [bürgerliche] characteristic, despite its difference and indeed because of it, expressed the same thing: the harshness of the competitive society. The individual who supported this society bore its blemish; his apparent freedom was the product of its economic and social apparatus.' A similar argument is developed in Anthony Arblaster, *The Rise and Decline of Western Liberalism*, Oxford 1984.

9. The failure to recognize the important historical shifts of meaning of the distinction is endemic to the literature on the subject. Examples include Andrew Arato, 'Civil Society Against the State: Poland 1980-81', *Telos*, 47, Spring 1981, pp. 23-47; Jean Cohen, *Class and Civil Society*; Boris Frankel, *Beyond the State? Dominant Theories and Socialist Strategies*, London 1983, especially part 1. The same weakness is evident in neo-Gramscian usages of the concept of civil society; see, for example, John Urry, *The Anatomy of Capitalist Societies. The Economy, Civil Society and the State*, London and Basingstoke 1981.

10. Thomas Hobbes, *Leviathan, or The Matter, Forme, and Power of a Common-Wealth Ecclesiasticall and Civill*, edited C.B. Macpherson, Harmondsworth 1972. All citations are from this edition.

11. Hobbes constantly describes the commands of the sovereign power, which is supposed to hold all individuals in awe, as 'authorized' by the subjects themselves. See ibid, pp. 265, 276, 279, 720-1.

12. Ibid, p. 215: 'Injustice, Ingratitude, Arrogance, Pride, Iniquity, Acception

of persons, and the rest, can never be made lawfull.'

13. John Locke, *An Essay Concerning the True Original, Extent, and End of Civil Government*, in *Two Treatises of Government*, edited Peter Laslett, New York 1963, pp. 305-541. All citations are from this edition.

14. These 'individuals' (as Locke says in the fourth of the *Essays on the Law of Nature*, edited W. Von Leyden, Oxford 1954, pp. 156-7) feel themselves 'urged to enter into society by a certain propensity of nature, and to be prepared for the maintenance of society by the gift of speech and through the intercourse of language'.

15. Cf. Thomas Hobbes, *Leviathan*, p. 313: 'The Soveraign of a Common-wealth, be it an Assembly or one Man, is not Subject to the Civill Lawes. For having power to make, and repeale Lawes, he may when he pleaseth, free himselfe from that subjection, by repealing those Lawes that trouble him, and making of new.'

16. The scope of Locke's strictures upon absolute sovereign power should not be exaggerated. They are weakened, even contradicted by his recommendations concerning the sovereign's *prerogative powers* – those very broadly defined, discretionary powers to provide for 'the public good'. As Locke says, this type of state power is unlimited; it can be exercised even against the positive laws of the day, and includes the legitimate right of preserving civil society by 'cutting off its corrupt or threatening parts (Two Treatises pp. 420; 424-5; 429). For the enfranchised, this prerogative power is threatening enough: in the name of the public good, sovereigns can well endanger the liberties of particular individuals (424-5). And for the great mass of disenfranchised, prerogative power, if judged according to Locke's trust principle, is equivalent to tyranny. The disenfranchised are the mere objects of rulers who have unlimited powers to define what is for their ('the public's') benefit. In this sense, the disenfranchised are in, but not of civil society. Civil society is a world to which they are obliged unconditionally, but from which they are excluded completely; without civil rights of any kind, they are playthings of a state power which can never be contested as illegitimate.

17. Locke refers explicitly to Richard Hooker's important distinction between 'sociable life' and a 'Common-weal' (*Of the Lawes of Ecclesiasticall Politie* (1632), 1, i, section 10; quoted by Locke, p. 403): 'Two Foundations there are which bear up publick Societies, the one a natural inclination, whereby all men desire sociable Life and Fellowship; the other an Order, expressly or secretly agreed upon, touching the manner of their union in living together; the latter is that which we call the Law of a Common-weal, the very Soul of a Politick Body, the parts whereof are by Law animated, held together, and set on work in such actions as the common good requireth.'

18. All citations are from Thomas Paine, *Rights of Man*, edited Henry Collins, Harmondsworth 1977.

19. All citations are drawn from G.W.F. Hegel, *Grundlinien der Philosophie des Rechts*, Frankfurt am Main 1976. Translations are my own.

20. All citations are drawn from Alexis de Tocqueville, *De la démocratie en Amérique*, preface by François Furet, Paris 1981, two volumes. All translations are my own.

21. See, for example, Herbert Spencer, *The Man versus the State*, London 1902; Karl Renner, 'Demokratie und Rätesystem', *Der Kampf*, xiv, 1921, pp. 54-67; G.D.H. Cole, *Guild Socialism Restated*, London 1920; Emile Durkheim, *Professional Ethics and Civic Morals*, Glencoe, Illinois 1958, and *The Division of Labour in Society*, New York and London 1964, p. 28: 'A nation can be maintained only if, between the State and the individual, there is intercalated a whole series of secondary groups near enough to the individuals to attract them strongly in their sphere of

action and drag them, in this way, into the general torrent of social life.'

22. Barbara Goodwin, *Social Science and Utopia. Nineteenth-Century Models of Social Harmony*, Hassocks 1978.

23. Alvin W. Gouldner, 'Civil Society in Capitalism and Socialism', in *The Two Marxisms. Contradictions and Anomalies in the Development of Theory*, London and Basingstoke 1980, p. 363: 'early sociology rejected the dominance of society by the state, saw the state as undermining society and as essentially archaic insofar as its characteristic form was domination by force.'

24. All citations are from Robert Owen, *A Developement [sic] of the Principles and Plans on which to Establish Self-Supporting Home Colonies*, London 1841.

25. All citations are from Ferdinand Lassalle, *Arbeiter-Programm. Über den besonderen Zusammenhang der gegenwärtigen Geschichtsperiode mit der Idee des Arbeiterstandes*, Leipzig 1919. All translations are my own.

26. The Hegelian roots of Lassalle's conception of the ideal state are evident throughout this essay, especially on pp. 67-8: 'In contrast to all previous states, a state which was ruled by the ethical idea of the working class would be driven no longer unconsciously and against its will by the nature of things and the force of circumstances. Rather, it would make this ethical nature of the state its mission, with the highest clarity of vision and consciousness. It would complete, freely and with perfect consistency, what until now has been derived imperfectly from reluctant and opposed wills ... It would thereby produce a soaring of the human spirit, a development of a quantity of happiness, culture, well-being and freedom without example in the history of the world.'

27. This programme is summarized in Mikhail Bakunin's letter to Nechaev, written 2 January 1870, and reprinted in Michael Confino, 'Bakunin et Nechaev', *Cahiers du Monde Russe et Soviétique*, vol. 7, 4, 1966, pp. 629-30: 'Total destruction of the world of the legal state and of all the bourgeois so-called civilization, by means of a popular revolution, directed not by an official dictatorship but by a collective, imperceptible and anonymous dictatorship of the partisans of the complete liberation of the people from all oppression, firmly united in a secret society and acting everywhere and always with the same goal and according to the same programme.'

28. Karl Marx, *Critique of the Gotha Programme*, in *Selected Works*, vol. 3, Moscow 1970, p. 26: 'Between capitalist and communist society lies the period of the revolutionary transformation of the one into the other. Corresponding to this is also a political transition period in which the state can be nothing but *the revolutionary dictatorship of the proletariat*.'

29. Carl Grünberg, 'Der Ursprung der Worte "Sozialismus" und "Sozialist"', *Archiv für die Geschichte des Sozialismus und der Arbeiterbewegung*, 11, 1912, pp. 372-9; Arthur E. Bestor Jr, 'The Evolution of the Socialist Vocabulary', *The Journal of the History of Ideas*, vol. 9, 3, June 1948, pp. 259-302; and G.D.H. Cole, *A History of Socialist Thought*, vol. 1, London and Basingstoke 1971.

30. 'On the Jewish Question', in *Writings of the Young Marx on Philosophy and Society*, edited Lloyd D. Easton and Kurt H. Guddat, Garden City 1967, p. 239.

31. Jenö Szücs, 'Three Historical Regions of Europe', in *Civil Society and the State*; Alvin W. Gouldner, 'Civil Society in Capitalism and Socialism', pp. 355-63. In a letter dated 29 August 1983 James O'Connor adds another reason for Marx's over-simplified view of early modern civil societies: '"Society" also included runaway serfs, free serfs, artisans, craftsmen and other independent commodity producers who tried to balance the moral and money economies. Marx failed to understand this because he saw capitalism ("society") as made up of only capital and labour ... Hence his one-sided view of "society".'

32. *Grundrisse: Introduction to the Critique of Political Economy*, translated Martin

Nicolaus, Harmondsworth 1973, p. 84.

33. Hannes Siegrist, ed., '*Bürgerliche Berufe*'. *Beiträge zur Geschichte der akade-mischen und freien Berufe*, Göttingen 1988.

34. See Karl Marx and Frederick Engels, 'The German Ideology', in *Writings of the Young Marx on Philosophy and Society*, Garden City, N.Y., 1967, p. 470; Karl Marx, 'The Eighteenth Brumaire of Louis Bonaparte', in *Selected Works*, vol. 1, pp. 394-487; and 'The Civil War in France', ibid, vol. 2, p. 219.

35. 'Preface to A Contribution to the Critique of Political Economy', *Selected Works*, vol. 1, p. 503.

36. Karl Marx, *Capital*, Moscow 1970, vol. 1, p. 703; cf. the critical discussions of Carey, Bastiat and the United States in *Grundrisse*, pp. 884-9 and p. 72: 'politi-cal conditions are only the official expression of civil society ... Legislation, whether political or civil, never does more than proclaim, express in words, the will of economic relations.'

37. These possibilities are neglected in Alvin Gouldner's call for the self-emancipation of civil society. He assumes that the state and civil society can only ever be in a zero-sum relationship; see 'Civil Society in Capitalism and Socialism', p. 371. More fruitful explanations of the different possible relationships between civil society and territorially bounded and centralized states include Michael Mann, 'The Autonomous Power of the State: its Origins, Mechanisms and Results', *Archives Europeénnes de Sociologie*, vol. 25, 2, 1984, pp. 185-213, and his *The Sources of Social Power. Volume 1: A History of Power from the Beginning to AD 1760*, Cambridge 1986; Theda Skocpol, *States and Social Revolutions*, Cambridge 1979; and Charles Tilly, ed., *The Formation of National States in Western Europe*, Princeton 1975.

38. *Critique of the Gotha Programme*, in *Selected Works*, vol. 3, p. 25.

39. See my *Public Life and Late Capitalism*, Cambridge and New York, 1984, chapters 5, 7; cf. Boris Frankel, *Beyond the State?* London and Basingstoke, 1983 chapter 13.

40. Karl Marx and Frederick Engels, 'Fictitious Splits in the International (1872)', in *Selected Works*, vol. 2, p. 285.

3

Work and the Civilizing Process*

Work for nought makes folk dead sweir [lazy]

(Eighteenth century English proverb)

The Civilizing Mission

Ever since the eighteenth century, European civil societies have been dominated increasingly by the fact of employment, and by the corresponding imperative that all individuals commit themselves fully to paid work and equate it with personal fulfilment. The modern injunction to work for pay within civil society was a vital ingredient of the morality of the bourgeoisie and its civilizing mission. As the entry 'Commerce' in the *Encyclopédie* (1751-72) observed, civilized nations were noted for their emphasis upon work and workhouses.[1] The connection between work and civil society is expressed in the term 'civilization', which appeared only during the second half of the eighteenth century. It refers to the process of taming and restraining the 'natural' proclivities of human beings, their adjustment to a politically regulated system of commerce and manufacturing based on the

---

* This essay was written for a course of lectures delivered to first year social science students at The Polytechnic of Central London in the autumn of 1984. Its background assumptions, supplementary arguments and wider political implications are elaborated in John Keane and John Owens, *After Full Employment* (London 1986), and 'The Political Dangers of a Statutory Right to Work', *Critical Social Policy*, 21, Spring 1988.

private ownership of property. In the view of its protagonists, the advancement of civilization requires the gradual intensification of social constraints, the development of 'mutual deference or civility' (Hume) among members of civil society. The first duty of civilized beings is to be as artificial as possible. They must accept that a fully civil society requires the cultivation of their production and exchange *and* their courteous capacities, feelings and tastes.[2]

Since genteel manners could not be expected to develop spontaneously among the lower orders, the advocates of civilization perforce became its missionaries. They insisted that the lack of refinement and slothfulness of the plebeian classes had to be checked; the crude and idle should be set to work. Employment is a mark of civilization, and therefore a moral duty for creatures endangered by their natural desires. The authoritarian effects of this bourgeois project of coupling employment and civilization quickly became evident to its victims. Among its first critics was Charles Hall. His half-forgotten classic, *The Effects of Civilization on the People in European States* (1805)[3] can be seen in retrospect as a forerunner of the utopian socialist tradition, which since its inception in the early years of the nineteenth century questioned the modern fetish of paid labour, and called for its reduction or outright abolition.

Hall's essay throbs with sympathy for the poor and indignation at the 'luxurious abundances' of the civilizing rich. The division of civil society into these two classes is seen to be among the defining features of the civilizing process. So too is the rapid growth of commerce and manufacturing, which forces independent cultivators off the land and into the employ of the rich. Liberty, whose essential condition is to enjoy the full fruits of one's own labour, and to labour briefly, is thereby destroyed. All the miseries of civil society – among which Hall lists European colonial expansion, war and military government – derive from its inequalities of property and, thus, from the power of the property-owning classes to force the propertyless into lengthy employment: 'Civilization we have defined to consist in the improvements of the sciences, and in the refinements of manufactures, by which the conveniences, elegancies, and luxuries of life are furnished. These things ... could have had no existence, unless the bulk of mankind had been reduced to be manufacturers; that is to say, till they were reduced to that degree of poverty as to be compelled to work at those trades for their subsistence' (106).

Employment Societies

The prescience of Hall's observations is remarkable. While *The Effects of Civilization* nostalgically preferred agriculture to manufacturing, it foresaw the growing dependence of the lower ranks of civil society upon paid labour. It pointed to a striking fact: that compared with all other past and present social systems, the modern capitalist civil societies that emerged in full force in Europe and North America during the eighteenth and nineteenth centuries have been most concerned – some would say obsessed – with employment and its converse, unemployment. These civil societies can be called *employment societies*, for it is only within them that the fact of paid work – being employed as a worker for a wage or salary within a labour market geared to agricultural, manufacturing or service production – emerges on a large scale and as an activity separate from the state and from the household and other institutions of civil society.

The emergence of employment societies, in which most people, for at least some of their lives, work for a wage or salary within a labour market, was a wholly new development. If one compares modern civil societies – post-eighteenth-century France or Britain, for instance – with hunting and gathering systems and late socialist systems of the Soviet type, to mention two randomly chosen examples, the contrast is striking. Anthropologists have pointed out that the members of hunting and gathering systems spent little time each day on subsistence activities – about four to five hours of intermittent and undemanding work in the case of the surviving Australian aborigines – and that, compared with our own employment societies, 'work' in these tribal systems did not at all have the same meaning for those who engaged in it.[4] Work – the production of the felt necessaries of life – was intermittent and discontinuous, ceasing at the moment when it was not required. It was not an activity performed for pay in a separate sphere of life – an 'economy' – because being 'a worker' was not a socially ascribed status in itself. Hunting and gathering systems did not simply lack an economy, they *refused* an economy. The tribal members worked, or produced, only in their capacity as mothers, fathers, brothers, sisters or as members of other kinship groupings. Whatever work the tribal members performed was an expression of pre-existing community relations, and not the reverse. Much to the anger of their European civilizers, these tribes deliberately rejected the notion that one's daily bread must be earned by the sweat of the brow – a refusal which often cost them their lives at the hands of their European masters. To work in hunting and gathering systems did not mean to engage in 'a job', and it certainly carried no positive status. Terms such as 'worker' and 'employee', or phrases such as 'the right to work', 'the dignity of labour' and 'the tragedy of unemployment' were simply meaningless to the members of these systems.

If we jump forward in time to late socialist systems such as Czechoslovakia or the German Democratic Republic, the contrast with employment societies such as France and Britain is also very marked.[5] It is true that, unlike hunting and gathering systems, both types of social systems are geared to constantly expanding production of goods and services. Late socialist systems nevertheless differ from employment societies in at least one crucial respect: they are characterized by the state's (attempted) control of every sphere of life and, hence, by the virtual liquidation of market mechanisms, private property and waged and salaried work (see essays 4, 6). In late socialist regimes, it makes no sense to speak of workers being employed for a wage or salary within an 'economy' separate from the state, for there is no officially tolerated labour market and, hence, no officially recognized unemployment (although various forms of 'hidden unemployment' are rampant). Producers neither contract with an employer for 'a job' nor, conversely, can they be fired or made redundant by management. Producers (and managers) are subject constantly to the commands of the state authorities, who routinely restrict the free geographic movement of producers, allocate them to particular projects and industries, conscript them into the army, and in extreme cases (the Gulag Archipelago is an example) confine them in institutions where they perform slave labour. In contemporary late socialist regimes, then, the absence of an institutionalized labour market and overt unemployment has a high price: producers are not allowed officially to bargain collectively or individually over their pay or conditions. Their pay and working conditions are determined for them by the Party-supervised state and, again in contrast to employment societies, producers cannot withhold their capacity to produce. Striking is considered by the political authorities as treasonable. At most, producers can withhold their capacity to produce from this or that enterprise for a time, or engage in such forms of guerrilla action as absenteeism, go-slows, 'homing' (producing objects for household use by utilizing the factory's machines and materials) and, especially, giving the appearance of working. (As the Russian novelist Zinoviev has observed, it is virtually impossible in these countries to tell the difference between a person who is working and a person who is pretending to work.)

By contrast with hunting and gathering 'systems and contemporary Soviet-type regimes, modern employment societies compel or induce large numbers of men and women to spend a considerable portion of their daily lives within an institutionally distinct labour market; in turn, this labour market functions as a vital (but not determining) component of the whole civil society (see essay 2). The development of employment societies in this sense dates only from the eighteenth and nineteenth centuries. From this time on, 'work' comes to have a special meaning. It ceases to mean (as it had done, say, in the vocabulary of old English) being engaged in any activity and effort, especially that aimed at satisfying the necessities of life (cf. Shakespeare's *Henry IV*: 'Fie upon this quiet life, I want worke'). Work instead assumes a special and much more restricted meaning: paid employment. Work comes to mean 'having a job', and those who are engaged in paid employment are from hereon described as workfolk, workpeople, workers or working-class. To be a worker, in other words, is to be employed, whereas the activity of a woman who runs a household, services men and brings up children, for instance, is consigned officially and arbitrarily to the category of non-work. There are some exceptions to this modern restriction of the sense of work to paid employment; even today, for instance, we still speak of 'housework', 'working around the home' or 'working in the garden'. But these are exceptions, which unfortunately (in view of their decisive importance in all people's lives) are not given official recognition or status. Within employment societies, household and other non-market forms of work such as cooking, cleaning and childcare are consigned by private employers and state policymakers to the shadowy realm of non-work, as if they did not exist. Work is seen officially as synonymous with employment in a labour market, and it thereby becomes a pressing fact in people's lives, regardless of whether they are inside or outside the labour market of civil society. As workers, individuals are compelled or encouraged to sell their capacities to private or public employers in return for a wage or salary. If they refuse, or if they cannot find paid work, and therefore remain unemployed, they risk going without income and, hence, without the basic necessities of life for themselves and their household dependants.

The development of civil societies shaped by labour markets separate from households was without historical precedent. Never before had work in the sense of paid employment existed on such a scale and intensity in any social system; never before or since has work and its traumatic converse, unemployment, come to be such a crucial factor in individuals' lives. Nor has 'work' ever been so celebrated, by the most powerful social groups at least, as the goal of life itself, and not merely its means. As employment societies began to emerge in full force during the eighteenth and nineteenth centuries, work came to be seen as a blessing. Many who believed in civilization celebrated the activity of work – Adam Smith and other writers within the new eighteenth-century discipline of political economy are among the best known – defined human beings as *homo faber*, as makers and users of tools. As the following passage from Benjamin Franklin's *Autobiography* makes clear, some writers went much further, regarding paid employment as not only natural, but as an ennobling and deeply satisfying form of activity: 'When men are employed they are best contented; for on the days they worked they were good-natured and cheerful, and, with the consciousness of having done a good day's work, they spent the evening jollily; but on our idle days they were mutinous and quarrelsome.'[6]

The official celebration of paid work as the goal, and not merely the means of life, distinguishes modern employment societies from all others. This fetish of employment within a labour market found its earliest expression in the so-called Protestant work ethic. As Max Weber showed in *The Protestant Ethic and the Spirit of Capitalism* (1904-5) the belief that (male) individuals had a 'calling' to serve God through their work was invented and popularized by the Protestant middle classes. From the seventeenth century onwards, the faithful Christian was seen by these classes as one who worked not in order to live, but who lived in order to work. No longer was work viewed as an undignified necessity (to be performed only by slaves, women and other non-citizens, as in classical Greece). Nor was it any longer interpreted (as it had been in the early Judaeo-Christian tradition) as the curse of Adam, as the consequence of human beings' fall from grace ('in the sweat of thy brow shalt thou eat bread'). Instead, work came to be regarded as the means of future salvation, as the most certain sign of genuine faith.

Guided by this deep conviction, the Protestant middle classes condemned the waste of time through idle talk, and they

despised both the frilly luxury and sexual indulgence of the
aristocracy, as well as the drunken laughter of idling commoners
in the public house. The hard-working Protestants insisted that
every hour squandered could have been an hour of work to the
glory of God. This celebration of work, Weber pointed out,
contributed crucially to the early development of employment
societies. Protestantism functioned to legitimize the new wealth
and power of the male, property owning classes; their attempts,
as private entrepreneurs, to accumulate wealth and make profit
within the market appeared to be the work of divine providence.
Protestantism also provided a justification of the poverty and
powerlessness of the lower classes, whose obedience to God was
said to be conditional upon hard work, low wages, sobriety and –
when necessary – confinement within workhouses which taught
them the virtues of paid work. Through time, Weber concluded,
it was not only the Protestants who regularly confirmed their
image of themselves in the mirror of employment. The Protestant
ethic also slowly became a conviction of the lower ranks, thereby
providing employment societies with conscientious, well-disciplined and punctual workers willing to work hard for an
employer's wage or salary: 'The treatment of labour as a calling
became as characteristic of the modern worker as the corresponding attitude toward acquisition of the businessman.'[7]

Towards Full Male Employment

Weber's conclusion presents a rather exaggerated picture of the
extent to which the less powerful social ranks of civil society
willingly or resignedly embraced the Protestant ethic. More
recent research indicates that well into the nineteenth century
the so-called working classes of modern employment societies
found ways of evading the pressures and moral imperatives of
regular and full-time employment. In fact, contrary to what is
commonly supposed, only a minority shared the crushing fate of
the early nineteenth-century factory workers who were often
employed up to eighty hours a week.[8] The less powerful social
groups *normally* had access to several types of employment during
the year; well into the nineteenth century, for instance, copper
workers in South Wales often abandoned their employers during
the summer months in favour of healthier open-air employment
such as stacking hay and fishing. These groups also *typically*
worked in the labour market only on a seasonal or sporadic basis,

and only until the point at which their traditionally-defined needs were met.* Many paid homage to 'Saint Monday' and most continued to work and to have access to food resources and 'an extra bob or two' *outside* the labour market. Work performed by men and women in households was especially crucial; activities such as domestic service, laundry work, homeworking for the textile trade and gardening operated as a kind of unemployment insurance system, ensuring that those who became unemployed were not necessarily without work and, hence, without the necessities of life.

This ability of individuals to subsist by moving, often on a seasonal basis, between the labour market and the non-market institutions of civil society (such as the household) began to decline rapidly in the second half of the nineteenth century. Consequently, employment and its converse, unemployment, loomed larger in the social lives of most workers. Henceforth, workers experienced increasing difficulties in making ends meet outside the labour market. These difficulties were due largely to the pressures of accelerating urbanization, the rapid growth of industrial manufacturing, new and stricter forms of factory discipline, and because the compulsory schooling of children and the exclusion of women from the labour market severely squeezed the earning capacity of households.[9] These factors can be seen as the decisive background against which demands for 'full employment' guaranteed by the state began to develop during the 1880s within the trade union movement and among various social and political reformers. This late nineteenth-century conviction that governments could do something to remedy unemployment, that they could reform employment societies so that they would no longer be societies of unemployment, had earlier roots.

The questioning of unemployment (in England, for example) was already prominent in the 1820s and 1830s among trade union associations and radical and socialist circles, which

---

* No doubt, this is why the eighteenth- and nineteenth-century advocates of industrial employment argued for keeping wages low. They feared, with considerable justification, that raising the wages of workers employed in the labour market would encourage them to work *less* in the labour market and *more* in non-market institutions such as households. The traditional (and misleading) view that full-time factory employment was the norm for nineteenth-century workers is discussed and criticized by J.D. Chambers, *The Workshop of the World* (London, 1961), pp. 21-2, and R. Samuel, 'Workshop of the World: steam power and hand technology in mid-Victorian Britain', *History Workshop*, no. 3 (Spring 1977), pp. 6-72.

attacked the view, associated with Malthus and others, that unemployment was either a natural problem or due largely to a 'surplus' of population among the lower classes of civil society.[10] These early nineteenth-century circles insisted, correctly, that unemployment is caused by the operation of modern civil societies themselves, and in so doing exposed a basic contradiction which has threatened the civilizing process (as it was conceived in the late eighteenth century) until today – that bourgeois civil societies have typically failed to generate enough of the paid work that they at the same time depend upon and celebrate officially.

What was new about the talk of 'full employment' after 1880 in Europe was the suggestion that this contradiction, and therefore the inconvenience or trauma of being unemployed, could be overcome by state policies aimed at guaranteeing every adult male a full-time job that provided a wage or salary sufficient for himself and his household dependants. In Europe, political support for the full employment welfare state gathered momentum, sometimes against considerable social and political resistance, between the years 1880 and 1940. The full employment consensus was stimulated by factors such as the increasing social power of the trade union movement, fears of social unrest among the powerful, two world wars, the experience of economic crisis, changing party policies and, by no means of least importance, pathbreaking proposals by J.M. Keynes, William beveridge and others for maintaining high levels of employment through welfare state regulation of the labour market. In the years after 1945, these factors combined to produce an entirely exceptional phase in the history of modern employment societies. Governments now attempted, for the first time ever, to provide full-time jobs for all adult men by policies designed to, first, stimulate private capitalist investment, second, provide a voice for trade unions in matters of collective bargaining and public policy-making and, third, define and secure the health, transportation and other social needs of citizens (see essay 1).

After Full Employment

In quite a number of west European countries, the commitment to high levels of male employment through welfare state intervention was attained only with great difficulty, and lasted for only a relatively brief period of two decades or less. While countries such as Sweden and Britain secured relatively low rates of unemployment after the Second World War, unemployment rates in other countries such as Italy remained quite high (around 10 per cent). Elsewhere, in Spain and Portugal for instance, full male employment was never achieved. And even during their heyday in the period 1955-65, the 'model' full employment welfare states such as Britain and Sweden were often criticized by employers, politicians and others advocating a return to less state regulation of the labour market.

Since the early 1970s, as levels of unemployment have risen dramatically, public concern about the future of paid work has increased greatly, both in volume and scope. There is a growing recognition that the orthodox post-war policies of guaranteeing full male employment through Keynesian welfare state regulation have lost ground. However, much less public recognition is presently being given to the problem of whether the once widely endorsed goal of full male employment *can* or *should* be restored. Indeed, in certain west European countries, public discussion of this problem is virtually taboo. In Britain, for example, public debate focuses only on the *means* of re-establishing 'full employment'. This goal, even when it is downgraded in favour of others (such as reducing inflation or increasing economic growth and international competitiveness) is simply assumed to be desirable and possible. 'Getting the jobless back to work', in other words, resembles something of a settled issue – it is part of the framework of unquestioned assumptions which guide the policies of political parties, trade unions, businesses and governments.

The evidence on which this optimistic consensus is based is thin and unconvincing – as I demonstrate (with John Owens) in *After Full Employment* – and this suggests that its confident expectations are supported by dogmatic premises, among the most important of which are a lamentable nostalgia for times past, and a belief in the primacy of political will.[11] Serious doubts can be raised about the feasibility and desirability of 'restoring' full male employment. There is much convincing evidence that the conditions that made possible full male employment in western Europe after 1945 are not repeatable, and that, consequently, there is an urgent need in the present period for democrats to develop new and unorthodox ideas and strategies for equitably remedying the present unemployment crisis.

The most stimulating attempt in western Europe to radically question the full employment consensus is that of André Gorz. His *Adieux au proletariat* (1980) and *Les chemins du paradis* (1983)[12] stand within the tradition initiated by Charles Hall and others.

Gorz's recent writings attempt to revive and popularize the old utopian socialist criticism of the grip of paid labour on civil society. They challenge the orthodox Keynesian and neo-conservative assumption that full-time paid labour is a necessary condition of a 'free' civil society. They suggest, correctly, that a democratic civil society cannot be based on full employment which 'crowds out' other social and political activities – as is assumed by almost all recent democratic theory.[13] Democracy instead requires that all individuals be guaranteed the right to (periodically) withdraw from the labour market without fear of going without. Consequently, Gorz points to the need to move towards a type of post-employment civil society in which individuals would be able to choose freely whether or not (or how much) they wished to engage in paid work.

Gorz's *Adieux au proletariat* and *Les chemins du paradis* are deliberately 'utopian' books. They rely upon the standard utopian technique of pointing to a future radically different from the present, and they do this by making exaggerated arguments which serve as standards against which present reality can be measured and judged as inadequate. As I shall show, the picture of the future presented by these books is also sketchy and inexact, and this too is a mark of their utopianism. Just as nearly every utopian island is shrouded in fog, so Gorz's utopian socialism is often lacking in clarity and definition. Gorz, therefore, does not pretend to have answered all of the many questions his books raise. He is concerned rather to mount an attack on what he describes as the prevailing nostalgic and unimaginative attachment, especially within the socialist tradition, to the goal of 'restoring' full employment. Five themes in Gorz's utopian socialist argument are of special relevance to a democratic theory of civil society and the state.

1. According to Gorz, political programmes based on the vision of maintaining or restoring the full employment welfare state are now exhausted. A society based on mass unemployment is coming into being before our very eyes; waged and salaried work is being abolished by the widespread introduction into the workplace of microelectronic systems. In each of the leading industrialized countries of western Europe, he argues, independent economic forecasts suggest that during the next decade automation ('the robot revolution') will eliminate up to 4-5 million full-time jobs. Unless there is a sharp reduction in the number of working hours as well as radical changes in the form

and purpose of productive activity, unemployment levels of 30-50 per cent by the end of the century seem not altogether unlikely.

Gorz could greatly strengthen his case against full male employment by examining the other, non-technological factors responsible for the present unemployment crisis. He does not consider, for instance, the crucial significance of changes in the international monetary and trading systems, the emerging new international division of labour, and the political problems and social conflicts generated by the welfare state; nor does he take into account the likely continuing expansion of the labour supply due to demographic and social factors (such as the baby-boom of the late 1950s and early 1960s, and the re-entry of increasing numbers of women into full-time or part-time employment).[14] Gorz instead emphasizes the revolutionary consequences of automation for the full employment welfare state. In both the industrial and service sectors of the economy, the increasing utilization of microelectronics is no longer creating but *destroying* jobs. This new technology revolutionizes the means of producing both material goods and non-material services; in all types of industrial and office employment, more goods and services can be produced with less investment, raw materials (especially energy) and waged and salaried labour. From hereon, Gorz concludes, the employment societies will experience 'jobless growth'; reflation through new investment, whether public or private, cannot be expected to create vast numbers of new jobs. Restoring full employment through accelerating quantitative economic growth is no longer a realistic goal.

2. The present long wave of rapid technological change not only generates mass unemployment. In Gorz's view, it also radically alters the socioeconomic class structure of the employment societies. Under pressure from quickening technological change, the workers' movement in particular loses whatever unity it once enjoyed. Not the capitalist system, but the 'working class' is disintegrating. It becomes subdivided into three distinct strata. First, there is an aristocracy of 'tenured workers'. Concerned to protect its own jobs and resist automation, this stratum forms the backbone of the trade union movement. Threatened by the advance of automation, this traditional working class is becoming little more than a privileged minority of full-time paid workers. (In Britain, to mention one indicator in support of Gorz's claim, more than 4 million jobs have been lost since the mid 1960s in manufacturing industry, the traditional heartland of this

stratum.) The political identity of this aristocracy of industrial labour is heavily shaped by its commitment to paid work; it is in this sense a compliment or 'replica' of capital, a group no longer capable of becoming an agent of radical social and political change. The second social stratum produced by the break-up of the working class is the growing mass of permanently unemployed. This group cannot be considered a 'reserve army' in Marx's sense for, as things stand, it is unlikely ever to re-enter the labour market. The mass of permanently unemployed find that there is little or no paid work available. The unemployed thereby become trapped in a vicious and ever expanding circle of poverty and idleness; they find that living on the dole is no holiday. Finally, there is a third stratum of the population, 'temporary workers', which is as it were trapped between the permanently unemployed and the aristocracy of tenured workers. This stratum of temporary workers is rapidly growing in the present period,[15] and it is employed in the least skilled and often most unsatisfying jobs. It has no job security and no definite class identity; it is engaged in casual, contracted, temporary and part-time employment. This stratum is frequently 'over-qualified' for the jobs it finds; unable to identify with 'the job', it endures paid work in order to earn a little money on which to exist. In the not too distant future, says Gorz, many jobs presently filled by temporary workers will be eliminated by automation.

3. Gorz uses the term 'non-class of non-workers' (or 'disaffected non-workers') to refer to the latter two strata of permanently unemployed and temporary workers.* Despite its present hetero-

---

* The term 'non-class of non-workers' is misleading because it gives the false impression that the permanently unemployed and temporary workers do not engage in types of work in the household and the informal economy. Gorz supposes that in employment societies work is synonymous with paid work, thereby forgetting that employment is merely one, albeit crucial form of work. Gorz's failure to discuss unpaid work (such as that performed in households, mainly by women) sometimes produces implicitly sexist conclusions in his writings. (In *Paths to Paradise*, for instance, he completely ignores the gendered work patterns of the era of full male employment, instead insisting that 'there can no longer be full-time waged work for all, and waged work cannot remain the centre of gravity or even the central activity in our lives' [p. 34]. His silence about unpaid forms of work also tempts him into highly romanticized accounts of life outside the sphere of the labour market (as in the following passage: 'Non-economic activities are the very fabric of life itself. They encompass everything which is done, not for money, but out of friendship, love, compassion, concern; or for the satisfaction, pleasure and joy derived from the activities themselves and from their end results' (ibid, p. 48)).

geneity and lack of organization, this non-class of non-workers is likely to succeed the old and decaying industrial working-class movement as the most powerful opponent of the capitalist system. This is because this non-class of non-workers shares the following social and psychological characteristics. (1) It is allergic to paid work. It experiences employment as an externally imposed obligation, and this is a correct perception, says Gorz. We are witnessing the final stage in the historic decline of the polyvalent skilled worker. Paid work is no longer the worker's own activity; whether in the factory or office, work has become a passive, programmed activity subordinated totally to machines and machine-like organizations which squeeze out any room for personal initiative. The present technological revolution only accelerates this deskilling and alienating trend. (2) Unlike the skilled workers of the age of industrial capitalism, the non-class of non-workers does not take pride in whatever employment it finds. Nor does this non-class acknowledge the actual or potential power paid work confers on workers. It therefore does not seek to appropriate collectively work and its tools; it simply is not interested in workers' control of production or class-based politics. For this non-class, it is no longer a question of finding freedom *within* paid work, but of *rejecting* work in order to act freely *outside* the labour market. (3) Although the non-class of non-workers is a fragmented and composite group, it is generally suspicious of established institutions (such as corporations, trade unions, political parties and state institutions). It experiences the whole of the existing capitalist system as 'something external, akin to a spectacle or show'. It has no single god or religion and, in definite contrast to the workers' movement of the nineteenth century, has no grandiose sense of historical mission.

Considered together, or so Gorz argues, these three characteristics of the non-class of non-workers endow it with great potential power to transform the existing capitalist system. This is not to underestimate the political difficulties facing this non-class. While its greatest strength lies in its reluctance to pose political problems in traditional ways – it is no longer in love with the idea of paid work or 'full employment', for instance – it presently suffers from a general lack of social and political consciousness. Until it develops this self-awareness – Gorz clearly sees his own writings as a contribution to this development – it stands in danger of remaining socially powerless and politically marginal.

4. According to Gorz, the present economic crisis – accelerating

automation, job loss and the growth of an impoverished non-class of non-workers – confronts employment societies with a fundamental political choice. This concerns whether the full employment welfare state will be superseded by *either* an authoritarian state-regulated capitalism ('living-dead capitalism'), in which full-time jobs will be scarce and most of the population will be segregated, regimented and reduced to powerlessness by various state-administered programmes, *or* by a democratic and post-capitalist society which equitably reduces socially necessary work to a minimum so as to maximize each person's 'free use of time'. Gorz has no doubt that only the second option is desirable and, in the long run, feasible. In his view it is high time that the old utopian socialist demand (which the contemporary trade union movement seems largely to have forgotten or ignored) be renewed: work less for pay, live more! The vision of a post-employment society must now be central to socialist politics. In the words of Gorz: 'Let us work less so that we all may work and do more things by ourselves in our free time. Socially useful labour, distributed among all those willing and able .to work, will thus cease to be anyone's exclusive or leading activity. Instead, people's major occupation may be one or a number of self-defined activities, carried out not for money but for the interest, pleasure or benefit involved.'[16]

This demand to work less does *not* imply the right to 'rest more'. Gorz rejects calls (those of Lafargue, for instance[17]) for more 'leisure'; he observes, correctly, that the enormous post-war growth of the manipulative 'leisure industry' paralyses the anti-capitalist and democratic potential of such calls. The demand to be employed less implies the right to 'live more'. It implies the right to do many more things than money can buy – and even to do some of the things that money presently *can* buy.[18] A politics of free time, Gorz argues, must aim at achieving a democratic civil society freed from the dominating imperatives of employment – in other words, developing a sphere of life regulated not by state institutions and/or by capitalist corporations and trade unions, but by networks of self-governing, small-scale institutions (such as non-patriarchal households, neighbourhood centres, rural community associations, repair and DIY shops, producers' and consumers' co-operatives, libraries, and places to make films or to record and play music) whose individual members consider each other as equals and exercise their unique productive powers in their own free time.

5. Gorz insists, correctly, that a multi-centred and self-governing civil society which maximized the free use of time could never do without state institutions (such as legislatures, civil administration, law courts, and the policy (see essay 1)). Contrary to most previous utopian socialists, centralized state institutions as we know them could not be abolished or somehow made to wither away. Gorz offers four overlapping reasons for this heresy. First, 'socially necessary' work (performed, say, by bus drivers, engineers, computer technicians and garbage collectors) cannot be eliminated once and for all. Gorz does not envisage a future Cockaigne, in which (as in Brueghel's painting of that name) there is no fear of want and no work to be done, and people can lie around with food literally flying fully cooked into their mouths, and with brooks of wine bubbling past their toes. This means that if 'socially necessary' work is to be shared equitably, performed efficiently and effectively and considerably reduced in quantity (Gorz suggests socially necessary work in this sense could be reduced to a mere two hours a day, ten hours a week, or fifteen weeks a year), it would have to be planned, and planning requires centrally co-ordinated state institutions. Second, Gorz observes that many of the tools, (e.g. telephones, video machines, bicycles, computers) which would enable individuals and groups to live freely within civil society *could* be produced at the level of small, self-governing groups equipped with the latest information technologies; however, this would sometimes be inefficient and time-consuming, and so in order radically to shorten the quantity of time given over to socially necessary work, these particular tools would be better produced within large-scale, centrally-organized state institutions. Third, Gorz insists that socialists (and others) who call for the abolition of the state dream the impossible; conflicts among different individuals and groups are unlikely to disappear, he insists, and future socialist society will therefore always require some means of conflict resolution, for which certain types of state institutions (such as courts of law) are uniquely suited. What is more, socialists who call for the abolition of state institutions nearly always defend 'socialist morality' – by insisting that each individual and group should identify with, and embrace, the whole social order. This morality, Gorz observes correctly, is antipathetic to individual and group liberty, and may even have totalitarian implications (see essay 2). Finally, Gorz points out that state institutions are not always a damper upon liberty. For example, the existence of a police force – whose strictly defined and politically controlled functions need not be

performed, as they are today, as a full-time career – makes it unnecessary for each individual to internalize a whole system of law and order. Similarly, the existence of a state-enforced traffic code makes it unnecessary to engage in tedious negotiations with every other road user at every intersection. These examples make it clear, or so Gorz argues, that certain state institutions may in fact be *enabling*, in the sense that they actually facilitate individuals' and groups' freedom in civil society.

Beyond Utopia

Gorz's attempt to revive and popularize the old utopian socialist criticism of paid labour is summarized only briefly here. These five themes nevertheless illustrate the main outlines of his very stimulating and quite justified attack on the present political consensus about the need to restore full employment.

Notice that a version of the distinction between civil society and the state occupies a central place in Gorz's polemic. The distinction between *civil society* (a non-state realm of voluntary co-operation among equal individuals and groups who have been released from socially necessary work) and *the state* (a sphere of compulsory, hierarchical institutions necessary for the efficient and effective servicing and co-ordination of civil society) is fundamental to Gorz's definition of socialism. Also fundamental to this vision, consequently, is the distinction between the 'self-determined' activity of civil society (Gorz prefers not to speak of this as work) and compulsory (if unpaid) work within the state sector. These distinctions lead Gorz to insist that socialism will not be equivalent (as it was for Owen, Fourier, Lafargue and many nineteenth-century socialists) to harmonious social co-operation without government, law and police. And contrary to neo-conservatives, he urges that socialism will not be equivalent to a Soviet-type regime which suffocates civil society under a canopy of state bureaucracy, red tape, party propaganda, secret police, centralized planning and compulsory work. Gorz rather insists that socialism means a type of system in which socially necessary work has been minimized and distributed equally by making the state sector as small, and the sphere of civil society as large, as possible. Socialism will be based on a type of *post-employment civil society* in which individual citizens will enjoy a maximum of free time, as well as determine, through periodic involvement in political activity, the broad guidelines and instruments of a centralized state planning system necessary for the survival and free development of civil society.

It should be evident from this sketch that Gorz's vision of a future socialist system is weakened by a number of untreated gaps and questionable claims. To begin with, Gorz has a disturbing tendency to ignore the need for more political democracy. How the voluntarily co-operating individuals and groups of civil society are to transmit their demands to the state or defend themselves against its power remains unclear from his account, which rests arbitrarily on the assumption – criticized throughout these essays – that state institutions are merely machine-like bureaucracies and, hence, inescapably heteronomous. Linked with this problem – the converse of it, in fact – is Gorz's overly simplified picture of the economic mechanisms of a democratic civil society. A theory of socialist civil society – here I disagree strongly with the ethereal views of Arato and Cohen – must give greater consideration to its main organizing principles of production, exchange and consumption.* Gorz insists, correctly, that the freedom and equality of all citizens requires the abolition of the monopoly grip of employment (and therefore the power of private capital) upon civil society. Yet the pluralist mixture of different types of economic activities necessary for the realization of a post-employment society guaranteed by the state – the dense network of households, individuals, small-scale private enterprises, co-operatives and large-scale socialized enterprises co-ordinated by carefully defined sectors of voluntary co-operation *and* bartered exchange *and* market mechanisms *and* state regulation – remains unclarified by Gorz.[19]

There are additional weaknesses. One such difficulty arises

---

* Andrew Arato and Jean L. Cohen's most recent interpretation of civil society ('Civil Society and Social Theory', New York 1986, manuscript) relies heavily on Habermas. They distinguish between the logics of the political and economic systems, regulated by administrative power and money, and civil society, or the life-world, which is based (potentially) on that of solidarity and communication. Concerning matters of production, exchange and consumption, two theoretical problems are generated by this view. First, civil society, because it is defined so narrowly, is left economically passive, and deprived of any property resources which would enable it to defend or enhance its power. Second, civil society, the realm of (potential) freedom, is viewed positively, while the economy is implicitly viewed negatively, as a realm of necessity in which only money speaks (cf. the neoconservative view). The material conditions of life in civil society are degraded to a mere instrument for the ends desired by civil society – just as the classical concept of civil society rested upon the silence and unfreedom of the *oikos*.

from Gorz's unstated assumption that socialism could be constructed within a specifically national context – despite evidence that the new international division of labour, changes in the global monetary and trading systems and superpower strategies would all loom large as obstructive factors in any single country's attempt to make a transition to socialism in Gorz's sense. A further difficulty arises from Gorz's belief (to be found also in Braverman's well-known account of the twentieth-century degradation of work[20]) that paid work has already become a passive and meaningless activity programmed from above, and that, for reasons of technical efficiency and effectiveness, this condition would persist in the state-organized sector of socially necessary production in future socialist society. This belief clearly exaggerates the degree of de-skilling, worker powerlessness and loss of work motivation in present-day employment societies.[21] More importantly, it underestimates the ways in which future state planning of socially necessary production could *not* function rationally without active workplace democracy.*

Gorz's discussion of transitional strategies to a future socialist system also suffers from a certain vagueness. Gorz does not provide a detailed picture of how to move from the present into the future. Consonant with his utopian mode of thinking, he emphasizes constantly that we must dare to ask questions about the present unemployment crisis which cannot be answered easily. He recognizes, correctly, that today's reality is often yesterday's utopia; and that tomorrow's reality is often today's utopia. His utopia is in this sense a deliberate provocation: it questions and rejects the apparently 'natural' ideal of full employment so as

---

* The most highly mechanized organizations – of the type envisaged by Gorz for minimizing the aggregate quantity of socially necessary work – are often high-risk systems and cannot operate automatically, that is, without active human input. Human skill, improvisation and collective judgements are required to prevent them from regularly malfunctioning in unexpected and dangerous ways (as at Chernobyl and Three-Mile Island). In addition, the latest machine systems (such as robots and computers) produce unstructured and open-ended problems which can only be solved by those who work with them. Finally, these new technologies' remarkable capacity to flexibly alter both the flow of work and the types of products can be maximized only through collective human decisions at the point of production. For further discussion of these points, see Charles Perrow, *Normal Accidents. Living with High-Risk Technologies* (New York 1984); Larry Hirschhorn, *Beyond Mechanization: Work and Technology in a Post-Industrial Age* (London 1984); and Mike Cooley, *Architect or Bee? The Human/Technology Relationship* (Slough 1983).

to stimulate public discussion about the future of paid work.

In my view, Gorz's utopianism is the greatest strength of his writings. It is indeed 'realistic' thinking about unemployment and paid work which in the present period has become unrealistic. Gorz is therefore right to point to the need for bold and impudent political claims, which help throw light on our present circumstances, showing just how unimaginative – and rooted in the early modern civilizing process – are the prevailing west European public policies and proposals for managing the present unemployment crisis. Gorz's arguments nevertheless provoke many questions about social and political *strategy*, that is, questions about which social and political means could facilitate his envisaged goal of a state-protected civil society no longer geared to the imperatives of paid labour. Three sets of strategic questions are especially important. They illustrate the types of difficulties to be overcome by democratic attempts to reduce and redistribute waged and salaried work.

1. *Is the 'non-class of non-workers' as allergic to paid work as Gorz claims, and is it capable of acting as a co-ordinated social movement in defence of free time?* Past experience suggests that the non-class of non-workers is unlikely to develop a common political identity, as Gorz anticipates. If anything the opposite will be true: unemployment has mostly depoliticizing and humiliating effects upon those who experience it. This was a clear lesson of the 1930s. As Middlemas explains, during that decade the unemployed found it extremely difficult to sustain membership of any social or political organizations through which they could define and defend their interests: 'The loss of workplace or union as a focus for activity, the onset of apathy, disorientation, undernourishment, combined with a lower level of political education, geographical fragmentation and incompatibility between stratified groups of unemployed workers, all militated against the creation of a mass movement *from below*.'[22]

Little has changed since that time. The trauma of being unemployed, the conviction that being employed is one of the main ways in which life can be made bearable and that, therefore, being flung into the ranks of the unemployed is a humiliating blow to one's very existence, persists. The consequences of being unemployed are often deeply personal, and are by no means restricted to the difficulties generated by a serious reduction of income and consumer spending power. Certainly, as in the 1930s, the traumatic effects of being forced into joblessness are highly variable, clearly depending upon such factors as gender, the type of occupation in which one was previously employed, the degree of unemployment in one's geographic locality, and whether or not other members of one's household are presently working for a wage or salary. Even when such factors are taken into account, however, it is clear that the unemployed often feel like passengers in an airborne plane with no landing gear. An acute sense of shock, panic, isolation, shame, lethargy, depression and fear of simply not being able to make ends meet is reportedly widespread among the unemployed; blood pressure, asthmatic difficulties, headaches, nervousness and other bodily ailments tend to increase; and young children of the unemployed are especially prone to disturbed feeding, sleeping difficulties and anxious behaviour.

The 'non-class of non-workers' typically finds itself humiliated and scared. It is isolated, deserted for the time being by trade unions, the main political parties and the employed majority. Under these circumstances, it is not surprising that the non-class develops not an allergy, but a passion to engage in paid work. Gorz wishes away these obstacles to the non-class of non-workers overcoming its own powerlessness by itself. He thereby fails to recognize the need for developing a strategy of *solidarity* between the unemployed and trade unions and reform-oriented political parties within civil society. Gorz instead falls back upon the very questionable (Marxian) idea of a single revolutionary group which is presently passing through a vale of tears en route to a mountain paradise of freedom. In view of the highly differentiated character of temporary workers and the permanently unemployed, Gorz's belief that there is presently developing a single revolutionary subject must be rejected. The prospects for a society based upon more free time depend not upon theoretical assumptions about a (potentially) homogeneous political subject, but instead upon the development in practice of solidarity between the non-class of non-workers and various other groups within civil society and the state. A solidarity of those in favour of freedom from employment cannot rest upon *ascribed* common interests (as it does in Gorz's analysis). It must instead begin with the difficult political problem of how to build co-operation among groups – the unemployed, the part-time employed, social movements and left-wing political parties – who would in turn respect each other's right to articulate their differences of opinion. Solidarity in this sense would not assume some 'essential shared interest' of the participants. It would instead be based upon a shared awareness among the various social and political groups that their needs are equally frustrated by mass unemployment, that a return to full employment is impossible, and that the reduction and equitable redistribution of paid work is therefore essential.

Developing this solidarity will not be easy. In western Europe, major political parties, including those on the left, remain deeply imbued with the ethos of full employment. In addition, a politics of free time is understandably developing at only a slow pace among trade unions. Under conditions of deindustrialization and declining (or new types of) investment, trade unions cannot easily press demands for the reduction and redistribution of paid work. When firms close or migrate to other countries, for instance, militancy is more likely to *encourage* rather than prevent disinvestment. The shift towards 'jobless growth' based on highly capital-intensive investment also undermines the power of trade unions, who find it difficult to guarantee employment for their remaining members, let alone support the unemployed and part-time employed. During the past five years or so, a push towards a standard thirty-five-hour week has been clearly identifiable among British and other west European trade unions; schemes for a thirty-two-hour week (e.g. the 'broad strategy' of the National Communications Workers' Union in Britain) are also increasingly common in wage and salary bargaining. While this suggests that the stratum of 'tenured workers' is not completely addicted to paid work, as Gorz claims, a more radical commitment to reducing and redistributing paid work − say, to a maximum twenty-four-hour/three-day week − nevertheless seems a long way off, even though it is clearly an essential condition of developing a viable and popular politics of free time.

2. The second type of strategic question prompted by Gorz's vision follows directly from this point. *Given that the demand to 'Work less, live more!' is desirable, which types of policies geared to reducing and redistributing paid work could help make it a reality for all people?* Gorz's discussion of the reduction of paid work is notably unclear about these specific policies. This is unfortunate, since there are serious difficulties in formulating viable policies for guaranteeing that those people who are able and willing to engage in paid work have the right to such work, but for fewer hours, thereby spreading paid work and its benefits more equitably throughout civil society. There are several possible types of policies. The main ones are summarized below. Each has its difficulties although,

depending on where and when they are utilized, they may be reduced or offset by combining two or more types of policies:

(a) *Reducing basic weekly hours*   A normal thirty-five-hour paid working week is given priority by trade union organizations in a number of employment societies. Some trade unions are already claiming an even shorter working week: for example, the British National Union of Bank Employees is claiming a twenty-eight-hour week spread over four days, already having enforced the thirty-five-hour week. Estimates of the number of jobs that might be preserved/created by a shorter paid working week differ greatly. According to a model designed by the German Institute for Economic Research in Berlin, an overall reduction of five hours in the paid working week in West Germany could lead to the creation of approximately 1 million new jobs within five years.[23] Others contest this estimate, pointing to the dismal failure of the Mitterrand government's legislated reductions in work time to provide even short-term relief from growing mass unemployment in France.[24] Regardless of which of these differing estimates is valid, it is clear that a reduction of basic weekly hours alone will not be a panacea for unemployment in the short term. There is also doubt as to whether employers will in fact create even part-time jobs to make up for the reductions in working time; employers' attempts to replace their labour requirements through automation and/or to compensate for the reduction of working time through productivity gains are more probable. And in the past, reductions of paid working time have been partly offset by employers' attempts to increase overtime working. This would clearly be counter-productive.

(b) *Reducing overtime*   The equitable expansion of freedom from employment clearly requires substantial cuts in overtime. Many paid workers, especially manual and service workers, still work long hours in the labour market. A sample survey conducted in 1977 in EEC countries indicated that average weekly hours for male employees in agriculture exceeded fifty hours in Britain and forty-five hours in seven other countries. In manufacturing industry, they exceeded forty-two hours in three countries, one being Britain. In the service trades, they exceeded forty-three hours in France, and forty-two hours in two other countries.[25]

   If overtime hours could be parcelled into full-time job

units, and if employers could be pressured to fill those jobs, this could absorb significant numbers of unemployed workers. The problems in discouraging overtime are, however, considerable. Employers usually oppose attempts to reduce overtime, on the grounds that it increases their costs of hiring and training new employees. Overtime is also a vital element of the weekly earnings of many in low-paid industries, and any attempt compulsorily to reduce overtime would fall hardest on such low-paid workers. As things stand presently, few full-time workers would be prepared to accept a permanent loss in their overtime pay in order to provide waged or salaried work for the unemployed – unless, perhaps, their basic pay level was raised by a proportionate amount.

(c) *Voluntary part-time employment* The proportion of full-time paid workers who are interested in working shorter hours is much higher than is commonly supposed. According to a number of surveys conducted during the 1970s, a majority of full-time employees would prefer to work less in the labour market, even if they thereby earned less. The most recent research in western Europe suggests this generalization still holds, despite the slowdown of wage increases during the past decade, and the corresponding rise in preferences among more workers for higher wages. Many surveys indicate that most people want to be employed and to earn more – but not to the point where other activities within civil society become 'crowded out'.[26]

Many workers want to be employed, say, five to six hours a week less, but do not wish to cut their working hours from forty to twenty hours a week. If this desire for voluntary part-time employment (preferably without a corresponding reduction in earnings) could be met, it might possibly have a modest impact upon overall unemployment figures. However, employers are reluctant to hire new workers due to the alleged costs of training. In addition, trade unions are deeply sceptical about voluntary part-time working arrangements. They suspect, correctly, that many part-time jobs are not secure, that the work is presently undergoing intensification (e.g. through speed-ups), and that part-time employees are usually discriminated against in such matters as promotion and entitlements. Trade unions also tend to assume that part-time workers will not support collective trade union policy, by strike action if need be. The conclusion drawn by many trade unions – that voluntary part-time employment undermines trade union solidarity and plays into the hands of employers – is arguably premature, however. Trade unions have barely begun to explore the possibilities of supplementing their collective strategies by bargaining vigorously in defence of the growing numbers of part-time employees (most of them women), and by demanding that every individual full-time employee be entitled to a right to work part-time *without* loss of entitlements or promotion opportunities.

(d) *Early voluntary retirement*   As an alternative to altering hours of employment, action could also be taken to reduce the size of the labour market, by considerably reducing the age of (voluntary) retirement, for example. The fight for a more meaningful and youthful existence at the end of one's employed life, instead of simply 'going for retirement' (or being forced there through compulsory redundancy), could create new jobs. The costs of this strategy are however considerable, not only in terms of increased pensions, but also through the possible loss of tax and national insurance contributions to state budgets. Many employees would also be reluctant to retire on their present pensions, preferring instead to achieve higher incomes by remaining within the labour market. If alternative forms of self-chosen work outside of the labour market were made more attractive, however, this reluctance to retire early from employment might be reduced greatly.

In view of the difficulties mentioned in this list of policy options, it is clear that an effective and equitable overall strategy for reducing paid working hours requires a *combination* of these partial strategies, varied according to local conditions. Ways must also be found of co-ordinating these strategies at the plant, office, local, regional and even international levels through state reforms from above and radical social initiatives from below. This would help prevent the present serious discrepancies of working conditions from developing further, and might even help to reverse them. It would also help counter the reactionary initiatives of conservative politicians and employers, who more and more present the so-called 'flexibility' of working hours – voluntary forms of part-time employment which are in practice poorly paid and often compulsory – as an individual solution to the collective problem of equitably reducing paid working time.

3. *Finally, does not Gorz's overall vision of a post-employment society suppose the need for a transitional strategy that guarantees a social wage be paid to all adult citizens? If so, are there not serious political obstacles to the popularizing and successful implementation of this citizen's wage?* Popularizing and implementing a guaranteed social wage is arguably one of the most crucial conditions of success of a policy of reducing and redistributing paid work, although Gorz gives it – and the barriers to its acceptance – insufficient emphasis. The basic principle of the citizen's wage, first developed during the 1920s in Europe, and revived during the 1960s, is simple: every adult citizen would be paid by the state a weekly or monthly income, adequate for subsistence, on no other condition than that except proof of citizenship. Assuming that paid work could not be abolished completely (as Gorz often implies), those citizens wishing to earn extra income from paid employment could do so, although those earnings would be taxed; those persons unfit for employment, such as the frail elderly and the differently abled, would be entitled to a supplement in order to protect their incomes from falling behind their fellow citizens'. The cost of operating the citizen wage system would be paid for by a single tax upon incomes deriving from employment and/or upon employers' profits deriving from the rapidly expanding productivity and output associated with the present wave of jobless growth. The collection of taxes and their redistribution in the form of a citizen's wage would be administered by a single state agency. Since the present jungle of state payments (e.g., unemployment and social security benefits, student grants, child allowances) and tax allowances would be combined into one computerized system, considerable savings on administrative costs would result.

Contrary to what is often thought, the citizen wage system would not have socially regressive consequences. It would instead guarantee all individuals the right *not* to engage in employment, and would at the same time distribute to everyone more equally the wealth created by civil society as a whole. Provided with an adequate social wage, individuals would no longer be forced to sell their capacity to work in the labour market; the right to an income (and therefore the choice between different ways of life) would be separated fully from the possession of a job. Individuals could more freely choose how much time they wished to spend either in employment or in other activities in civil society, including work in the household and the informal economy comprising individual activities (such as plumbing or freelance writing), small-scale private enterprises (such as restaurants) and co-operative ventures. A guaranteed citizen's wage would also effectively weaken the undemocratic power of surveillance of welfare state bureaucracies over many claimants: all individuals would be entitled to the citizen's wage regardless of their employment or social status. In addition, a guaranteed wage for all individuals would effectively terminate the present system of 'the family wage' (whereby men are alleged by state and private employers to be the sole 'breadwinners' of households) as well as the financial dependence of women upon men within households. *For the first time under modern conditions, all women would be treated as equals of men in civil society.* The citizen's wage to which all women, regardless of their marital status, would be entitled automatically would make it possible for them to escape their present financial dependence upon men, and to move much more freely between the realms of paid and unpaid work.

In *Les chemins du paradis* and subsequent essays, Gorz considers for the first time the need for a guaranteed income for life. When linked with the demand for reducing and redistributing paid labour, he observes rightly, the guarantee of a citizen's wage could greatly enhance all individuals' liberty to choose different ways of life within civil society. Gorz fails to consider, however, the very serious strategic obstacles working against the acceptance of the citizen's wage principle, especially among private capital, trade unions and socialist political parties. Capitalists are likely to object to increased taxation, and to the feeling that they would no longer be members of the select few who receive a handsome income without being employed. They may therefore engage in a politically motivated capital strike – although this opposition could be anticipated and assuaged by restricting the free movement of financial capital, by giving high tax relief on new investment and other schemes. Among socialist political parties, there is presently a deep hostility to this principle, partly due to a simple reaction against its appropriation by anti-socialists, especially neo-conservatives.[27] It is also partly due to the failure of advocates of the citizen's wage to publicize the significance and viability of certain short-term measures (such as improved maternity/paternity leave and sabbatical schemes) which might stimulate widespread public acceptance of the broader citizen's wage principle.[28] There are further serious objections to the idea of a citizen's wage, raised especially by trade unions. Under conditions of high unemployment and a deepening 'dualization' of employment societies, public sector trade unions do not respond warmly to citizen's wage proposals that would inevitably involve the elimination of jobs in the social policy bureaucracies of the state. Private sector trade unions also object to citizen's wage proposals on the grounds that they would weaken trade unions' power to defend their members' livelihoods. If all citizens were entitled to a subsistence wage, these trade unions argue, collective bargaining would inevitably be confined to the matter of supplementary income derived from employment, thereby adding to the present difficulties trade unions encounter in preserving solidarity and attracting new members.

This trade union and political party opposition to the idea of the citizen's wage is understandable, and yet troubling for Gorz's thesis. It is symptomatic of an irony – that the present labour movement is committed strongly to defending full-time paid work, whereas, as in the nineteenth-century campaigns for Sunday rest, the ten-hour day and the prohibition of child labour, large sections of the labour movement struggled *against* paid work – that will only be resolved and overcome in practice if creative strategies ensuring solidarity among the employed, unemployed and part-time employed can be invented and popularized by democratic forces within civil society and the state.[29]

After Full Employment

These types of strategic questions and problems prompted by Gorz's analysis remain unresolved in his writings. As a confessed utopian, Gorz justifiably does not apologize for these strategic weaknesses and gaps in his vision. This commitment to bold conjectures is nevertheless both the greatest strength and a major source of weakness in his case against compulsory employment. Sooner or later – better sooner than later – the democratic vision of breaking the grip of employment upon civil society will have to confront and resolve hard political questions concerning *how* this vision can be achieved in practice. The development of viable employment policies – workable and popular strategies for reducing and equitably redistributing paid work – is required urgently, and is certainly necessary for combatting the inequitable, nostalgic and self-contradictory neo-conservative and social democratic strategies for 'returning' to 'full employment'. Questions about ends *and* means must become central to contemporary democratic politics. For one of the most telling counter-arguments with which democrats must deal in the debate about unemployment is the oft-heard charge that the social and political costs of reducing and redistributing work are too high; that is, that the democratic goal (of maximizing the complex freedom and equality of all individuals by abolishing their compulsory dependence upon employment) is contradicted by the lack of clarity about the means for achieving this goal.

The present unemployment crisis provides the democratic tradition with a once-in-a-lifetime opportunity of overcoming its recent loss of energy and direction. But if democrats are to seize this historic opportunity to change the course of the civilizing process, they not only will have to convince others publicly that a new ideal is needed to replace the undemocratic and unrepeatable, and therefore obsolete ideal of full male employment. They will also have to resolve an equally formidable problem: that of inventing viable strategies for ending the tyranny of paid work, thereby making possible a post-employment civil society which maximizes individuals' choice of whether, or how much, they work for pay.

Notes

1. Denis Diderot and Jean d'Alembert, *Encyclopédie, ou Dictionnaire raisonné des sciences, des arts et des métiers, par une société de gens de lettres*, Elmsford, New York 1984, vol. 3, p. 697.

2. This theme is summarized in *Political Dictionary*, London 1845, vol. 1, pp. 516-17: 'The fundamental ideas ... contained in the word Civilization are – the continual advancement of the whole society in wealth and prosperity, and the improvement of man in his individual capacity.' See also the contributions of Helmut Kuzmics and Norbert Elias in John Keane, ed., *Civil Society and the State*, London and New York 1988; Pierre-François Moreau, 'Société civile et civilisation', in François Chatelet, ed., *Histoire des idéologies savoir et pouvoir du XVIIIe au XXe siècle*, Paris 1978; Lucien Febvre, '*Civilisation*: evolution of a word and a group of ideas', in *A New Kind of History*, edited Peter Burke, London 1973, pp. 219-57; and Zygmunt Bauman, 'On the Origins of Civilisation: A Historical Note', *Theory, Culture and Society*, vol. 2, 3, 1985, pp. 7-14.

3. All citations are from Charles Hall, *The Effects of Civilisation on the People in European States* (1805), London 1850. Little is known about Hall. He practised as a physician in western England, and his book was evidently based on a wide reading of Smith, Paine, Godwin and others, as well as on personal observations of the negative effects of industrialization. He died around 1820, penniless, in prison.

4. See, for example, Marshall Sahlins, 'The Original Affluent Society', in his *Stone-Age Economics*, London 1974, pp. 1-40; and Pierre Clastres, *Society Against the State*, Oxford 1977, chapter 11.

5. The best recent discussion of the functioning and limits of these regimes is Ferenc Fehér et al., *Dictatorship over Needs*, Oxford 1983. See also the important

criticisms of their argument in Mihàly Vajda, 'East-Central European Perspectives', in *Civil Society and the State*.

6. Benjamin Franklin, *Autobiography*, London 1886, p. 170.

7. Max Weber, *The Protestant Ethic and the Spirit of Capitalism*, New York 1958, p. 179.

8. The brutal, time-governed exploitation of factory workers by private employers in early nineteenth-century civil societies was described with great passion by Marx in the first volume of *Capital. A Critical Analysis of Capitalist Production*, Moscow 1970, pp. 252-3: 'In its blind unrestrainable passion, its were-wolf hunger for surplus labour, capital oversteps not only the moral, but even the merely physical maximum bounds of the working-day. It usurps the time for growth, development, and healthy maintenance of the body. It steals the time required for the consumption of fresh air and sunlight. It higgles over a meal-time, incorporating it where possible with the process of production itself, so that food is given to the labourer as to a mere means of production, as coal is supplied to the boiler, grease and oil to the machinery. It reduces the sound sleep needed for the restoration. reparation, refreshment of the bodily powers to just so many hours of torpor as the revival of an organism, absolutely exhausted, renders essential. It is not the normal maintenance of the labour-power which is to determine the limits of the working-day; it is the greatest possible daily expenditure of labour-power, no matter how diseased, compulsory, and painful it may be, which is to determine the limits of the labourers' period of repose. Capital cares nothing for the length of life of labour-power. All that concerns it is simply and solely the maximum of labour-power, that can be rendered fluent in a working-day. It attains this end by shortening the extent of the labourer's life, as a greedy farmer snatches increased produce from the soil by robbing it of its fertility.'

9. See John Keane and John Owens, *After Full Employment*, London 1986, chapter 1.

10. See E.P. Thompson, *The Making of the English Working Class*, Harmondsworth 1972, pp. 853-4n. Thompson here criticizes the view of G.M. Young (*Victorian England*, Oxford 1936, p. 27) that 'unemployment was beyond the scope of any idea which early Victorian reformers had at their command, largely because they had no word for it'.

11. This nostalgia is arguably strongest within the socialist tradition. A typical example is to be found in a recent booklet issued by the Communist Party of Britain, Marxist-Leninist, *Unemployment*, London 1984, p. 15: 'No labour movement today can claim to be moving in the direction of socialism if it does not have as the first inscription on its banner 'an end to unemployment – we *will* work'. No amount of alternative plans for coping with new technology can act as a substitute for the struggle in the workplace to safeguard jobs.' Political voluntarism (combined with inaccurate statistics) is a defining feature of Göran Therborn, *Why Some Peoples are More Unemployed Than Others*, London 1986, which interprets unemployment as primarily a consequence of the bad faith of neo-conservative governments. The weaknesses of this position are discussed in John Keane and John Owens, 'The Political Dangers of a Statutory Right to Work', *Critical Social Policy*, 21, Spring 1988.

12. All citations are from André Gorz, *Farewell to the Working Class. An Essay on Post-Industrial Socialism*, London 1982, and *Paths to Paradise. On the Liberation From Work*, London 1985. Also relevant are his 'Qui ne travaille pas mangera quand même', *Lettre internationale*, 8, Spring 1986; and 'The American Model and the French Left', *Socialist Review*, 84, November-December 1985, pp. 101-8.

13. Most recently, see Robert A. Dahl, *A Preface to Economic Democracy*, Cambridge 1985. The classic social democratic statement of this position is T.H.

Marshall, 'Citizenship and Social Class', in *Sociology at the Crossroads*, London 1963, pp. 67-127: 'the basic civil right is the right to work.' The same argument is repeated in Mike Rustin, 'A Statutory Right to Work', in *For a Pluralist Socialism*. London 1985, pp. 147-72. Of course, some contributions to recent democratic theory remain wholly silent about the whole issue of paid and unpaid work. A case in point is Benjamin Barber's *Strong Democracy; Participatory Politics for a New Age* (Berkeley and Los Angeles, 1984).

14. See *After Full Employment*, chapter 1 and passim.

15. This trend appears to be more long-standing than Gorz supposes. According to R.E. Pahl, *Divisions of Labour*, Oxford 1984, p. 335, between the 'full employment' years of 1960 and 1980, the number of full-time employees in Britain fell by over 2 million, whereas that of part-time employees doubled to 4.4 million, of whom 3.8 million were women. According to other estimates, only 5 per cent of paid workers in 1951 had part-time employment in Britain, compared with 21 per cent today, most of these being located in the service sector. Consistent with this trend, the workforce of British companies such as Sainsbury's and Marks and Spencer's is now over 60 per cent part-time, and employers in general talk more and more of the need for greater 'flexibility' in their labour requirements.

16. From a television interview, London, August 1983.

17. Paul Lafargue, *The Right to Be Lazy* (1883), Chicago 1975, p. 35: 'Let us be lazy in everything, except in loving and drinking, except in being lazy.'

18. According to Gorz, extensive urbanization, the dominance of capitalist consumerism and the growth of state-directed services such as health and education have together resulted in a collapse of traditional networks of mutual aid as well as in a general decline in individuals' capacity for self-reliance. He claims that this decline of mutual aid and self-reliance is a major source of unfreedom in employment societies, and that it is likely to be strengthened by the new long wave of information technology-based accumulation. He consequently argues against this bureaucratizing trend, and for a renewal of popular know-how and self-reliance in matters of health, housing, food consumption and childcare. If implemented, this recommendation would undoubtedly lead to an *expansion* of the quantity of unpaid work performed by individuals outside the formal labour market.

19. The most important available sketch of the form of economic activities appropriate to a democratic civil society (and the best corrective to Gorz's blindspot) is Alec Nove, *The Economics of Feasible Socialism*, London 1983. Nove's attempted break with the economic assumptions of both statist and 'self-managing' conceptions of socialism is laudable, and certainly compatible with my attempts to provide radically different terms for thinking about the subject of democracy and socialism.

20. Harry Braverman, *Labor and Monopoly Capital*, New York 1974.

21. See Birgit Mahnkopf, *Verbürgerlichung. Die Legende vom Ende des Proletariats*, Frankfurt am Main and New York 1985.

22. Keith Middlemas, 'Unemployment: the Past and Future of a Political Problem', in *Unemployment*, edited Bernard Crick, London 1981, p. 141.

23. Fritz Vilmar, 'Reduction in Working Hours – a Way to Full Employment?', in *The Future of Work: Challenge and Opportunity*, edited by Gabriel Fragnière, Maastricht 1984, p. 78.

24. F. Walz, 'Shorter Working Hours and Their Impact on Overall Employment', *Swiss Bank Corporation Economic and Financial Prospects*, 1, February/March 1984, p. 5; Rolande Cuvillier, *The Reduction of Working Time*, Geneva 1984.

25. *Eurostat: Labour Force Sample Survey, 1977*, Brussels 1978, table 21, p. 31. According to a British TUC report, only 35 per cent of manual workers do not

work overtime. The real average for those who do is therefore approximately ten hours per week, in other words, a working week of about fifty hours (European Trade Union Confederation Campaign for Reduced Working Time, *TUC Progress Report No. 1*, November 1979, p. 9).

26. OECD, *Labour Supply, Growth Constraints and Work Sharing*, Paris 1982; *Europäische Wirtschaft*, 10, October 1985, pp. 1-9.

27. Friedman's proposed negative income tax is an example of this; another version is sketched in Keith Roberts, *Automation, Unemployment and the Distribution of Income*, Maastricht 1982. In the hands of advocates of the 'strong state, free market' strategy, the social wage principle is understood as a mechanism for simplifying social policy arrangements as well as for improving the mobility of paid labour and generating greater 'flexibility' (read: reduction) of wages and salaries. The social policy institutions of the state, it is said, could be run more efficiently and cost effectively. Above all, the market mechanism could be rejuvenated. The state's provision of a guaranteed subsistence income to citizens would allow employees to adjust to the demands of employers. Old industries presently in decline and new enterprises, especially those linked to the new microelectronics technologies, would be able to reduce their wages and salaries bill by paying workers less. Job-sharing and part-time employment, especially in poorly paid and insecure jobs, would also be likely to increase; supported by a subsistence income, and offered the option of a part-time job, the presently unemployed would have an incentive to enter the labour market in order to supplement their state-provided income with earned wages.

28. See Karl Hinrichs, Claus Offe and Helmut Wiesenthal, 'Time, Money and Welfare State Capitalism', in *Civil Society and the State*.

29. Some stimulating suggestions are developed in Robert J. van der Veen and Philippe van Parijs, 'Universal Grants versus Socialism', *Theory and Society*, 15, 1987, pp. 723-57.

4

Party-centred Socialism?

Reflections on Contemporary European Socialism and its Party Forms

> Faction is ever ready to seize all occasional advantages; and
> mankind, when in hazard from any party, seldom finds a
> better protection than that of its rival.
>
> Adam Ferguson (1767)

A 'Law' of Party Oligarchy?

Many issues of vital importance to the contemporary socialist
tradition – the recent electoral setbacks of socialist parties on the
'parliamentary road', the failures of Eurocommunism and the
crises of 'real socialist' regimes – are inseparable from considerations of party politics. Contemporary socialism seems thinkable
only in terms of parties, party leaders and their leading role as
agents in the struggle for state power.

This close affinity between socialism and political parties has
older roots. During the course of the past century and a half, the
socialist tradition has been marked by a deep process of 'politicization'. Modern socialism originated in Europe during the first
quarter of the nineteenth century as a heterogeneous social
movement on bad terms with the fledgling European party
systems. It has since become, with few exceptions, closely dependent upon various types of political parties and party systems.
Early nineteenth century socialism developed as a social
movement within the most hidden interstices of civil society. In
those European countries where civil liberties were virtually non-
existent, it was forced to operate entirely within the hidden

subsoil of civil society. The practical struggles of the first socialists were wholly outside the party system, which was viewed, with great hostility, as a mechanism for ensuring the political dominance of the wealthy aristocratic and bourgeois social classes.

Early socialists organized themselves through a variety of contestatory strategies. No doubt, some of their tactics (e.g., Blanqui's Society of Families and the Society of the Seasons in France, and the Society of the Despised and the League of the Just in Germany) were statist and authoritarian in style and intention; they aimed at emancipating workers from wage slavery and bourgeois political domination through the armed conquest of political power by a group of tightly disciplined conspirators. Other socialist strategies – the formation of educational circles, self-help and corresponding societies, co-operatives, trade unions and groups for petitioning and pressuring legislatures – had more openly democratic effects, inasmuch as they contributed to the pluralization of power within civil society and the state's subjection to its demands. Until the final years of the nineteenth century, the established systems of party government typically reacted against these initiatives with various forms of political repression, including the imprisonment, execution or exiling of the leadership of the socialist movement. In its early years, socialism was not a subject, but a mere object of party government.

The contrast with our times, when socialism appears to be almost a perfect synonym for parties and their struggle to achieve and maintain state power, is very striking. From being a social movement deeply antagonistic to aristocratic-bourgeois party government in the first half of the nineteenth century, socialism has become obsessed with parties, party systems and state power. For reasons of space, I cannot examine how and why this long-term shift from an anti-party perspective to a cultish party-centred conception of the 'road to socialism' came about. I can only note its contemporary effects, among the most debilitating of which is the serious decline of socialist theorizing about political parties – certainly if compared with the early decades of this century, when fierce battles were waged over the socialist party form and its participation in 'bourgeois' party systems.* For

---

* These controversies matured during the two decades after 1905 when, broadly speaking, three different party models vied for support within the socialist movement: (a) the *parliamentary social democratic party*, defended, for instance, by J. Ramsay MacDonald's *Socialism and Society* (London 1905), especially chapter 6. Capitalist societies are seen to be subject presently to 'non-catastrophic and non-

more than half a century, and despite deepening uncertainty about its future, the socialist tradition has permitted its parties to function in a twilight zone, as primarily a matter of practice rather than of theory. During this time, serious discussion about parties has declined seriously, to the point where questions concerning the origins, consequences and possible future of socialist parties have fallen into obscurity.

While this development is proving to be a short-lived phenomenon – or so I shall argue later in this essay – it is important from the outset to understand why, for some decades now, the subject of socialist political parties has been something of a settled issue. Critics of the socialist tradition often argue that the observation that the socialist tradition is now deeply politicized is self-evident and trivial, inasmuch as there is a 'natural', that is inevitable, affinity between socialism and political parties. These critics usually pin their claims on Robert Michels's *Zur Soziologie*

---

revolutionary laws'. These laws stimulate social cleavages and unrest, as well as a corresponding decline of bourgeois parties and the rise of socialist political parties and organizations (such as the Labour Representation Committee, formed in Britain in 1900) aiming at 'political readjustment'. According to MacDonald's evolutionary socialism, the labour movement must work for the formation of socialist parties and organizations whose aim is the realization of 'a positive view of the state' – one which recognizes that the modern parliamentary state in civilized countries is already democratic and that, hence, through party-political organization, pressure can be brought on this state to enact legislation which removes poverty, creates a 'hive of busy workers', reinforces the 'social instinct' and, in general, promotes social order and fairness; (b) this parliamentary road to socialism is challenged directly by *revolutionary syndicalism*. In the view of writers such as Georges Sorel (*Réflexions sur la violence* (1908)) only spontaneous, militant proletarian solidarity – as it is expressed in the form of the general strike – can dissolve the bourgeois domination crystallized in parliamentary politics. The possibility of socialism is seen to be the work of civil society itself. The workers' movement, initially in but not of civil society, summons itself against the power of capital and its state apparatus without the mediation of the party form or the party system; (c) the *vanguardist party-dominated road to socialism*, evident, for example, in Georg Lukács's *Tactics and Ethics. Political Essays 1919-1929* (London 1972). Especially from the time of the failure of the factory councils in Italy in 1920, Lukács criticized various aspects of syndicalist politics, insisting that only the centralized, tightly disciplined cadre party is capable of seizing, organizing and directing political power, thereby initiating the leap forward into socialism. The general strike alone – the tactic of folded arms, as Lukács called it – is insufficient. Only the revolutionary party could prevent the degeneration of the workers' movement by raising its spontaneous actions to the plane of class-conscious activity – in other words, to the level of awareness the movement would have if it were able to comprehend its true position within the relations of production of civil society. The revolutionary party, equipped with absolute knowledge of history, is the midwife of the proletariat – the organizational expression of the proletariat's (imputed) revolutionary will.

des Parteiwesens in der modernen Demokratie (1911).[1] According to this classic interpretation, all large-scale organizations, including modern socialist political parties, necessarily give their officers a near monopoly of power over both their rank-and-file members and the social movement(s) they nominally serve. Michels argued that the swallowing of social movements by the party form, and the concentration of power in the hands of party leaders and administrators, flows not only from what he called the 'essential incompetence' of the masses,[2] and from their pathological, sheep-like desire for 'tried and trusted' charismatic leadership.[3] Party oligarchy and dominance of social movements is propelled mainly by the factors of technical complexity and tactical skill. Social movements locked in battle with opponents who are already organized in political parties can defend their perceived interests only by forming party organizations as well. In turn, these party organizations can function efficiently and effectively only if they are organized hierarchically and led by a permanent staff of expert officials, executive committees and bold, energetic, adroit and charismatic leaders. Michels posited a 'general rule': 'The growth of the power of leaders is directly proportional to the expanding scope of the organization.'[4]

For these reasons of mass psychology, complexity and tactics, direct, inner-party democracy declines. Party representatives become dominant over the represented. And socialist parties inevitably come to resemble military organizations dominated by a permanent oligarchy. Viewing the party machine as a hammer in its own hands, the party oligarchy skilfully harnesses a variety of power resources which its privileged position makes available to any leaders. Among these power resources are party funds and information, which can be used to silence dissenters as well as to secure consent for leadership policies; acquired occupational skills, such as organizing meetings, speechmaking and writing articles; control over the party's day to day administration; and threats to resign and, hence, to disrupt severely the normal functioning of the party organization. These resources greatly strengthen the hand of the party hierarchy over its rank and file, the social movement from which it emerged, as well as its more distant electoral supporters. The caesarist party oligarchy becomes driven increasingly by the instinct of self-preservation, even if this instinct contradicts the original ideals of the social movement which the party was established to defend. The party oligarchy comes to live *off* (rather than *for*) the social movement within which it was born.

As a consequence, the party oligarchy becomes convinced that only a compact and well-disciplined party is capable of translating the lofty ideals of socialism into action. It develops an allergic reaction to any socialist struggles conducted by freelances, amateurs and 'rebels' inside and outside the ranks of the organized party. Under pressure from 'the law of the historical necessity of oligarchy',[5] the external form of the party, its bureaucratic, machine-like organization, gains the upper hand over its inner soul. The doctrinal and theoretical substance of the party is sacrificed whenever it interferes with the needs of the smooth-functioning party machine. From a means of struggle, the socialist party becomes an end in itself. It comes to resemble a state within a state, a miniature copy of the state organization it opposes: 'Generated to overthrow the centralized power of the state, starting from the idea that the working class need merely secure a sufficiently vast and solid organization in order to triumph over the organization of the state, the party of the workers has ended by acquiring a vigorous centralization of its own, based upon the same cardinal principles of authority and discipline which characterize the organization of the state.'[6]

In several ways, Michels's account of the growing discrepancy between the ideals and strategies of the early twentieth century oppositional socialist party remains unsurpassed. It raises questions of fundamental importance to the analysis of the subsequent history of socialist parties and their oligarchic tendencies. His analysis also provides a rich catalogue of techniques used by party leaders to manipulate those whom they claim to serve. And there can be little doubt that its iconoclastic and disturbing conclusions still make it compulsory reading for democrats of every persuasion. Nevertheless, Michels's assertion that there is a 'natural' affinity between socialism and oligarchic political parties must be contested, especially when it forms the basis of contemporary explanations for the prevailing party-dominated conception of socialism mentioned at the outset. More obviously, *Zur Soziologie des Parteiwesens in der modernen Demokratie* needs revision, if only because it was written within an earlier political and social conjuncture, which differs greatly from our own, and therefore renders some of Michels's theses obsolete. For example, his assumption that the socialist party leadership would always become integrated into the established order prevented him from anticipating the emergence of the revolutionary vanguard party (of the Bolshevik type). His conviction that the masses would always be clay in the hands of party leaders – a conviction inspired by the work of Le Bon and others – also blinded him to the contemporary complexity of the European workers' movements and their relationship to different party systems.[7] Less obviously, the 'natural' affinity between socialism and political parties which Michels postulates is better described as a type of 'elective affinity', that is, the wholly conventional (and therefore potentially reversible) outcome of specific historical developments. The prevailing party-centred conception of the 'road to socialism', I shall argue in the first half of this essay, has been fostered primarily by the dominance, in the European socialist tradition, of two different types of political parties: the west European compromise party and the totalitarian party of central-eastern Europe. Despite clear signs that they are presently losing their grip on the democratic imagination – a theme pursued in the second half of this essay – these two party forms, and not a supposed 'law of the historical necessity of oligarchy', have greatly reinforced the 'politicization' of the socialist movement, securing its transformation from a social movement within civil society to a more or less blind defender of party systems and state institutions.

The Compromise Party

This thesis can be illustrated initially with reference to late capitalist systems such as Britain, West Germany and Austria, where the influence of party-centred socialism has been secured and greatly extended in recent decades by the compromise party. The socialist compromise party – examples include the British Labour Party, the German SPD, the Austrian SPÖ and other member parties of the Socialist International – predominated after 1945 in most west European countries. Its roots are traceable to the crisis of the oppositional socialist mass party during the decade prior to the First World War.[8] In contrast to its class-based, extra-parliamentary predecessors (such as the SPD, which was regarded widely in the late nineteenth century as the prototype of a 'pure opposition' socialist party),[9] the compromise party explicitly abandons its revolutionary fervour and hostility to the existing party-political system. Wrenching political power from the government of the day, and ending once and for all the class-based system on which that government rests, are no longer its declared aims.

Throughout the post-Second World War era, no doubt, the

metamorphosis of the socialist party was a contested development. Bitter resistance came either from within the party (examples include the Jusos's criticism of the Bad Godesberg
programme of the SPD; struggles within the British Labour Party
over Gaitskellite revisionism; criticism of the SPÖ by the Scharf-
Hindels Left), or from without (e.g., from its trade union allies).
Especially after the active reform period of the early post-war
years (as in Britain) and the onset of the Cold War, the general
trend is nevertheless clear: the socialist struggle against the
dominant classes and their parties is no longer one of principle,
but mainly one of competitive jostling and bidding. The compromise party is not, as the early modern (Burkean) definition would
have it, a group of persons who intend to promote the public
welfare 'upon some principle on which they are all agreed'. The
compromise party is instead committed to the 'game of alterna-
tion' (Kirchheimer) characteristic of parliamentary democratic
systems. The compromise party assumes that socialism can be
achieved by instalments, each instalment being accepted without
serious opposition from other, non-socialist parties. Defeat at the
polls is therefore met with good temper. It is not regarded by the
party as a permanent or fatal surrender of its fundamental interests or aims. The party ceases to be a *Weltanschauungspartei*. It
becomes locked into the relatively narrow framework of oligopolistic competition with one, two or several other, non-socialist
parties. Oligopolistic party competition resembles a three-legged
race, in which the socialist party, in anticipation of similar
responses from its competitors, defends policies nearly identical
to those of its opponents, areas of disagreement among all parties
being confined to matters of product differentiation: to the ordering of priorities among policies as well as to the methods to be
relied upon in their implementation. The class enemy, whose
defeat was once viewed as the condition of socialist triumph,
becomes the political opponent, and coexistence with that
opponent is accepted as a precondition of political democracy.
This logic was well summarized by Willy Brandt during the
heyday of the compromise party: 'In a sound and developing
democracy, it is the norm and by no means exceptional that the
parties put forward similar, even identical demands in a number
of fields. Questions to do with priorities, the rank order of tasks to
be solved, as well as methods and accents thereby more and more
become the substance of opinion formation.'[10]

More or less in harmony with its non-socialist party
opponents, the compromise party becomes committed firmly to

defending and expanding Keynesian welfare state arrangements. Its overriding concern is to temporarily mobilize all strata of civil society and, on election day, to win a maximum number of votes and parliamentary seats. In pursuit of this end, the compromise party generally observes five fundamental rules.

First, it engages in constant publicity efforts to present a 'moderate' self-image to voters. The party works hard at becoming a purveyor of middle-of-the-road consensus: it strives to shake off its old (allegedly vote-losing) image as an intense, sectarian defender of specific clientele, such as the industrial working class. The contrast with, say, the late nineteenth century SPD tactic of 'pure opposition' is clear. Between the time of the Erfurt Programme of 1891 and 1905, when the Party was divided increasingly by the rise of reformist and revolutionist factions,[11] the SPD consistently used the Reichstag more as a platform of proletarian agitation than as a (potential) legislative mechanism (refusing either to vote for the national budget or to acknowledge the authority of the Kaiser, for instance). Outside the parliamentary arena, it aimed to popularize the *sozialistische Geist* – the principles of internationalism, full political democracy (including votes for women, proportional representation, direct election of officials and referenda and recall mechanisms) and a socialist economy based on common ownership of the means of production – through unsparing criticism of the capitalist order and its *Klassenstaat*. The compromise party, in stark contrast to this strategy of pure opposition, tries to abandon its old image of itself as an uncompromising 'workers' party' dressed in a cloth cap. Instead it represents itself as a 'people's party' capable of competently and responsibly managing the political system in the public interest.

Secondly, the compromise party seeks to bolster its middle-of-the-road image by concentrating on settled issues, that is, upon relatively uncontroversial themes (such as continuous economic growth, the 'defence of the nation', expanded social welfare and educational opportunities) that do not meet resistance from the major power groups within civil society and the state. Especially when in opposition, and close to election day, the compromise party may well be critical of the inept handling of matters by the governing party of the day. But even then it must continuously reaffirm its support both for the established way of doing things, and for the goals upon which 'the majority' agrees. The compromise party (as the 1951 Frankfurt Declaration signed by western Europe's socialist parties makes clear[12]) neither anticipates nor desires advance toward a fully socialized society. In fact, no radical transformation of the existing political and social order, even as a distant goal, is envisaged. The party's 'basic' programme limits itself to settled issues: the conservation and extension of social security, public housing, full employment of labour and capital, improvement of the standard of living, the acceptance (reluctantly or enthusiastically) of NATO.

Thirdly, the compromise party attempts to capture a nationwide audience by becoming chameleonic. It adopts policies which are both vague and flexible enough to permit the most variegated interpretations, as well as sufficiently attractive to rally many groups and individual voters around the party. A compulsory optimism based on vague and generalized assertions of humane sentiments and concern for the national welfare is very useful in this respect. Preserving a good measure of policy indeterminacy and elasticity is always a good thing, for when party proposals and policies are too concrete and specific, their defects can be exposed more easily, thereby becoming weapons in the hands of the party's competitors.

Fourth, the compromise party expects most voters and other social power groups to be passive admirers of the party's well-executed electoral campaigns. The old oppositional socialist parties embraced their electoral supporters more closely. They functioned simultaneously as a channel of social protest, as a source of solidarity and protection among their supporters, and as a custodian of the memory of past struggles and a defender and popularizer of future visions. The German SPD, for instance, developed tight (if tense) links with the rapidly growing trade-union movement. Almost every German town and city had its party sporting club and cultural association, its socialist youth organizations, daily newspaper, consumer co-operative and *Parteikneipe*. The SPD functioned as a kind of secular chapel, uniting its expanding membership and sympathizers in the active pursuit of a vision of a better, more just life under post-capitalist conditions.

The compromise party, by contrast, is much less concerned with the moral and political *encadrement* of civil society. Instead of feverishly channelling supporters into its ranks, it concentrates mainly on achieving electoral success, on temporarily capturing a nationwide audience for its claims. It thereby reduces most citizens to passive involvement in party affairs, to gazing upon its skirmishes and manoeuvrings within the electoral or parliamentary arenas. The degree to which the socialist party can become a party of compromise aloof from particular interests is definitely limited (as the trade-union 'block vote' within the British Labour Party indicates) by the extant patterns of social organization and resistance within civil society. This factor explains why the socialist compromise party cannot entirely abandon attempts to align itself with trade unions and other social power groups, particularly those which serve as important reservoirs of financial and electoral support. The party nevertheless strives to temper its relations with particular social power groups (and their supporters within the party), for fear of dissuading voters whose sympathies lie with *other* social power groups. This strategy was evident, for instance, in the 'party of government' course adopted by the British Labour Party between 1964 and 1970, when the leadership emphasized the need for being tough with the party's traditional supporters, and especially the trade unions (as during the seamen's strike of 1966, and the government's 'In Place of Strife' proposals for the reform of the trade unions). As a consequence, by actively discouraging and suppressing conflict within its ranks, and by keeping its distance from voters and other power groups within civil society, the compromise party functions less and less as an open, two-way transmission belt between civil society and the state. It rather comes to resemble an upright funnel connected with the state, a funnel whose channels are less than fully open, and therefore less than fully responsive, to pressures from below from the sphere of civil society.[13]

Finally, the compromise party attempts to steady itself by relying heavily on the dynamics of charismatic leadership. The process of nominating and appointing leadership comes to occupy a crucial place in the life of the compromise party. So also does the image of the party leader, who becomes a (partial) substitute for the lack of agreement upon goals within the party. Since the strategic aim of the compromise party is to maximize its votes on election day, a prominent and well-liked leader (such as Willy Brandt, Olof Palme, Harold Wilson or Bruno Kreisky) can help to firmly implant a positive image of the party in the minds of millions of voters – just as a good advertising campaign can help secure a commodity's dominance of a market for mass-produced, standardized consumer goods. No doubt, there are desirable limits upon the zeal and idiosyncracies of the party leader. Since the aim of the party is electoral victory, its leader must seek prominence without 'saying the wrong thing' or 'going too far'. Ideally, the leader should be an uncommon person of common opinions. On television, in the newspapers and at public gatherings, the successful leader must be sufficiently distinguished in looks, style and content so as to make his/her party plainly recognizable. But the difference must never be so great as to frighten off potential customers, thereby driving them into the ranks of a competing producer of a similar, but not identical product.

The One-party System

Questions concerning the possible instability and future of the socialist compromise party can be set aside momentarily, in order to introduce into the discussion its main contemporary counterpart, the totalitarian party of late socialist regimes such as Poland and Czechoslovakia.[14] The roots of this one-party system are traceable to the Bolshevik Revolution (although, arguably, they run deeper, to the practice of party discipline, the calculated use of promotions, demotions and expulsions, and the sometimes life or death struggles for organizational control within the oppositional socialist parties of the nineteenth and early twentieth centuries). Its geographic scope and influence was extended by Stalin into the countries of central-eastern Europe in the aftermath of the Second World War, and always (as in the *coup de Prague* of 1948) at the expense of compromise parties, socialist and non-socialist alike.

In these late socialist regimes of central-eastern Europe, the basic organizing principle of life is the leading role of the Party. The Party is sovereign – it is the central nervous system of the political order. All important powers of decisionmaking and administration are concentrated in its hands.[15] The Party organization is itself pyramid-shaped; all Party members are formally equal, but the higher echelons – the senior *nomenklatura* – are definitely 'more equal' than the rest. Having carefully climbed the ladders of power within the Party, the senior member enjoys wide-ranging privileges, including a special kind of non-monetarized wealth attached to the leadership roles. The leading members of the Party choose the Party membership, and also structure the outcomes of the Party Congress. Constitutional changes must be approved by the Party leadership before going through the mere formality of acceptance by the parliamentary bodies. The Party executive monopolizes key decisions concerning investment, production and consumption. In matters of law, legislative and judicial powers are also supervised closely by the Party executive; and in particularly important cases, it directly determines sentences, the courts functioning only as executive bodies. In the field of communications, the hand of the Party leadership is omnipresent as well. The editorial 'We' cultivated in the socialist party presses of the Second International (a development noted by Michels[16]) is finely tuned and extended continuously to the population at large. The Party seeks to encase the whole political order within an ideological pyramid of highly clichéd and often bizarre language ('Socialism is a young, dynamic social order, which is seeking and testing in its stride ways of making even better use of its advantages, of organizing and controlling social development most efficiently',[17] etc.). The army and police are also supervised closely by the Party executive; in central-eastern Europe, the secret police (who are, according to a Polish quip, the beating heart of the Party) are even supervised directly by their Party-controlled Soviet counterparts.

The monopoly of the Party leadership in matters of state policymaking and administration, production and consumption, communications, law and policing leads unavoidably to arbitrary decisionmaking. It also produces a constant widening of the discretionary powers of the Party authorities. The line of the Party leadership is always correct. Even when it contradicts itself or changes course markedly, the Party has a sibylline quality, representing itself as wise and omniscient. Its 'scientific' pronouncements are assumed to be incontrovertible, even if onlookers often find them mysterious, confused and unfathomable. The standpoint of the Party, especially its leadership, is synonymous with life itself: 'Life is with the Party, the Party is the heart, the soul of Life.'[18]

The overall function of the Party and its leading echelons is to determine the substantive aims and formal methods to be followed by all subsidiary organizations and personnel. The leading echelons of the Party seek to penetrate, strictly subordinate and centrally unify the vast labyrinth of state ministries, which perforce have distinct chains of bureaucratic command, interact with each other at various levels, and develop and defend (partially) divergent interests. In this task of centrally co-ordinating and synthesizing the various state bureaucracies, the sovereign Party leadership is reinforced by a complex network of subordinate Party structures (e.g., trade unions, youth and women's organizations) staffed by middle- and lower-level Party members. The task of these ancillary Party organizations is to enforce the primary objectives of the ruling pinnacle of the Party and, thereby, to monitor, regulate and discipline each and every organization within the political order.

Their function is also to maintain the Party's firm grip on each and every individual citizen. Since proportionately few citizens are Party members, the vast majority of the population are considered second-class citizens. The life chances of a young person who fails to join the Party, for instance, are extremely limited, for s/he thereby refuses to accept the principle that only Party members can and should govern. That person also refuses to acknowledge the converse of this principle: that the programmes and actions of the Party are always binding upon its individual subjects, who must therefore be prevented systematically from developing alternative policies, organizations and forms of expression in matters of politics, production and culture. These policy areas are the exclusive prerogative of the Party, its ministries and ancillary organizations. Their goal is unchallenged hegemony, the complete subordination and incorporation of all individuals into the crystalline structures of the Party-dominated state. The vast majority of the citizenry of late socialist regimes has no say at all − not even legally − in the decisive question of who will rule them. This question is always decided in advance. Since the Party is always right, even retroactively, it must lead, limit and teach its citizens. The one-party system is in this precise sense totalitarian: its action programmes are directed constantly at preventing the formation of a pluralistic, self-organizing civil society opposed to the Party-dominated political order.

The one-party system is described here (and throughout this essay) in an ideal−typical manner, since the totalized control it seeks has neither been achieved fully nor assumed the same form in every country and every period since 1945. Thus, the designs of the sovereign Party are to a limited degree elastic, due to resistance emanating from within − and without − its ranks (as in Czechoslovakia in 1968). Depending on the calculations of the Party leadership, the one-party system can also display a degree of tolerance towards its subjects (as in Hungary, where it is today possible for subjects to open a private restaurant, but not a private publishing house). Such concessions are nevertheless always tenuous; democratic pluralism is always considered illegitimate.

The mode of control exercised by one-party systems has also varied during the years since the Second World War. In the immediate post-war years, for instance, the pro-Stalinist parties of central-eastern Europe carried through programmes aimed at completely extinguishing civil society through tactics (such as purges, arrests, torture, labour camps and show trials) that were wholly capricious, delirious and brutal. During this period, neither ordinary citizens nor Party members were safe from their own Party's tactics. More recently, as in post-1968 Czechoslovakia or the Soviet Union under Gorbachev's programme of *perestroika*, the one-party system has come to display some decidedly novel characteristics.[19] The Party continues to rely ultimately upon government by fear and brutal repression, but in considerably more anonymous, selective and calculated form. Furthermore, while the Party still attempts to asphyxiate civil society under an ideological tent of images of the past, present and future world, almost nobody (probably not even senior Party apparatchiks) believes any longer in its pantomime of ritualized claims. There are even attempts to remedy this situation by renovating these claims from above with more believable slogans – such as openness, democratic change, performance – as well as talk (in Hungary, for instance) of 'a free civil society' (Imre Poszgay). The Party's utter disregard for efficiency, characteristic of the delirium of the Stalin period, has also been abandoned. Especially in matters of administration and production, much emphasis is given to efficiency, productivity and the need for permanent reform. Finally, no longer do the parties of late socialist regimes strive to control fully the bodies and souls of their subjects, to embrace everything in depth, to magnetize everyone so as to produce a single will, crystallized in the caesarist leader. One-party systems are no longer guided by the old totalitarian formula, *L'état, c'est nous*. The Party is instead now content with the regulation and control of *apparent* behaviour; so long as its subjects quietly conform and only grumble among themselves, they are probably safe.

Under these more recent conditions of post-Stalinism, the citizens of one-party systems are expected to join the 'community of the defeated' (Ivan Klíma), to abide by its basic unwritten rules: that 'the embodiment of the policy of the Party in the activity of the State has been and remains the most important condition ... for widening and deepening socialist democracy' (Gorbachev); that there will only ever be one governing Party, to which everything, including truth itself, belongs; that the world is divided into enemies and friends of the Party and, accordingly, that compliance with Party policies is rewarded, dissent penalized; and, finally, that the Party no longer requires the complete devotion of the citizen, only the quiet acceptance of its dictates. This means that the Party only recognizes or insists upon discipline, caution, respectability, self-censorship, resignation, and moral flaccidity among its citizens ('far better not to know and not to think'). Conversely, the Party fears and actively discourages independence of mind and judgement, excellence, boldness, perspicacity, courage, public commitment to democratic principles and the pagan distrust of official jargon and bureaucratic regulations. These basic unwritten rules of one-party systems specify that no citizen is ever fully innocent before the Party apparatus. In effect, this apparatus subjects each citizen to a form of permanent internment. And since the Party is always right, even retroactively, those citizens who cease being humble and obedient Party followers are automatically considered to be its deserters and, therefore, enemies of socialism. Citizen opposition to the Party is always regarded by its top echelons as 'decadent' and seditious, which is also why the (potential) opponents of the Party are to be found not only among the intellectuals, but also in every cafe, street queue, factory and church.

Anti-Party Politics

> Two Poles are travelling by train between Lodz and Warsaw. One groans constantly, apparently in pain: 'Ooh! Ooh!' The other Pole, losing patience completely, erupts: 'Can't you talk about anything else but politics!'

Among the deeply ironic and (for contemporary western socialists enamoured with party politics) puzzling consequences of the one-party system is the manner in which it is presently generating a deep popular hostility to the ideal of the leading role of the Party – and to the 'socialist' ideology in which it envelops its subjects.[20] The rigid totalitarian one-party system is proving to be the gravedigger of the idea of socialism achieved through the vanguard party form. Among its democratic opponents, it is also stimulating a profound questioning of party politics per se; in this sense, or so I shall argue, it stimulates a type of anti-party activity reminiscent of sections of the early socialist movement during the first half of the nineteenth century.

The contours of this anti-party activity – described through terms such as 'independent civic initiatives', 'second culture', 'parallel politics', 'second economy' and 'parallel society' – are difficult to summarize because of their heterogeneity and protean quality. Anti-party activity may operate within middle and upper echelons of the state apparatus, or it may be 'underground' and invisible. It can be tightly co-ordinated or structured loosely. It may require a full-time or part-time commitment. Anti-party activity encompasses spontaneous individual acts of resistance, the actions of particular groups (such as Charta 77), and more broadly-based social movements. It may comprise underground enterprises, *samizdat* publishing, conversations among friends and relatives, underground music and poetry, and movements for women's rights, ecological protection, the defence of the poor and free trade unions. But in every case, the hostility of anti-party activity to the domination of the Party is a guiding theme. This massive and deep reaction against the one-party system can be measured in a preliminary way by comparing it with earlier twentieth-century eulogies of the monopolistic vanguard party. Consider, for instance, the following verse of Louis Aragon from the Stalin period:

Mon parti m'a rendu mes yeux et ma mémoire,
Mon parti m'a donné le sens de l'époque,
Mon parti, mon parti, merci pour tes leçons,
Et depuis ce temps là, tout me vient en chanson,
Le colère, l'amour, la joie et la souffrance.

The attitude of the democratic opposition in central-eastern Europe bears almost no similarity to this image of the party – indeed, there is a deep revulsion against its totalitarian implications. The one-party system is defined by its opponents as synonymous with 'politics'. In this totalitarian world organized by a single party, the opposition prefers not to speak of politics as a form of collectively based speech and interaction oriented to the attainment of the good life (as in the Aristotelean tradition). Rather, politics is viewed as a type of impersonal and unprincipled activity typical of sombre-suited Party apparatchiks, generals with tinted glasses, military-uniformed bureaucrats, leather-jacketed secret policemen and other cogs in the machinery of the party-dominated state. Politics is shrewdness and violence, the struggle of the few to win and exercise state power over the many. To be political is to be caught in the delirium of state power, despite political actors' rhetoric to the contrary. The appeals of the politician, for instance, are only so many means to the end of gaining and maintaining power over others. 'A politician for whom the exercise of power is not an end in itself is a contradiction in terms.'[21] Politics is inherently absolutist. Its field of operation, human beings living together in complex societies, is infinitely deep and wide, and this means that its hunger for seducing, manipulating and subsuming others is never satisfied fully.

The view of politics as the art of fraud, manipulation and control, as therefore no business of ordinary citizens, has a long history in central-eastern Europe. It is evident, for instance, in Thomas Mann's discussion of the 'terror' of politics in *Betrachtungen eines Unpolitischen* (1918). Even so, the restrictive definition of politics being developed among the democratic opposition is not simply a cultural product of that region. Its growing popularity is a direct effect of the one-party system itself. Some protagonists of the term venture further by denying that its use should be restricted in scope to one-party systems. These systems are viewed (by Václav Havel, for example[22]) as an ominous and grotesque trial model of a type of state power already implicit in the so far less developed and 'softer' forms of impersonal politics presently sweeping the whole of the globe. The party-dominated 'real socialist' regimes, in other words, are viewed as the possible shape of things to come, as the most complete and devilish expressions so far of the attempt of modern states to transform citizens into subjects who are compelled to act as if they were mere casts of extras in a fully politicized stage performance directed from above.

The nightmarish dystopia of totalizing politics drives the present-day democratic opposition to one-party systems into the preparation of a new antidote – anti-party politics. From the standpoint of anti-party politics, exemplified in the pathbreaking strategy developed after 1976 by the Komitet Obrony Robotników (KOR) in Poland, the one-party systems of late socialism are excessively political. Late socialism means too much political power, too little freedom from meddlesome politicians. Anti-party politics accordingly involves attempts to leave the fully politicized stage of the one-party system. It involves questioning and refusing that system at its deepest foundations, at the level of the everyday life of the individual and small group. To engage in anti-party politics is to deny the insatiable power-hunger of those who presently govern, to stop them in their tracks, and thereby to put politics in its proper place of securing and enhancing the existence of an independent, pluralist, self-organizing civil society. Anti-party politics aims to make political rulers more humble and polite. It is the practice of constructing a democratic civil society, of limiting and 'socializing' political power in its favour.

Anti-party politics is envisaged by its protagonists as essentially a slow and drawn-out process. Compared with the drama of a military coup d'état, the sudden proclamation of a curfew, or the scuffles of police and demonstrators, anti-party politics appears to be banal, a non-event. Deeply suspicious of organized attempts at grabbing power, it is both cautious and acephalous. In its fight against totalitarian power, anti-party politics often bases itself on networks of 'secret societies' (here there is an evident parallel with the eighteenth-century struggle against despotism[23]). It is concerned not to sharply define itself too quickly into rigid and highly visible institutional forms, which it knows can be spotted, 'decapitated' and eliminated more easily by the political authorities. The effects of anti-party politics are therefore often hidden, indirect, hard to measure and long-term. It is patient and does not easily give up, for its sense of time is quite differently organized than that of the traditional revolutionary left or right. It knows that it cannot succeed in days, weeks or months, and anti-party politics is convinced that there is no such thing as total defeat. Because of this different sense of time, it can, if necessary, wait a very long time and endure considerable setbacks. The main keyword of anti-party politics is solidarity, a type of pluralistic co-operation among previously isolated individuals and groups who, though they have been bruised and abused badly by the one-party system, remain convinced that a life devoid of meaning and independence is simply no life at all. Defenders of anti-party politics call for a 'solidarity of the shaken' (Patočka), and they reaffirm some old-fashioned European principles: sympathy and respect for others; the dignity and autonomy of the individual; honesty; and democratic self-determination.

It is not clear from this sketch of the anti-party reaction how (or indeed whether) the demands of an independent, self-organizing civil society could best be projected into the sphere of state institutions.[24] What is clear is that the democratic opponents of one-party systems are usually not concerned to form oppositional parties. Reminiscent of the early socialist movement, defenders of anti-party politics are deeply cautious about the party form, and when (as in Hungary) they are concerned with such issues, their aim is to publicize their conviction that electoral politics in the one-party system is a fraud, that official elections under totalitarian conditions have a regimenting function, in which citizens are sent to the ballot box like soldiers to the front.

It is important to understand the reasons for this refusal to form new political parties. It is not simply a matter of sour grapes or sober judgement concerning geopolitical realities. These realities are that the Soviet Union, equipped as it is with weaponry capable of annihilating the whole earth several times over, cannot be forced to withdraw militarily and politically from central-eastern Europe, and that, within the framework of Yalta, it therefore cannot acknowledge the legitimacy of open challenges to the one-party system, upon which its empire depends.

There are less obvious, more subtle and positive reasons why the democratic opposition shuns the party form. Those who work for anti-party politics know that the development of forms of social solidarity, though they can be driven underground easily by the state apparatus (which is specialized in the art of eliminating competing political organizations), are much more difficult to eliminate in root and branch than political parties. Under the extremely adverse conditions of the one-party system, anti-party politics minimizes the likelihood of a crushing, total defeat and, conversely, maximizes the chances of 'victories in defeat'. Those engaged in anti-party politics are also convinced that the possibility of democracy is conditional upon abandoning the traditional (Lukácsian–Leninist) aim of forming a revolutionary party in order to capture and then overthrow the machinery of state power, thereby forcibly dissolving the separation of state and civil society. Democratization is seen to be contradicted by revolutionary politics. The principle of revolution is not 'the irruption of the masses in their own destiny' (Trotsky), but the lust for power among jostling minorities of professional manipulators, who seek the ultimate prize summarized during the French Revolution by Joseph Fouché: 'Those who act in the spirit of the revolution are allowed everything.' Certainly, it is recognized that revolution is a transformative experience, an adventure of the heart and soul. Citizens initially feel strengthened by it. Their inner feelings of emptiness momentarily disappear. Astonished, they discover boundless energies within themselves. They experience joy in their determination to act and to change the world. Participation in the revolution becomes a giddy exploration of the unknown. The democratic opposition acknowledges all this. But it also recognizes that there comes a moment when disappointment, paralysis, melancholia, and vengeance replace the turbulent thrill of revolution. It is also suspicious of the unintended consequences of revolutionary politics. The old discourse of party-guided revolution, military discipline, heroic sacrifice and all-or-nothing victory – a discourse which supposed the existence of a knowable logic of History – is viewed as a dangerous anachronism of the early modern period. It is rejected as an undemocratic political ideology from the days of swords, guillotines and simple firearms which, if repeated nowadays, would likely lead to a frightening concentration of the means of power into the hands of the victorious few.*

The Limits of Revolutionary Syndicalism

The defenders of anti-party politics also reject the old revolutionary syndicalist recipe – defended most eloquently in Georges Sorel's *Réflexions sur la violence* (1908) – for dramatically toppling the state by means of a mass social movement from below. Since parallels are sometimes drawn (in western Europe, at least) between anti-party politics and Sorel's revolutionary syndicalism,

---

* This point can be illustrated by comparing the caustic, but light-hearted nineteenth-century scepticism of Théophile Gautier's *Les Jeunes-France*, Paris 1878, p. xv; 'What is a revolution? People fire guns in a street; that breaks many windows; scarcely anyone profits but the glaziers. The wind blows away the smoke. Those who stay on top push the others under ... It is worth the suffering to turn up so many good paving stones, which otherwise could not be moved!' with the sober warning of Adam Michnik that democracy is rarely born out of bloody upheavals, and that the strategy of putchism is likely to have totalitarian consequences: 'Taught by history, we suspect that by using force to storm the Bastilles of old we shall unwittingly build new ones ... The experience of being corrupted by terror must be implanted upon the consciousness of everyone who belongs to a freedom movement. Otherwise, as Simone Weil wrote, freedom will again become a refugee from the camp of the victors' ('Letter from the Gdansk Prison', *The New York Review of Books*, 18 July 1985, p. 44). A cursory glance at the history of modern revolutions from the late eighteenth to the late twentieth centuries suggests that Michnik is correct. From the French to the Iranian Revolutions, power struggles between political factions have always broken out. Groups of 'professional revolutionists' (Arendt) possessed of great initiative, organizational talent and elaborate doctrines have always made their appearance. At first, they appear to have listened to their fellow citizens who are rebelling. Later, these revolutionary groups claim to represent them. Eventually, they supplant them, always through violence. This dynamic of unintended consequences of revolutionary politics was seen clearly during the French Revolution by the greatest German liberal, Georg Forster. See his *Kleine Schriften und Briefe*, edited Claus Träger, Leipzig 1961, p. 344: 'The Revolution is a hurricane; who can harness it? Galvanized by its spirit, human beings find it possible to commit actions that posterity, out of sheer horror, will be unable to comprehend.'

their deep and important differences are worth spelling out in more detail.

Réflexions sur la violence belongs to a quite different historical context, of course. Amidst the growing involvement of the socialist tradition in party politics, and inspired by a wave of anti-parliamentary activity throughout western Europe after the 1902 Belgian general strike,[25] this classic syndicalist work is driven by the expectation of a profound crisis of both parliamentary socialist politics and the capitalist system. It is intoxicated with the apocalyptic idea of an 'absolute revolution' of the workers' movement against private property, the state and political parties.

Sorel expressed nothing but contempt for the 'democratic stupidity' of socialist party politics. The parliamentary road to socialism contributes blindly to the growing power and legitimacy of the state. The parliamentary socialist struggle against social slavery fosters the formation of new forms of political slavery (Sorel specifically draws upon Tocqueville's account of the rise of democratic despotism). By strengthening and legitimating the state machinery, parliamentary socialism contradicts its declared aim of eventually abolishing the state. Furthermore, parliamentary socialism masks the contradictory interests of labour and capital. Charmed and seduced by the pettifoggery and chicanery of electoral politics, and especially by promises of social welfare legislation enacted through the state, parliamentary socialism deepens the degeneracy which drags the bourgeoisie and the proletariat far from the path assigned them in Marx's theory. Enfeebled classes, Sorel observes, foolishly always put their trust in the protective powers of the state.

Finally, the parliamentary socialist tradition is deeply implicated in the spirit of Robespierre. Sorel argues – and most advocates of anti-party politics would agree – that every (attempted) political revolution from the time of 1789 has strengthened the repressive powers of the state. He also argues that, despite their good intentions, a parliamentary socialist government would likely continue and worsen this trend. There are no greater protagonists of order than victorious revolutionaries. In office – here Sorel anticipates the later argument of Michels – parliamentary socialism would institute a kind of dictatorship of the politician over his/her own followers. A parliamentary socialist government would be no different from other political revolutionaries, who have always pleaded 'reasons of state' – and accordingly employed repressive legal sanctions and police methods – against their enemies as soon as they came to power.

Sorel reasoned that these disastrous political outcomes could be prevented only if the socialist movement relied upon the resolute class separatism of the proletariat. Its refusal of centralized political leadership, its native sympathy for violent action and its growing belief in the efficacy of strikes exposes the fraudulence of ruling-class attempts to mediate state and civil society through parliamentary democratic politics. The violent direct action of the proletariat sharply polarizes civil society, which comes to resemble a field of battle between two antagonistic armies. The new middle class of salaried bureaucrats crumbles, capitalist employers are forced back into their class role, and class divisions are deepened and simplified, just when they seemed in danger of rotting in the marsh of parliamentary politics. Proletarian direct action, which originates in the small-scale, face-to-face *sociétés de résistance* of the trade unions, exposes and undermines the force organized by the bourgeoisie in the property and state systems. It also snaps the bonds of bourgeois habit and cowardice, and produces a new culture of solidarity in civil society. No longer blinded by party politics, the proletariat is ever more guided and inspired by myth, by learned bodies of shared, emotionally charged mental pictures (such as the idea of a general strike) which sharpen its determination to work towards a distant socialist future. The proletariat, initially in but not of civil society, ceases to be acted upon. It becomes a living social movement in possession of itself, and therefore capable of directing itself against the power of capital and its state apparatus – without the mediation of the party form or the party system. This process crystallizes in the actual drama of the general strike, likened by Sorel to a Napoleonic battle which crushes its adversary outright. The general strike of workers makes it clear, Sorel concluded, that only two historical options remain open to the socialist movement: either bourgeois decadence, in which the movement is swallowed up by a degenerating ruling class of property owners, administrators and politicians, or the violent revolutionary struggles of the proletariat to seize productive property from private capital and, thereby (note Sorel's reductionism) to abolish the state.

Notwithstanding their wholly different vocabularies, the protagonists of anti-party politics evidently share with the Sorelian strategy a deep antipathy to party politics and state power. But here the parallel comes abruptly to an end. Defenders of anti-party politics are deeply suspicious of ideological myths (see essays 6 and 7). They reject the Sorelian assumption that a single revolutionary class, arising out of the heart of civil society, could ever embody *la volonté générale*. Anti-party politics, stated simply, is a pluralistic and not a monistic type of opposition, which is also why – again in contrast to Sorel – it rejects the myth of the abolition or withering away of the state. A democratic civil society, one containing many and often conflicting elements and therefore subject constantly to controversy, innovation, the unknown and unintended, is seen to require a framework of state institutions, which can help prevent the outbreak of serious domestic conflict as well as negotiate with other states in the international arena. Hence, anti-party politics aims not to abolish political power, but to 'socialize' some portion of it in order to prevent its encroachment upon matters which are, simply speaking, none of its business.

The democratic opposition to one-party systems also rejects Sorelian-type myths of brave and heroic violence. Living under a heavily armed regime which ensures that surveillance, military parades, prison and fears of violence are constant everyday companions of the whole population, it understandably develops a deep antipathy towards the deployment of violence.[26] It associates bravery not with heroic acts of violence (such as terrorism, assassinations or kidnappings) against its perceived enemies, but with the civilized patience of citizens who seek to live decently in an indecent regime and therefore remain unmoved by acts of violence directed against them. It sees an inner connection between violence and politics, and therefore rejects the view that 'violence is the midwife of every old society pregnant with a new one' (Marx). Violence is the enemy of all societies, old and new. Again in contrast to Sorel, the democratic opposition develops a fundamentally different sense of time. It rejects fantasies of apocalyptic revolution because it knows that a precondition of a democratic civil society is that citizens acquire a measure of patience. It envisages a peaceful transformation of the one-party system by means of a *slowly ripening* development of civil society underneath the edifice of state power.

Finally, the defenders of anti-party politics shun the party form because – analogous to sections of the early socialist movement, such as Owenism – they sense that the possibility of democracy depends upon shaking off the presence of the one-party system within each and every individual by altering the relations of power 'closest' to them. Those who live a life of anti-party politics reject the innocent fiction that power in the one-party system is a thing to be grasped or abolished. Power is not concentrated in a single place (e.g., in the leading echelons of the Party or, in Sorel's version, within the ruling class). The regime is not divided between those who have power and those who are powerless. The one-party system is viewed as omnipresent, as a labyrinth of control, repression, fear and self-censorship which swallows up everyone within it, at the very least by rendering them silent, stultified and marked by some undesirable prejudices of the powerful. Since the lines of power organized by the one-party system pass through all its subjects, the latter can defend themselves against it only by being different in the most radical sense, that is, by driving the system out of their own personal lives. Democratic opposition is seen for this reason to be most éffective when it keeps its distance from politics. Democratization is not merely a matter, say, of replacing party-appointed officials with a government or head of state elected once every few years. Democratization rather depends on successfully cultivating mechanisms of self-protection, individuation and social co-operation in areas of life 'underneath' the party-dominated state: in the household, among friends, in the citizens' initiative, the workplace, the parallel economy and in the sphere of unofficial culture.

Problems of the Socialist Compromise Party

Due to their quite different institutional environments, organizational form and mode of operation, socialist compromise parties and one-party systems of the Soviet-type are not faced currently with identical problems, or even with problems of a similar magnitude. The crucially different contemporary fate of these two types of socialist parties must be kept constantly in mind when comparing their relative viability and popularity. Having noted (but not yet explained) that difference, it is nevertheless legitimate to ask – analogous to the line of enquiry examined above – some basic questions of the socialist compromise party: How durable or unstable is the prevailing compromise party-centred definition of socialism in the political systems of western Europe? Are there signs that the reign of the compromise party in those systems may be coming to an end or, at least, losing its grip? If so, can the decline of the compromise party effectively be reversed? If, on the contrary, the leading role of the compromise party is being eroded seriously, might socialists instead need to develop fresh perspectives which help question, as well as provide positive alternatives to, the prevailing party-centred conception of the 'road to socialism'?

These basic questions are appropriate and timely, since these are difficult times for the socialist compromise party. One index of these difficulties (which vary according to such factors as the type of party competition, electoral system and socialist tradition of each western European country) is the general spate of electoral losses suffered by compromise parties during the 1970s – a trend that has been reversed, and then only shakily, in Norway and Sweden, and Mediterranean countries (Portugal, Spain, Greece) formerly governed by military despotisms. Another index of these difficulties is the way in which the political party form is ceasing to be a relatively settled issue within the socialist tradition, as it was during the period after 1945. There are signs not only of a growing anxiety about the serious electoral vulnerability of compromise parties, but also of a decline of Panglossian confidence in the compromise party and the 'parliamentary road'.

No doubt, some part of this electoral anxiety and reduced confidence of compromise parties derives from their identification with Keynesian welfare state policies, such as the full employment of labour and capital, social welfare policies and defence of the nation-state under American supervision. As these policies have encountered increasing practical difficulties during the past two decades, socialist compromise parties' identification with the welfare state has proven to be an electoral and policy liability. Bereft of fresh theories and policies, compromise parties tend to suffer bouts of defensiveness and nostalgia; they lack coherent explanations of the failures of the Keynesian welfare state and how they might be remedied. This trend has been deepened by the (not unrelated) fragmentation of the old electoral alliance of trade unions and working-class and middle-class voters, upon which compromise parties typically depended after 1945.[27]

These developments – the crisis of Keynesian welfare state arrangements, the dimsightedness of policymaking and the fragmentation of old constituencies – help explain the general spate of electoral losses incurred by compromise parties during the 1970s. The reasons for their present problems nevertheless run deeper and wider. These difficulties affect not merely the policy content and patterns of electoral support for the compromise parties, but also their *organizational form*. Particular mention can be made of four interrelated factors which are presently working against the continuing stability and effectiveness of the compromise party form, and are therefore of particular relevance to my argument here concerning political parties and the future of socialism.

(a) The first destabilizing factor concerns the growing loss of centrality of the party form as the representative of civil society. The actual role of political parties, including the socialist variety, is rather more limited than is apparent from the generous media attention lavished upon them. Compromise parties can no longer be considered plausibly as the central intermediary structure (or 'messenger') between civil society and the Keynesian welfare state. They are rapidly ceasing to be the 'buckle' (to appropriate Bagehot's classic description) linking governmental authority and its citizens. In fields such as industrial and energy strategy, the determination of wages and salaries, and welfare and taxation policies, the interaction between civil society and the state is being determined increasingly by processes beyond the reach of the parliamentary arena – and therefore beyond the direct control of the governing party, whether of the socialist or anti-socialist type.

An important example of this trend is the steady (if periodically interrupted) expansion of corporatist arrangements specializing in functionalist forms of representation of social interests. Although these date from the last quarter of the nineteenth century, they have since expanded considerably in many policy areas and at various 'levels' between the state and civil society.[28] In consequence, the Keynesian welfare state can be described as a 'dual state', in which certain key operations of the state apparatus are permanently insulated from party politics and parliamentary control (see essay 5). There develops, in other words, government alongside and underneath elected party government, an infrastructure of subsidiary powers or 'sub-government',[29] comprising a matrix of unelected state institutions and social power groups or 'voluntary associations' which in fact function as quasi-governmental organizations.

To point to the growth of the dual state is not to repeat the point that mechanisms of decisionmaking running parallel to political parties and outside parliamentary structures have existed since the beginnings of socialist parties. This is a familiar point within the socialist tradition. Indeed, one of the crucial sources of momentum of the nineteenth and early twentieth century socialist movements consisted in their ability to publicize successfully the enormous power of both political factors (e.g., state bureaucracies) and social forces (such as that of private capital) in predetermining the outcomes of 'bourgeois' party politics. This same insight has been resurrected during the present crisis of the Keynesian welfare states. Socialists correctly emphasize, for instance, that there is limited room for manoeuvre for incoming socialist governments in matters of economic, social and foreign policy, owing to the immense obstructive power of private capital and states at home and abroad.[30] However, what is new and of equal significance about corporatist arrangements is that formal and informal, extra-parliamentary transmission belts are being established to ensure that key social power groups and state authorities negotiate and implement policies on a wide range of issues affecting many groups who have limited or no access to these bargaining processes.

Neo-conservatives have been quick to publicly criticize this growth of corporatist relations between civil society and the state (essay 1). They point, for instance, to the downgrading of parliament, the 'privileged' position accorded trade unions, and the neglect of small business interests. In recent years, a sizeable body of socialist literature on the subject of corporatism has also developed. Yet it remains a curious fact that the implications of corporatist trends for the socialist compromise party remain largely unexplored. Many west European socialists still cling to a conception of party politics which exaggerates the role socialist parties do or could play in present-day state policy formulation and implementation. The fundamental point here is that defenders of the compromise party have always assumed that access to the centre of state power would follow directly from victory at the national polls. This assumption is becoming ever more misleading and anachronistic and, if corporatist processes expand, they are bound to produce growing frustration among rank-and-file activists and electoral supporters of socialist parties, who are likely to sense that the power potential and significance of voting is currently in decline, that the number and size of pots of gold at the end of the parliamentary rainbow are dwindling.

(b) Compromise parties are being destabilized not only due to their decentring in the complex network of interactions between civil society and the state. Another factor is the widening power gap between their leadership and their rank-and-file activists, especially those who remain committed to the old-style, class-based politics of 'pure opposition', and who therefore resist the drift towards compromise with the 'bourgeois' party system.

Contrary to some recent accounts,[31] a power gap between the leadership of socialist parties and their rank-and-file leadership is not a new phenomenon. A similar tendency was observed by Sorel and Michels, who pointed during the period of the uncompromising socialist parties to the bureaucratization of party decisionmaking and to the deactivation of rank-and-file party membership. Since the early years of the twentieth century, this process has continued and, during the era of the compromise party, it has been perceived as a necessary condition of the electoral success of socialist parties. In contrast to the extra-parliamentary agitation of socialist parties in the late nineteenth century, the successful compromise party must strive to formulate policy programmes which offend no major social power group, and which therefore tend to have no principle except that of appearing to cater for everyone. This means, in effect, that the compromise party must more strictly control and exclude from its ranks policies and activities which threaten its compromise role. In other words, it must try to deal with the contradiction (spotted by Michels) between the centralized bureaucratic means upon which it relies and the democratic ends for which it stands by eliminating or downplaying certain traditional socialist policies (such as common ownership and control of the means of production) and confrontational tactics which come to be viewed as an electoral liability. In practice, this means building a party which, despite its professed hostility to one-party socialist systems, resembles the democratic centralist model,[32] as well as weakening or silencing – and thereby alienating – its active 'left-wing' elements, with which the relatively unprincipled, non-programmatic, omnibus compromise party cannot live easily.

These attempts by the compromise party leadership to deradicalize the party, to separate it from its oppositional past, and to deactivate (some sections of) its membership base – symptomatic of the widening power gap between the leadership and the base of the party – increase the likelihood of inner-party conflicts as well as the party's loss of legitimacy among the media. These leadership tactics also tend to decrease the legitimacy of the party among its grassroots activists. They point to the party's loss of direction, its increasing inability to define clearly the meaning of 'socialist' goals and, thus, its loss of distinctiveness and mission. The consequent wrenching of compromise parties is a well-known dynamic, one that becomes especially virulent whenever the compromise party is in office (as in the serious controversies of the late 1960s between the Jusos and the SPD leadership over the latter's *Mittelklassestrategie*), or whenever the party has suffered a serious electoral defeat (as evidenced by conflicts during the early 1980s between the leadership of the British Labour Party and the *ouvrierist* Militant Tendency).

(c) The growing emphasis of the compromise party upon its leadership is also proving to be a source of its destabilization. During the early days of the compromise party, writers such as Schumpeter and Kirchheimer singled out the nomination of candidates for popular legitimation as officeholders as the most important function of political parties.[33] However, they failed to fully anticipate the strong present-day trend, stimulated by the mass communications industry, towards *leadership-dominated* parties. The tremendous growth of the mass communications media, especially television, has operated as one of the most important factors contributing to leader-centred politics – to the point where the organizational machinery of the compromise party becomes less central to its campaigning strategy. During the early years of the compromise party, leaders had to rely more directly on the strategy of mustering the party's organizational strength to communicate with voters – by means of party-organized handshaking, leafletting, baby-kissing and other forms of stumping. Nowadays, it is increasingly possible for leaders to bypass these tactics, and to establish direct contact with voters by means of the mass media and the new information technologies (so-called 'computer caging' and 'credit card politics').

No doubt, this development does not assume the form of a simple switch from party-centred to leader-centred party politics. The continuing dependence of compromise parties on media such as campaign literature, posters and local rallies necessitates strong party organization. Nevertheless, such older, more labour-intensive forms of advertising are steadily undergoing replacement by capital-intensive media, especially television. Consequently, it is increasingly the image of the leader, and less the abstraction known as 'the party', which is sold to the electorate. There develops a deep media – and party – preoccupation with the compromise party leadership. In what amounts to a permanent media-directed campaign, with all its rumours, razzamatazz and drama, the compromise party leadership's every move is recorded and commented upon endlessly, and its style, sex appeal, nervousness and dressing habits become crucial factors in determining the fortunes of the party as a whole. This is why intra-party struggles for or against the leadership become such a vital characteristic of socialist compromise parties. It is also the reason why, conversely, these parties become ever more dependent for their survival and success upon their own leadership, who therefore exercise enormous power, possibly unprecedented when situated within the wider history of socialist parties. It is a rare compromise party leader who resists the temptation to think and act and to say, in the manner of the Le Roi Soleil, *Le parti, c'est moi*. The deep media preoccupation with party leadership, finally, is the reason why the salience of the party for electorates begins to decay. A strong trend towards 'voting for the leader' or 'following the leader' rather than the party develops.[34]

The aggregate consequence of these three factors presently destabilizing the compromise party − its reduced role as a transmission belt between civil society and the state; the growing power gap between its leadership and traditional rank-and-file; and its growing dependence upon leadership − is to increase the sense of ambivalence towards it among many groups within civil society. In particular, the salience of the party among the voting electorate decays and, contrary to Michels, its grip over its supporters and rank-and-file members is weakened.

This loss of legitimacy of the compromise party is only a tendency, of course. Global statements about the decomposition or decline or end of compromise parties should certainly be avoided. The time of the socialist compromise party has certainly not ended. And its weaknesses might well be remedied by future events (such as war or political crisis) which shock late capitalist systems in a party-strengthening or party-redefining manner. Here the contrast with the fate of the one-party system, presently suffering an overwhelming loss of respect and anti-party challenges, is clear. The decline of the compromise party has definite limits. It is not simply being rejected outright by voting electorates. A more subtle and, from the point of view of compromise parties, more troubling development is involved. It takes the form of a creeping weariness towards the party form, with activists' and electorates' attitudes shifting from a strongly positive identification with the party (in the earlier years of the compromise party) to a type of diffuse, resigned indifference towards, or merely tactical support for, the compromise party. And even when identification with the party remains stable, the strength of feeling for it declines. The socialist compromise party may pride itself on remaining a 'broad church', yet it functions less and less as a secular chapel which binds together the party faithful and its supporters in the pursuit of common ideals.

(d) This heightened public indifference and calculativeness towards the compromise party is responsible not only for the much discussed recent increase in tactical voting and volatile electoral behaviour. It is also the soil in which social movements grow. Social movements may be considered as both the unintended effect of the compromise party, and a fourth factor in its present destabilization.[35] Developing networks of visible as well as 'submerged' public spheres of discussion and action largely outside and 'underneath' the party system, social movements (such as feminism, ecology and the black movement) raise important questions not only about the distribution and legitimacy of macro-social power relations. Such movements also challenge and reverse the established deep patterns of social interaction in civil society. They publicize grievances and uncertainties about everyday life; they redefine its shared sense of time, space and 'normality'; and they operate on the assumption that it is possible to expand and democratize civil society in accordance with these unconventional rules of space, time and interpersonal relations. Western social movements are in this precise sense the counterparts of the democratic opposition and social movements in Soviet-type regimes. They are marked by a definite anti-political quality, inasmuch as their activities are governed neither by the epic fantasy of seizing and transforming state power nor by the more humble desire to get involved in party politics. They instead concentrate on the apparently banal task of publicizing and transforming the less visible fields of micro-power relations within which they emerge and operate.

This is why social movements challenge the assumption (defended during the heyday of the compromise party by Anthony Downs, for example[36]) that it may well be rational for voters to delegate part or all of their political decisionmaking to compromise parties, no matter how important the decision or its degree of correctness. The new movements up-end this assumption: If the compromise party cannot provide desirable alternative solutions to the problems ordinary citizens deem important and feel strongly about, it is reasonable for those citizens to view the compromise party either as irrelevant or as obstructive and, hence, in need of correction by initiatives *outside* the party system. Social movements stimulate public awareness of two key points: that not every important conflict can be traced ultimately to a single centre of power (such as class antagonisms); and that, conversely, no single, unified class, movement or political organization can defend all particular interests. Accordingly, social movements tend to be on bad terms with the compromise party. It is accused of devaluing grassroots activity in the life of the party and, in the name of 'realistic programmes', of screening out certain controversial issues which the movements consider vital.[37] Here the commitment of the compromise party to the three-legged race of oligopolistic competition with anti-socialist parties rebounds against itself. The compromise party, by projecting a moderate self-image, concentrating heavily on settled issues and formulating policies that are vague and highly flexible, stands accused of fudging the issues and of abandoning its egalitarian and libertarian socialist policies. It is seen to exchange its former function of actively representing civil society for that of ordering, controlling and limiting the demands civil society can feed into the state. The compromise party is perceived as dwarfing its clientele, reducing them to docile instruments of its media- and money-backed manoeuvrings and opportunistic policies.

The Uncertain Future of the Compromise Party

The challenge to the compromise party from the new social movements is very important. This is not only because, by pressuring from below, they force the compromise party to again take seriously demands arising independently from within civil society. No less important is the fact that the demands of the social movements crystallize a wide range of social complaints about the *form* of the compromise party; they raise questions about its structural problems and limits, as well as posing some difficult normative and strategic issues about its future.

Broadly speaking, three main types of proposals concerning the future of the compromise party are being canvassed presently among west European socialists.[38] I shall consider, and reject, each in turn with the aim of discussing and defending a possible fourth strategy – a fully democratic socialist strategy which recognizes the limits of the party form and which, although appropriate only to late capitalist systems, makes possible a convergence of perspectives between democrats in both halves of Europe.

(a) The renewal of the compromise party by means of its 'modernization'
The main outlines of this response to the structural problems of the compromise party are evident in sections of the West German

SPD and, especially, the British Labour Party, and are summarized in the words of Neil Kinnock: 'What we need to do is to ensure that every word, every action, every attitude, every statement, everything that we do to educate, agitate, and organise is geared completely to victory.'[39] From this standpoint, the compromise party can be rejuvenated through better researched, more tightly managed and carefully targeted public relations campaigns that communicate with 'ordinary people'. This necessitates, in turn, the streamlining of the party organization, rectifying its inadequacies, a reliance upon the 'latest' techniques of fundraising, and the expulsion or silencing of those party activists who employ the tactic of 'impossibilism' (Kinnock). The party must aim to renew its appeal among those sections of the electorate (such as the unemployed, the old manual working class, sections of the new middle class and the new social movements) which have become indifferent or hostile towards the party. In effect, this strategy amounts to an attempt to form a majority compromise party by gearing everything to winning elections through a permanent campaign which stresses the need for less policy and more presentation of the party's moderate self-image.

Proponents of this strategy have considerable starting advantages. Not only the burdens but also the inertia of a whole era are on their side. Much is therefore to be said for it as a pragmatic strategy. Important factors working in its favour include the extant fundraising, administrative and campaigning structures of the party, as well as its legitimacy and officially recognized presence within many branches of the state apparatus. What is less certain, however, is whether, and how, the streamlined and 'modernized' compromise party can effectively and lastingly overcome the four destabilizing factors analysed above. For instance, the revamped compromise party will further widen the power gap between its leadership and traditional rank-and-file. It will also fail to address the complaints against the party form made by participants within the new social movements. The revamped compromise party *could* campaign for official recognition and public sanctioning of functional forms of representation in the form, say, of a social parliament (an old proposal of Guild Socialism and Austro-Marxism – see essay 5). The choice to follow this course, and thereby to attempt to give the party a more pronounced guiding role vis-à-vis functional forms of representation, would seem nevertheless to violate and challenge some basic givens of the existing party system – a violation which it carefully wishes to avoid in the name of moderation. Dealing adequately with these various destabilizing factors appears to be fraught with problems, especially considering that several core policy elements of Keynesian welfare state capitalism – price stability, economic growth and full male employment within the framework of free collective bargaining – can no longer be restored simultaneously, and cannot therefore serve as a reservoir of consensus upon which the party could renew its appeal to electorates.

(b) *The formation of an uncompromising socialist party* The limits of the strategy of modernizing the compromise party have recently prompted proposals for the formation of new, class-defined and less compromising socialist parties resembling their oppositional predecessors.[40] From this second viewpoint, the idea of achieving socialism (defined usually as the collective ownership and control of the means of production) by competing respectfully with other parties for control over the ballot box and, hence, over state power, is illusory. Compromise parties, it is argued, are not worth fundamentally reforming from within (say, by means of 'entrism'). Having fudged and compromised the fundamental principle of class conflict, they become oblivious to the panoply of class power relations which surrounds all parties and elected governments, either of the left or right. Compromise parties turn a blind eye to the immense pressures upon any party which holds office. Consequently, they are incapable of effecting a radical transformation of the existing relations of class power through class struggle.

In view of this basic defect of the compromise party, what is now required is a new socialist party, even if this results in short-term electoral costs to existing compromise parties. The new party must endeavour to pressure and outflank the latter by constructing and popularizing an authentic socialist programme energized and informed by militant grassroots actions: factory occupations, peace campaigns, blacks' and women's resistance. The new extra-parliamentary party would take seriously the context of 'bourgeois democracy', for instance by fighting elections at the local and national level. Yet it would avoid being absorbed into 'electoralism' and 'parliamentarism' (Miliband) by linking itself organically with the working-class struggles of civil society. Only in this way would the extra-parliamentary party be capable of politically linking the immediate preoccupations of the working class with the longer term process of fundamentally altering the balance of class forces in favour of working-class socialism.

It is unclear in this proposal for an uncompromising extra-parliamentary socialist party whether its fundamental opposition to the existing party system could result in *political* gains, that is, changes at the level of state policies. A fundamentalist 'no compromise' party strategy is sooner or later likely to be self-paralysing. Its moralistic refusal to succumb to 'electoralism' and 'parliamentarism' would likely be interpreted – negatively – by its own (potential) electoral supporters as a decision *not* to work for practical, if small reform measures.[41] The extra-parliamentary socialist party, if it participates in electoral competition, and if it is not to risk losing popular support, would be forced to tread a narrow path between fundamental 'pure opposition' and self-compromising co-operation with other parties; the choice of either extreme would be perilous, and possibly fatal. This strategic problem would likely be exacerbated by the fact that fundamentalist opposition would surely be met with political repression and hysterical media campaigns, neither of which would work in favour of the party's electoral popularity.

No less problematic is the 'classism' of this second proposal. Its proponents seem to suppose that they are living in the late nineteenth century. They believe, or hope, that there currently exists a large, 'objectively homogeneous' and growing workers' movement which can serve as the driving force of the new party. When this supposition is brought to bear upon the new social movements, a species of vanguardism (i.e., the familiar problem of 'substitutionism') becomes evident. These movements are posited as 'working-class'.[42] On the basis of this theoretical sleight of hand, the party would happily represent itself as the mouth-piece of a unifiable subject – analogous to the early Lukács's view of the Party as the organizational expression of the proletariat's (imputed) will.[43] Thus, it would preserve intact the ultimate (classical Marxian) goal of abolishing, in the name of socialism, the separation between civil society and the state – with all its probable despotic consequences.

It is difficult to envisage how this strategy can escape the telling criticisms of vanguardist party politics made by the advocates of anti-party politics in central-eastern Europe. And whether the new social movements, or other sections of the electorate, will recognize this vanguardist strategy as legitimate is doubtful. As Manuel Castells suggests, the attempt to incorporate the new social movements into an uncompromising extra-parliamentary party might well heighten these groups' suspicion that the new party is bent on defusing their particular demands, as well as smothering their anti-political and decentralized form in the name of a socialism which is defined in a wholly abstract and elusive manner.[44]

(c) Privileging the role of the new social movements Faced with a choice between joining an ailing compromise party and the flawed option of building a new socialist party, many socialists have abandoned party politics altogether, and in recent years have invested their energies in the campaigns of the social movements. In the view of these participants, the socialist compromise party has largely followed the script written by Michels. It is said to leave little or no room for meaningful citizen participation. Citizens are reduced to the role of occasional voters and/or to debaters of branch-level resolutions that hardly ever have any direct effect on overall party policy or structure. The party is seen to be dominated by specialization, expertise, organization, bureaucracy and leadership which resembles a blind and arrogant monarch when it comes to the 'real issues'. Party government and politics are seen to be deeply inimical to genuine democracy, in the sense of self-government. In arguing this, movement activists retrieve Rousseau's warning, in *Du contrat social*, that 'the instant a people allows itself to be represented it loses its freedom'. The mandate or representation principle, upon which all parties thrive, robs citizens of all significant responsibility for their judgements and actions. In the act of voting, meaningful citizenship drops with the marked paper into the ballot box – both disappear simultaneously.

Ultimately, the compromise party transforms ordinary citizens into passive clients of party manipulators and their expensively-packaged campaigns and slick public-relations work. Government by parties – here the movements concur with Schumpeter's observation[45] – allows citizens to select only from among the elites who are to govern them. From this observation, some movement activists conclude that the foremost site of political activity must be civil society itself. Here, outside the party system, and beyond the reaches of the centres of state power, public spheres of interacting citizens can project into the political arena problems and issues untreated or compromised by the party system and the state. Here, in what remains of civil society, the movements demand that hitherto neglected interests be articulated and served. It is here also that the individual pleasure and self-confidence gained through participation in public spheres can be maximized, at the same time reinforcing the principle that there are no 'amateurs' in public affairs because there can be no professionals.

This line of argument against compromise party politics provides the important reminder that there is no 'natural affinity' between socialism and parties, and that the party form is not necessarily privileged as a way of articulating social interests. Yet it is unconvincing in regard to the problem of *how* the movements' demands on the party system and the state will be recognized, conceded and processed effectively – or, indeed, whether they will be tolerated at all by the political authorities. The anti-party fundamentalism of this third proposal does not reckon properly with the possibility that a personally meaningful, authentically self-co-ordinated activity can be diverted, dispersed or dissolved by macro-power arrangements. One basic flaw of this third strategy, in other words, is that it underestimates the role parties *can* still play in articulating and defending the interests of the presently less powerful groups in civil society.

In principle, as the 'parties do matter' literature has reiterated in recent years,[46] parties can function as effective aggregators of social interests. They can serve as addressees, advocates and protectors of groups in civil society (such as women, the unemployed, ethnic and sexual preference minorities) who presently are not as well organized as other social interests, and who therefore are unable to make their voices heard in the sphere of political institutions. In principle, parties can also function as political platforms for popularizing the visions of things to come invented by social movements themselves, as well as for formulating a corresponding set of coherent policy programmes suitable for realizing such visions. Furthermore, parties can recruit and nominate public office holders, and present them, together with their visions and policy programmes, for confirmation or rejection by voting publics.

Finally, parties can function as arbitrators and co-ordinators of functional power groups in civil society. They can partly compensate for the particularistic and fragmented interests of civil society, helping mould them into a relatively coherent (if always contingent) political coalition based on solidarity.[47] In this respect, parties can be seen as a solution to the peculiarly modern problem of how to overcome the dangers of social faction and 'anarchy' without succumbing to the perils of political unaccountability and tyranny. In other words, parties are a vital mechanism for rendering grassroots democracy workable in a large-scale

republic. By seeking to reconcile popular control and accountable government with effective and efficient state policymaking
and implementation, political parties can function, to borrow
from Madison, as representative bodies which can 'refine and
enlarge the public views by passing them through the medium of
a chosen body of citizens'.[48] Political parties are a vital prerequi-
site of representative government, which is to say – against the
ambivalence of the second and third proposals towards competitive party systems – that the achievement and stabilization of
socialism, understood as a fully modern type of sociopolitical
order in which civil society and the state are separated, and each
is subject to democratic mechanisms for limiting and regulating
the exercise of power, requires and supposes political opposition.
That is, it supposes a competitive party system consisting of two
or more democratic parties, free not only to express themselves
within state institutions, but also to legitimately agitate and
organize within the permanent, free and recognized structures of
civil society.

Democracy and Party Organization

Democratic party competition of this type was first signalled in
the non-violent transfer of control over governmental office from
the Federalists to the Jeffersonians in America in 1801.[49] It was a
unique achievement of the modern world. Modern democratic
party systems developed only slowly, against great political odds,
and despite widespread hostility to their allegedly factious and
seditious effects.* Their birth dates only from the early years of
the eighteenth century and their growth – exemplified by the

---

* Prior to assuming leadership of the Republican Party, Thomas Jefferson
quipped: 'If I could not go to heaven, but with a party, I would not go there at all'
(quoted in Benjamin R. Barber, 'The Undemocratic Party System: Citizenship in
an Elite/Mass Society', in Robert A. Goldwin, ed., *Political Parties in the Eighties*,
Washington 1980, p. 34). This remark typifies the almost universal official distrust
and outright resentment expressed toward the fledgling political parties of the
early modern period. For a century after Bolingbroke's famous defence of a 'country party' (a type of anti-party party designed to end once and for all the patronage and corruption that he saw to be associated with the form of government-
by-party exercised by the new Whig regime of Robert Walpole – see 'A
Dissertation upon Parties' (1733-1734)) in *The Works of Lord Bolingbroke*, Philadelphia 1841, vol. 2, pp. 11, 21, 167), early modern political thought, both conservative and liberal, was virtually unanimous and persistent in its condemnation of

small parties that took shape in the House of Commons in England during the long reign of George III[50] – is linked with the struggle against despotism and the appearance of nascent forms of representative government. At first, they assumed the form of 'honorable connections' of gentlemen (Burke) whose role was to criticize, restrain or support ministers of state in the name of dominant class power groups of civil society. Until the first quarter of the nineteenth century, these fledgling parties consisted mainly of loosely organized groupings of the parliamentary representatives of the aristocratic and bourgeois classes. Situated exclusively in the legislature, they neither engaged in open electoral competition nor solicited members outside of the legislature. Nor did they discipline themselves by means of party rules and regulations.

These practices, usually associated with mass membership and competitive party systems, only emerged during the course of the nineteenth and early twentieth centuries. Their growth was encouraged by pressures from social power groups (the bourgeoisie, workers and women) hitherto excluded from parliament, as well as by political reforms from above, such as the effective widening of the male suffrage (after 1832 in England, the middle of the 1830s in the United States, and after 1870 in France, Germany and other west European countries). As Ostrogorski's classic account makes clear,[51] the nineteenth-century ideals of the open, democratic and competitive party system were never in practice realized. The development of mass-based, competitive political parties was a highly uneven, sometimes violence-ridden and usually tenuous and incomplete process. Throughout the second half of the nineteenth century, parties' membership was far from massive. Their elitism and the restricted franchise effectively insulated them from the pressures of the powerless in civil

parties and party conflict. A lasting political commonwealth, in which civil and political liberties are guaranteed by ordered conflict among parties, was considered (in the theory of constitutional government developed from Locke and Montesquieu to the Federalist papers and Tocqueville, for instance) as a contradiction in terms. It was viewed as a recipe for government by faction based on passion, conspiracy, greedy ambition and disrespect for the national interest ('the best kind of party', as Halifax said, 'is in some sort a conspiracy against the nation'). See Erwin Faul, 'Verfemung, Duldung und Anerkennung des Parteiwesens in der Geschichte des Politischen Denkens', *Politische Vierteljahresschrift*, March 1964, pp. 60-80; and Caroline Robbins, '"Discordant Parties": A Study of the Acceptance of Party by Englishmen', *Political Science Quarterly*, December 1958, pp. 505-29.

society. Party organizations also continued to be weak and poorly co-ordinated, while their programmes were not always binding upon their own representatives. And, of decisive importance, the workers' movement, although solicited increasingly to vote, remained largely outside the existing systems of party government, a mere object of their restrictive and often repressive operating rules.

This deep discrepancy between the democratic ideals and the stunted practice of the early modern party system, and between the widening social power of the workers' movement and its exclusion from party politics, proved to be the catalyst of attempts by the early socialist movement to develop its own party forms. Working outside and through the established party systems, the early socialist parties helped defend the civil liberties of the powerless (their rights to combine in trade unions, for example). In addition, they fought to expand the population's right of entry into the parliamentary political arena through, for instance, the extension of the franchise; and contributed, directly or indirectly, to changes of state policy in matters of economic and social policy. While these civil, electoral and state policy successes of the early socialist parties also entailed serious costs –highlighted in the analyses of Sorel, Michels and others – they invite the conclusion that, far from simply being a means of bourgeois control, modern competitive party systems are a vital mechanism for guaranteeing peaceful and democratic exchanges between civil society and the state.

Democratic party systems are an early modern invention of bold and pathbreaking dimensions. They opened up the possibility that elections would not degenerate into acts of conquest, and that the elected would seek to retain the loyalty of the electorally defeated to the political system. This is why democrats must relinquish the chiliastic hope that one day, when private property is abolished, parties will wither away, to be replaced by an undifferentiated, classless, conflict-free socialist order. It is also the reason why democratic party competition should not be allowed to pass away slowly – choked by legislative restrictions and altered methods of policing, for example – or to die suddenly at the point of a bayonet or tank gun barrel. In the late twentieth century, we should frown upon George Washington's view – typical of the early modern aristocratic and bourgeois traditions – that party government is 'alternative despotism of one faction over another' that has 'perpetrated the most horrid enormities' and 'frightful despotism'.[52] We know, on the contrary, that the most frightful despotism – based on torture, legal arbitrariness, concentration camps and forced exile – more likely results from the suppression of party competition, and that a partyless democracy is a contradiction in terms and in practice.

Alas, unhappy consciousness sets in at this point in the argument. For the reasons sketched earlier in this essay, I must admit that the reality of the compromise party falls dismally short of the ideal of democratic party competition sketched here. The discrepancy between the ideal and the reality of late capitalist party systems can be summarized by contrasting the main type of criticism of the compromise party form with the dominant criticism of the fledgling parties during the early modern period. During the eighteenth and early nineteenth centuries, parties were charged with gratuitously provoking political and social strife and threatening the unity and harmony of the state and civil society. Nowadays, the characteristic criticism of the compromise party (among the new social movements, for example) is precisely the *inverse*. Compromise parties are accused of promoting the unity and harmony of civil society and the state, blocking the pores of civil society, and frustrating and screening out political dissent. The compromise party, having degenerated into a bureaucratic quasi-state apparatus (when in office) or a ladder for party elites aspiring to the office of government, fails to acknowledge or to pose the 'real' issues with clarity and conviction.

Pressured by this type of criticism, the ideal of competitive democratic party government (sketched above) today remains just that: a neglected hope, a thwarted ideal, a yet-to-be-realized utopia. In my view, two broad types of transformations of the compromise party are required if west European reality is to be brought a step or two closer to this ideal image. Needless to say, whether and how these changes are brought about depends upon the structure of the party system, the prevailing matrix of power forces within civil society and the state, and upon the capacity of the compromise party for internal reform. If these changes could be brought about, they would lead either to the radical restructuring of the compromise party or to the formation of a new party capable of supporting the democratization of civil society and the state. In either case, the resulting democratic party would pursue a 'dualistic' strategy, reflecting the two required changes summarized below.

First, the development of a fully democratic party would require a far-reaching transformation of the internal structures and parliamentary tactics of existing compromise parties. It seems unlikely, to be sure, that temporary oligarchic tendencies within political parties can be eliminated completely. The choice to participate in parliamentary-electoral politics often necessitates the making of policy decisions under great time constraints, which in turn tend to undermine time-consuming consensual procedures. Nevertheless – contrary to Michels – there is no fundamental 'law of the historical necessity of oligarchy' in political parties, only a dialectic of attempted oligarchy and, from below, counter-pressure exerted by independent public spheres within and without the party.[53] Again contrary to Michels, disunion in parties does not always work in favour of existing party oligarchs or their successors. Nor is it true, as Michels claimed,[54] that the party rank-and-file rarely succeed in either controlling their leaders or fragmenting and reducing their power.

Internal democratization of the compromise party's decision-making structures is in principle possible (as mandatory reselection of MPs by their constituency parties and other constitutional changes within the British Labour Party since 1980 suggest). It is crucial to the contemporary renewal of democracy. Concretely, internal democratization would require reversing the wholly *conventional* trend, commonly observed of the compromise party in recent years, of choking off inner-party discussions and controversies, embracing and exploiting the power of office, fetishizing leadership and allowing the life of the party to die a slow death – as if these were somehow due to 'technical imperatives' or the natural passivity of the masses.

A new type of democratic party (where necessary) would also work for the replacement of electoral systems (of the first-past-the-post variety, for instance) which disenfranchise minority parties and would-be parties by alternative systems (such as the single transferable vote form of proportional representation) which more accurately reflect the voting preferences of civil society. It would work for majority rule with minority rights, the election of preferred individual candidates and strong and stable government. Radical changes in legislative tactics would also be required, principally along the lines of abandoning the faith that parliaments are presently the centres of political power. In its parliamentary work, the party would precisely try to work for the practical realization of this textbook principle (see essay 5). This change would entail abandoning the passive parliamentarization of the compromise party. It would involve questioning and obstructing the polite etiquette and often restrictive rules of the parliamentary game (instead of accepting them, like a regular party, as an objective necessity). It would necessitate becoming highly skilled at committee work, defining clearly the party's own demands and veto positions, exploiting weaknesses in opposition parties' tactics, and uncovering and publicizing the distortions and blindspots in their policies. To sit in parliament would mean recapturing something of the spirit and tactics of 'pure opposition' of the extra-parliamentary socialist party. Inevitably, this change would make parliament a more interesting and important place, and the permanent object of the media and public attention and controversy.

This active parliamentarism of the fully democratic party would *not* mean retreating into vague, overly generalized political principles. Nor would it involve treating parliament as merely a public stage on which already decided socialist principles would be acted out in full view of a passive public who remained uncertain of their practicability. Active parliamentarism would instead involve tackling, through hard discussion, compromise and tactical agreements, the difficult strategic questions of how to formulate concrete and workable policy programmes which have democratizing effects and therefore point beyond both neoconservatism and the ailing system of Keynesian welfare state capitalism.

A second necessary condition of creating a fully democratic party points beyond the party-centred definition of socialism that today has a strong grip on the socialist tradition. The types of changes in the internal structures and tactics of the compromise party sketched above could not be achieved by party work alone or by travelling exclusively on the parliamentary road. Their necessary condition – their source of energy and dynamism, as well as their means of resistance to obstruction by the ruling powers – is the pressure of a plurality of social forces *outside* the party. A democratic party would need to recognize the limits of the competitive party form. It would thereby acknowledge a basic insight of the anti-party politics presently being developed in central-eastern Europe: that changes in civil society cannot always or best be attained or preserved by means of the state apparatus; and that encouragement therefore must be given to the development and maintenance of a *creative tension* between movements and voters, on the one side, and the party and the state on the other.[55]

If the democratic party could become self-limiting – an 'anti-party party' – it could resolve at least three problems well known to the socialist tradition. First, it would recognize clearly that participation in competitive party systems is a sharp double-edged sword that must be brandished with caution, since it courts the twin dangers of party oligarchy and unprincipled reformism. Secondly, the self-limiting perspective of the democratic party would maximize its chances of resolving a chronic strategic dilemma of democratic socialism.[56] A democratic party intent on socializing a capitalist civil society would be faced inevitably with the difficult task of steering a course between two incompatible strategies. These are: the naive exclusive reliance upon parliamentary politics and the (highly dangerous and self-contradictory) resort to authoritarian and violent political methods to reach its objectives. By adopting an anti-party strategy, the democratic party could in principle avoid this dilemma. On the one hand, it could prevent itself from being blinded by the old parliamentary socialist illusion that participation in the process of competitive party politics enables democrats to beat the dominant political and social power groups at their own game. By shedding this illusion, the party would instead recognize the force of Laski's insight that a 'capitalist democracy will not allow its electorate to stumble into socialism by the accident of a verdict at the polls'.[57] On the other hand, the self-limiting course of the democratic party could help it avoid the opposite temptation (when in governmental office) to resort to violent, authoritarian methods. It could resist this temptation precisely by encouraging the development of a powerful infrastructure of *social* support groups capable of defending the party and resisting the obstruction and backlash that would inevitably accompany it into the offices of government. The tactical dualism of the party, in other words, would recognize plainly (with Machiavelli) that whoever undertakes to govern civil society without securing its flanks against bitter and determined opponents establishes a government of very brief duration.

Finally, the democratic party would abandon the false assumption that social development is always decided by parties and states. It would instead acknowledge that further democratization of civil society – the building of a socialist civil society – depends ultimately on changes in the way people live, love, work and socialize, and that social initiatives and movements, and not parties or governments, are more capable of effecting these changes democratically.

No doubt, active parliamentarism could help stimulate *political* awareness within social movements themselves. It could force them to peer beyond their own particular concerns towards the great complexity of social and political problems and events, considered as a moving and open-ended totality (see essay 7). By offering public recognition and funding to groups in civil society, the new democratic party could also help prevent attempts by opposition parties and governments to marginalize or criminalize these groups. But this is not to conclude (with Lukács) that the party would become the organizational expression of the movements' (imputed) will. On the contrary, the democratic socialist party would admit the serious dangers of this view – summarized long ago by Walt Whitman as 'the never ending audacity of elected persons' and by Rousseau as 'the tendency of all government to degenerate'. For the first time under modern conditions, the democratic party would explicitly recognize the necessity *and* limits of parties. It would acknowledge openly that its fundamental source of energy and strategic protection lies in a *non-party realm* – in the self-governed enterprise, the democratic trade union, the rape crisis centre, the gay and lesbian collective, the housing co-operative, and other public spheres of civil society.

Notes

1. All references to this work are drawn from the original edition (Leipzig 1911). Also valuable is his earlier attempt to analyse the sociological composition of the German Social Democratic Party in 'Die deutsche Sozialdemokratie. Parteimitgliedschaft und soziale Zusammensetzung', *Archiv für Sozialwissenschaft und Sozialpolitik*, XXIII, 1906, pp. 471-556.

2. Michels, *Zur Soziologie des Parteiwesens in der modernen Demokratie*, p. 338.

3. Ibid. The pathological obsequiousness of the masses was exemplified, Michels argued, in a variety of contemporary socialist customs, from the popularity of 'Karl Marx liqueurs' and 'Karl Marx buttons' to the late nineteenth century Italian practice of naming children Lassallo or Marxina.

4. Ibid, p. 33.

5. Ibid, p. 383.

6. Ibid, p. 353.

7. See Carl E. Schorske, *German Social Democracy 1905-1917. The Development of the Great Schism*, Cambridge, Mass. and London 1955; and David Beetham, 'Michels and his Critics', *Archives européennes de sociologie*, 22, 1981, pp. 81-99.

8. Some important analyses of socialist compromise parties include: K.L. Shell, *The Transformation of Austrian Socialism*, New York 1962; Frederic S. Burin and K.L. Shell, *Politics, Law and Social Change. Selected Essays of Otto Kirchheimer*, New York and London 1969, especially part two; William E. Paterson and Alastair H. Thomas, eds, *Social Democratic Parties in Western Europe*, London 1977; Anton Palinka, *Social Democratic Parties in Europe*, New York 1983; Claus Offe, 'Konkurrenzpartei und kollektive politische Identität', in R. Roth, ed., *Parlamentarisches Ritual und politische Alternativen*, Frankfurt 1980, pp. 26-42; and *Contradictions of the Welfare State*, edited John Keane, London 1984, chapter 8.

9. Carl E. Schorske, *German Social Democracy 1905-1917*, chapter 1.

10. Willy Brandt, *Plädoyer für die Zukunft*, Frankfurt am Main 1961, p. 17.

11. Carl E. Schorske, *German Social Democracy 1905-1917*, chapters 1-2.

12. *Die Zukunft*, VI, July 1951, pp. 177-80.

13. On the role of parties in 'clogging' the channels between civil society and the state see Wolf-Dieter Narr et al., *SPD – Staatspartei oder Reformpartei?*, München 1976, pp. 91, 132-3; and Gianfranco Pasquino, 'Party Government in Italy: Achievements and Prospects', in Richard S. Katz, ed., *Party Governments: European and American Experiences*, Berlin and New York 1987, pp. 202-42.

14. The case of Yugoslavia is special and highly complex. The interaction of eight Communist Parties, functioning as regional oligarchies, produces strong decentralization trends which are not, however, synonymous with democratization. See my interview with Tomaž Mastnak et al., 'Yugoslavia's Permanent Crisis', *East European Reporter*, vol. 2, 2, 1986, pp. 46-50. On the historical background of the rise to dominance of the League of Communists, see Vojislav Koštunica and Kosta Čavoški, *Party Pluralism or Monism. Social Movements and the Political System in Yugoslavia 1944-1949*, Boulder 1985. Other recent considerations of the political system include April Carter, *Democratic Reform in Yugoslavia. The Changing Role of the Party*, London 1982; Zagorka Golubović and Svetozar Stojanović, *The Crisis of the Yugoslav System*, Köln 1986; Frane Adam and Darka Podmenik 'Predgovor', in Tomaž Mastnak (ed.), *Socialistična Civilna Družba*, Ljubljana 1985, pp. 13-28; and the stimulating and important analyses of the growth of an independent civil society and the need for a constitutional state in Tomaž Mastnak, 'De la démocratie en Yougoslavie', *Problemi*, vol. 23, 7, 1985, and 'Socialisticvna civilna družba. Skica aktualnega stanja diskusije', *Katedra*, vol. 28, 6-7, January 1987. In a letter dated 26 July 1987, Mastnak writes: 'In Yugoslavia, we are experiencing a process of the withering away of coherent state institutions. They are being absorbed by the emerging civil society. This represents one decisive respect in which Yugoslavia differs from the Soviet bloc, and yet it leads to the same unbearable situation – the absence of a civil society independent of legally circumscribed and coherent political institutions. The irony is that this result is fully in accord with a key proposition of scientific socialism.'

15. Ferenc Fehér et al., *Dictatorship over Needs*, Oxford 1983, especially chapter 5.

16. Michels, *Zur Soziologie des Parteiwesens in der modernen Demokratie*, p. 129.

17. Gustav Husak, 'May Day Speech', in *Information Bulletin of the Central Committee of the Communist Party of Czechoslovakia*, 4, June 1984, p. 9.

18. Ferenc Fehér et al., *Dictatorship over Needs*, p. 198.

19. See, for example, Václav Havel et al., *The Power of the Powerless*, edited John Keane, London 1985; and Milan Šimečka, *The Restoration of Order. The Normalization of Czechoslovakia 1969-1976*, London 1984; Mihály Vajda, *The State and Socialism*, London 1981. On the Gorbachev reforms, see Adam Michnik, 'Gorbachev – as seen from Warsaw', *East European Reporter*, vol. 2, 4, 1987, pp. 32-4.

20. See John Keane, ed., *Civil Society and the State: New European Perspectives*, London and New York 1988, part 3; Adam Michnik, *Letters from Prison and Other Essays*, London 1986; Jan Józef Lipski, *KOR. A History of the Workers' Defense Committee in Poland. 1976-1981*, Berkeley 1985; György Konrád, *Anti-Politics*, London 1984; Václav Havel et al., *The Power of the Powerless*. Good surveys of the variety of anti-political initiatives include H. Gordon Skilling, *Samizdat and an International Society in Eastern Europe*, London and Basingstoke 1988, and Elemér Hankiss, *The 'Second Society'*. Budapest 1986.

21. György Konrad, *Anti-Politics*, p. 95.

22. Václav Havel, 'Anti-Political Politics', in *Civil Society and the State*; and my

interview, 'Doing Without Utopias', *The Times Literary Supplement*, 23 January 1987, pp. 81-3.

23. The fundamental importance of secret societies in the Enlightenment battle against absolute monarchy is well-documented in Reinhart Koselleck, *Kritik und Krise. Eine Studie zur Pathogenese der bürgerlichen Welt*, Frankfurt am Main 1973, p. 76, where Koselleck notes: 'Against the mysteries of the superstitious and political *arcana* there stood the secret of the Enlightened. "Why secret societies?", asks Bode, their protagonist in northern Germany. "The answer is simple: Because it would be foolishness to play with one's cards down when your opponent has them up."'

24. This issue has become important since the amnesty of September 1986 in Poland. It was also crucial during the second year of Solidarity's existence, although there was no agreement reached within its ranks; see Gábor Demszky, 'Parliamentarism in Eastern Europe – The Chances of the Independent Candidate', *East European Reporter*, 1, 3, Autumn 1985, pp. 23-5. The view that Solidarity 'should fight with every means at its disposal for the election of a new Sejm and new local government bodies' was defended by its Upper Silesian leaders. They urged that if the Sejm was unwilling to declare new elections, the union itself should organize such elections. More moderate union leaders such as Jan Rulewski rejected this proposal as too strong. According to Rulewski, the goal was indeed parliamentary democracy, 'because this is the rational framework for political confrontations'. However, before pursuing this goal, Solidarity should first call for a referendum to decide whether the population had confidence in the existing system; only if the response to the referendum was negative, would new elections be called. A third proposal strongly paralleled the old Guild Socialist idea of a social parliament. According to the supporters of self-management, a representative democracy founded on the workers' councils required that the Polish legislature become bicameral. In the so-called Self-Managing Lower House, the trade unions, workers' councils and consumers' representatives would be represented. The Lower House would have played the role of the actual controller of the means of production, whilst the so-called Upper House would function to represent civil society's political interests, as well as to secure the leading role of the Polish United Workers' Party. A parliamentary reform of this type would have attempted to synthesize a functional form of representation with the more traditional territorial system of representation. All three proposals were silenced temporarily by the 1981 military coup d'état.

25. Henriette Roland-Holst, *Generalstreik und Sozialdemokratie*, Dresden 1906, especially pp. 53-69; Phil H. Goodstein, *The Theory of the General Strike from the French Revolution to Poland*, New York 1985.

26. This experience is expressed sharply in a Polish anecdote dating back to the early 1950s, when Polish industry was restructured to produce arms. A father badly needed a pram for his newborn child. Unable to find one anywhere in the shops of Warsaw, he approached a friend, who happened to be working in a factory which manufactured prams – or so he thought. This friend promised to fetch him a pram, piece by piece. Each day, the pram factory worker brought his friend bits and pieces, carefully smuggled out of the factory by stuffing them into his heavy winter overcoat. A fortnight later, the two friends decided that they now had a complete set of parts. But, according to the anecdote, when they came to assemble the bits and pieces they found that they had actually built a machine-gun.

27. For the British case, see Gareth Stedman Jones, *Languages of Class. Studies in English Working Class History 1832-1982*, Cambridge 1983, chapter 5. On the French case, see Stanley Hoffman and George Ross, *The Mitterrand Experiment*.

Continuity and Change in Modern France, Cambridge 1987. The complex patterns of erosion or stagnation of working class electoral support for Scandinavian socialist parties is discussed by Diane Salisbury, 'Scandinavian Party Politics Re-examined: Social Democracy in Decline?', *West European Politics*, 7, October 1984, pp. 67-102, and 'The Electoral Difficulties of the Scandinavian Social Democrats in the 1970s', *Comparative Politics*, vol. 18, 1, October 1985, pp. 1-19; and Gösta Esping-Andersen, *Social Class, Social Democracy and State Policy*, Copenhagen 1980, chapters 1, 4, 11.

28. See Keith Middlemas, *Politics in Industrial Society*, London 1979; Alessandro Pizzorno, 'Interests and parties in pluralism', in Suzanne Berger, ed., *Organizing Interests in Western Europe – Pluralism, Corporatism and the Transformation of Politics*, Cambridge 1981; and Claus Offe, 'The Attribution of Public Status to Interest Groups', in *Disorganized Capitalism*, edited John Keane, Cambridge 1985.

29. Norberto Bobbio, 'Italy's Permanent Crisis', *Telos*, 54, Winter 1982-3, pp. 123-33; cf. Claus Offe, *Disorganized Capitalism*, pp. 7-8, 221-58.

30. See, for example, Barry Hindess, *Parliamentary Democracy and Socialist Politics*, London 1983; and the conclusion to the study of economic policymaking in Britain by A.M. Gamble and S.A. Walkland, *The British Party System and Economic Policy 1945-1983: Studies in Adversary Politics*, Oxford 1984, p. 174: 'The adversary politics thesis in its well-known version exaggerates the role of parties in policy formulation and implementation and underplays the role of other bodies and institutions, and still more the constraints which circumstances, administrative procedures, events, and outside forces impose on any government.'

31. For example, Claus Offe, *Contradictions of the Welfare State*, edited John Keane, London 1984, pp. 185-6.

32. R.H.S. Crossman, 'Introduction' to Walter Bagehot, *The English Constitution*, London 1963.

33. Frederic S. Burin and K.L. Shell, *Politics, Law, and Social Change. Selected Essays of Otto Kirchheimer*, p. 369; cf. Joseph A. Schumpeter, *Capitalism, Socialism and Democracy*, London and New York 1942, chapter 22 and p. 283: 'Party and machine politicians are simply the response to the fact that the electoral mass is incapable of action other than a stampede, and they constitute an attempt to regulate political competition exactly similar to the corresponding practices of a trade association. The psycho-technics of party management and party advertising, slogans and marching tunes, are not accessories. They are of the essence of politics. So is the political boss.'

34. This would appear to be a more general trend in late capitalist systems, affecting socialist and non-socialist parties alike. The trend towards a 'candidate-centred' politics seems strongest in the United States, where the general hoopla and razzamatazz of media campaigns centred on candidates has rendered parties less institutionally relevant and salient to the voting public. According to Martin P. Wattenberg (*The Decline of American Political Parties 1952-1980*, Cambridge Mass., and London 1984. p. xv): 'For nearly three decades the American public has been drifting steadily away from the two major parties. Once the central guiding forces in American electoral behaviour, the parties are now perceived with almost complete indifference by a large proportion of the population.' This indifference would appear to be warranted for, in striking contrast to their (socialist and non-socialist) counterparts in western Europe, American parties project much more limited programmes, and unite their members against their opposition less markedly. They also impose much less discipline on their elected members; whether in office or in opposition, they perform far fewer functions between elections; and they are rarely considered accountable as parties for the successes and failures of their incumbents. It is worth observing that a deep ambivalence

towards political parties has much older roots in America, as has been argued by
Austin Ranney (*Curing the Mischiefs of Faction: Party Reform in America*, Berkeley
1975, chapter 2), and Richard Hofstadter (*The Idea of a Party System. The Rise of
Legitimate Opposition in the United States, 1780-1840*, Berkeley, Los Angeles and
London 1970).

35. Plausible interpretations of contemporary social movements as forms of
collective action based on solidarity, conflict and a capacity for breaking the limits
of the institutions within which they emerge, include: Alberto Melucci, 'Social
Movements and the Democratization of Everyday Life', in *Civil Society and the
State*, and his *Challenging Codes. Social Movements in Complex Societies*, edited John
Keane and Paul Mier, London 1989; Alain Touraine, *The Voice and the Eye. An
Analysis of Social Movements*, Cambridge 1981; and Claus Offe, 'New Social
Movements: Challenging the Boundaries of Institutional Politics', *Social Research*,
52, 4, Winter 1985, pp. 817-68.

36. Anthony Downs, *An Economic Theory of Democracy*, New York 1957, p. 233.

37. This type of criticism is discussed in Joachim Raschke, ed., *Bürger und
Parteien. Ansichten und Analysen einer schwierigen Beziehung*, Opladen 1982.

38. Here I am excluding consideration of the work of dedicated revolutionary
vanguardist sects, which appear to have no chance of political success and are
likely to have totalitarian effects (as Michnik and other advocates of anti-party
politics emphasize).

39. *The Observer*, 14 July 1985; cf. Kinnock's earlier comments: 'For a democratic political party, the only effective discipline is the self-discipline of the will to
win.' (*The Guardian*, 21 January 1985.)

40. See, for example, Ralph Miliband, *Parliamentary Socialism*, London 1961;
and David Coates, 'The Labour Party and the Future of the Left', in Ralph
Miliband and John Saville eds, *The Socialist Register 1983*, London 1983, pp. 90-
102.

41. This self-paralysing tendency, as carl E. Schorske has argued (*German
Social Democracy 1905-1917*, pp. 7-27), was strongly evident in the early German
SPD, which is otherwise conventionally considered as the prototype of a 'no
compromise' socialist party. From the early 1890s, the SPD's tactic of pure opposition was pursued less rigorously – and the hand of reformism within the Party
strengthened accordingly – in the less industrialized regions of south Germany,
where any long-term success of Social Democracy was felt to depend upon
winning support among the independent peasantry and the peasant–artisan class.
Reformist trends were further strengthened by the growing power of the trade
unions, which concentrated, understandably, not on organizing the proletariat for
revolution, but rather on the 'positive work' of achieving immediate economic and
political gains for their members. More recently, the claim that fundamentalist
parties have a built-in self-paralysing tendency has become central in discussions
concerning the future of *die Grünen* in West Germany. See, for example, Joachim
Hirsch, 'Between Fundamental Opposition and *Realpolitik*', *Telos*, 56, Summer
1983, pp. 172-9; and Claus Offe, 'Zwischen Bewegung und Partei. Die Grünen in
der politischen "Adoleszenskrise"?', in Otto Kallscheuer, ed., *Die Grünen – Letzte
Wahl?*, Berlin 1986, pp. 40-60.

42. Cf. Adam Przeworski, 'Social Democracy as a Historical Phenomenon',
New Left Review, 122, July–August 1980, pp. 41-2: 'There is no reason to doubt
that today the working class together with its allies comprise around eighty per
cent of the population of France or the United States. If to industrial workers we
add white-collar employees, petty bourgeois, housewives, retirees, and students,
almost no one is left to represent interests antagonistic to socialism. Exploiters
remain but a handful: "the businessman with a tax-free expense account, the

speculator with tax-free capital gains and the retiring company director with a tax-free redundancy payment", in the words of the 1959 Labour Party electoral manifesto.'

43. Georg Lukács, *Tactics and Ethics. Political Essays 1919-1929.*

44. Manuel Castells, *The City and the Grassroots. A Cross-Cultural Theory of Urban Social Movements*, Berkeley and Los Angeles 1983, part 6. The failure to address this point constitutes a basic flaw in neo-Gramscian arguments for extending the power and influence of the socialist party form. See, for example, Mike Rustin, 'Different Conceptions of Party: Labour's Constitutional Debates', *New Left Review*, 126, March–April 1981, pp. 17-42. According to Rustin, 'for all the potential costs one can see, there seems to be no socialist progress possible without the creation of stronger political forms, capable of widely challenging for power, of proposing changed goals and priorities for institutions, and of aiming to democratize and disseminate authority more consensually and equally in society' (p. 42). While acknowledging the problem of 'substitutionism', Rustin's argument comes very close to reproducing its main elements, for instance by referring (against Miliband and others) to the British Labour Party as 'the major political vehicle of working-class interests' (p. 35) and, consequently, by indirectly privileging the competitive socialist party form over grassroots social movements – as if the latter could function as the 'raw material' of socialist party politics.

45. Joseph A. Schumpeter, *Capitalism, Socialism and Democracy*, pp. 269-83. Carried to its extreme, this judgement leads to the bitter indictment of parties as 'a counterproductive tool, ... a trap into which life energy disappears, indeed, where it is rededicated to the spiral of death' (Rudolf Bahro, 'Statement on My Resignation From The Greens', in *Building the Green Movement*, London 1986, p. 211).

46. Klaus von Beyme, 'Do Parties Matter? The Impact of Parties on the Key Decisions in the Political System', *Government and Opposition*, 19, 1, Winter 1984, pp. 5-29.

47. This indispensable mediating function of political parties is underestimated in the classic treatise on the rise of modern parties by M. Ostrogorski, *Democracy and the Organization of Political Parties*, London 1902. Ostrogorski's exhaustive examination of parties in the United States and Britain proposed the abolition of parties and their replacement by voluntary associations for the temporary promotion of particular aims. Yet what remains unclear in his account is precisely how representative government in large, complex societies could function without the mediating role of a plurality of permanently organized parties.

48. *The Federalist Papers*, New York 1964, no. 10, p. 82.

49. Richard Hofstadter, *The Idea of a Party System.*

50. See Lewis B. Namier, *The Structure of Politics at the Accession of George III*, second edn., London and New York 1957; and *Monarchy and the Party System*, Oxford 1952; Eric J. Evans, *Political Parties in Britain. 1780-1867*, London 1985; and Harvey Mansfield Jr, 'Party Government and the Settlement of 1688', *American Political Science Review*, December 1964, pp. 937, 945. The emergence of parties in the United States is best analysed by William N. Chambers, *Political Parties in a New Nation: The American Experience 1776-1809*, Oxford 1963; and Richard Hofstadter, *The Idea of a Party System.*

51. M. Ostrogorski, *Democracy and the Organization of Political Parties.*

52. Quoted in Harold J. Laski, *Parliamentary Government in England*, London 1938, p. 100.

53. This argument is elaborated in my *Public Life and Late Capitalism. Towards a Socialist Theory of Democracy*, Cambridge 1984.

54. Robert Michels, *Zur Soziologie des Parteiwesens in der modernen Demokratie*, pp. 150-57.

55. See Nicos Poulantzas's discussion of the need for recognizing 'une certaine tension irreductible entre les partis ouvriers et les mouvements sociaux' in his 'La crise des partis', *Repères. Hier et aujourd'hui*, Paris 1980, pp. 163-83. Poulantzas here criticizes the proposal of Pietro Ingrao (*La politique en grand et en petit, ou les chances de la troisième voie*, Paris 1979) to view the socialist/communist party as the synthesizer or 'moment of globalization' of the new social movements.

56. Peter Gay, *The Dilemma of Democratic Socialism. Eduard Bernstein's Challenge to Marx*, New York 1952.

57. Harold Laski, *Democracy in Crisis*, London 1933, p. 77.

5

Dictatorship and the Decline of Parliament

Carl Schmitt's Theory of Political Sovereignty

> Nowadays the representative system is associated with the
> republican form of state. But originally it arose in monarch-
> ies, wherever the monarch, representing the unity of the
> state, opposed the estates, representing the diverse private
> interests which had to be rewoven constantly into a unified
> whole. This dualism is basic for the system of representative
> government. In modern political life it appears in the polar-
> ity of 'state' and 'society', of the unity and diversity of inter-
> ests of a people.
>
> Otto Hintze

The Age of Liberalism

The representative assembly, or parliament as it is called most
often, is one of the oldest, most commonplace and – for the
socialist tradition – most controversial democratic institutions.
Suspicion of parliament is certainly not confined to the socialist
tradition. The modern history of parliament – the ultimate political symbol of peaceful compromise and quiet agreement – has
been littered with bitter conflicts, paralysis and open violence. In
the early decades of this century, these trends reached something
of a climax. With the Bolshevik Revolution, the severe political
crises that followed in the aftermath of the First World War, and
the rise of syndicalism and fascism, parliament appeared to have
little or no future. This period saw not only the first successful

large-scale attempts, within the socialist and fascist movements, to dismantle parliamentary government. It also witnessed a deep loss of confidence in the spirit of parliamentarism among its closest supporters, many of whom publicly lamented the declining legitimacy and effectiveness of representative assemblies.[1]

Carl Schmitt, whose political writings are little known outside his native Germany, was undoubtedly the shrewdest and most controversial European critic of parliament during this period. His writings on parliament directly address the subject of civil society and the state. They cast serious doubts on the capacity of parliament to regulate the relations of power within and between civil society and the state. Schmitt's rejection of parliament raises fundamental political questions concerning state sovereignty, civil war, dictatorship and the future of democracy, and these in turn have a strikingly contemporary ring about them. For these reasons, his writings on parliament deserve careful reconsideration, freed from the highly personalized and bitter reaction they typically evoke in West Germany today.[2]

Schmitt situates his criticism of parliament within a wider account of the grip of liberalism upon nineteenth-century European politics. The essence of modern liberalism, in his view, is its deep antipathy to state power. In its struggle against the arcane power of absolutist states, liberalism developed a deeply negative distrust of political power without, however, defining a positive political view of its own. Liberalism admits the need for state and governmental power – suitably subdivided into legislative, executive and judicial branches – but only inasmuch as it serves the specific purpose of enhancing individuals' freedom within civil society. Every transgression by political rulers of their properly limited prerogatives is therefore denounced by liberals as tyranny, as *eo ipso* evil and unjust.

Schmitt does not consider the objection that liberal individualist thinkers from Hobbes to Bentham, Guizot and Mohl were often driven, by the force of their liberal individualism, to support strong state measures in matters of domestic rule, colonization or military conquest.[3] He instead emphasizes that the central preoccupation of liberalism is the protection of individuals' rights of property ownership and freedom of speech. The liberal schema supposes that free competition among freely speaking and propertied citizens within civil society neutralizes state power and renders it nearly superfluous. In contrast to the notion of politically enforced unity and balance of its absolutist predecessor, liberalism views social and political equilibrium as a consequence of the *absence* of political regulation – as the effect of 'perpetual competition and perpetual discussion'[4].

From this perspective, Schmitt views parliament as a key liberal mechanism for ensuring equilibrium between the state and civil society.[5] Parliament is supposed to openly, fairly and peacefully resolve differences of expressed opinion within civil society, as well as subjecting the state apparatus and its governmental executive to processes of deliberation and legislation. Parliament is the fulcrum between civil society and the state, the guarantor of non-violent and unforced social and political harmony. 'The essence of liberalism is negotiation, a cautious half-measure, in the hope that the definitive dispute, the decisive bloody battle, can be transformed into a parliamentary debate which permits the decision to be postponed forever in an unending discussion.'[6] The 'essential principles' of parliament are openness and discussion. According to Schmitt's strict definition, tussles among conflicting interests, and mere negotiation and compromise, are not features exclusive to parliament. They are clearly evident, for instance, in private meetings between company directors and political party or trade union officials, and at diplomatic conferences. Open parliamentary discussion is essentially different. It rests on a shared commitment to principled argument and counter-argument. It supposes the willingness to be persuaded of another's point of view and, hence, freedom from particular loyalties and selfish interests. 'Discussion means an exchange of opinion that is governed by the purpose of convincing one's opponent through argument of the truth or justice of something, or allowing oneself to be convinced of something as true or just.'[7]

In the liberal view, various parliamentary arrangements are supposed to facilitate this form of open and principled discussion. These include unrestricted parliamentary proceedings, the rights of free speech and legal immunity of representatives, as well as their freedom from party or constituency instructions, their obligation being only to their own principled conscience (as in article 21 of the Weimar constitution). Parliamentary arrangements of this kind ensure that opinions are formed not by a noisy clash of jostling interests, but through an unhindered exchange of reasoned arguments. Every matter before parliament is supposed to be discussed, negotiated and agreed in a process of calm and open deliberation. According to Schmitt, Bentham's observation that in 'parliament ideas meet, and contact between ideas gives off sparks and leads to evidence'[8] correctly summarizes the liberal parliamentary principle. On this view, legislators seek the truth together honestly and openly. Political truth, as it crystallizes in universal norms and promulgated, generally binding laws, consists neither in the discovery of transcendental standards nor blind compromises among dogmatists defending their selfish interests. Rather, it is a function of unrestricted competition among freely expressed opinions within the legislative assembly. In this sense, liberal parliamentary government, in contrast to its absolutist predecessors, is visible government, openly reported by a free press. Parliamentarians find themselves under the watchful eye and attentive ears of the citizenry, whose access to a free press (here Schmitt draws upon a central theme of Guizot's *Histoire des origines du gouvernement représentatif en Europe*) enables them in turn to ascertain the truth of matters and express it to their parliamentary representatives.[9]

The Spiritual Crisis of Parliament

Schmitt's account of the nineteenth-century liberal era of parliamentarism is brief and overly simplified. Yet it serves the deeper purpose of foregrounding and defending his claim that twentieth-century parliament is facing a profound crisis. In his view, classical liberal parliament and its ideals are degenerating into a rump parliament without ideals. This process is likened to the slow disappearance of monarchy. Just as the end of the epoch of European monarchy was signalled by growing criticisms and outright rejections of the monarchic principles of kingship and honour, so the loss of legitimacy of parliamentary ideals indicates that the hour of parliament has tolled, even if, like monarchy, it survives indefinitely as a crippled and hollow figure from the past.

Symptomatic of the loss of reality and spiritual crisis of parliament is the militant rejection of parliamentary institutions by communists, fascists and anarcho-syndicalists.[10] Among its staunchest defenders, Schmitt observes, the old intellectual arguments for parliament have also run out of steam. They appear ever more antiquated and idealistic and, in their place, purely pragmatic reasons are adduced in favour of parliament. Compared with the untried and risky – experiments in direct democracy, for instance – parliament is said to ensure a minimum of political order and governmental continuity. Or parliament is favoured on the equally pragmatic grounds (spelled out in Schmitt's time by Max Weber, Hugo Preuss and others)[11] that it functions primarily as a means of screening and selecting competent political leadership – as a testing ground for a future political class. Schmitt reasons that such pragmatic defences of parliament are frail and unconvincing, since they fail to explain the essential principles upon which it rests. The distinction between essential principles and pragmatic considerations is basic to Schmitt's argument that contemporary parliament is suffering a deep spiritual crisis: 'Parliamentarism consists today of a method of government and a political system. Just like every-thing else that exists and functions tolerably, it is useful – no more and no less. It counts for a great deal that even today it functions better than other untried methods, and that the minimum of order that is today actually maintained would be endangered by frivolous experiments. Every intelligent person would concede such arguments. But they do not carry weight in an argument concerning principles.'[12]

This spiritual crisis has several causes. Among the most vital is the growing influence of democracy. Schmitt argues that the struggle for greater political democracy pressures governments to expand their scope and power in order to satisfy growing social demands. Thereby, the nineteenth-century trend toward a non-interventionist liberal constitutional state is reversed. By increas-ing the strategic importance of state power, the struggle for democracy also makes a mockery of the old parliamentary princi-ples. The open deliberations of parliament are destroyed by mass democracy, and especially by the concomitant growth of compet-itive party politics.

Schmitt's analysis of this trend thinly veils his well-known lifelong disdain for party politics. The masses are subjected to a constant barrage of party campaigning, which utilizes propa-ganda geared to voters' passions and immediate interests, in order better to manipulate and govern them. Parties 'create electoral propaganda, process the masses, and dominate public opinion'.[13] Elections become a plebiscitary contest among sectional interests, 'a roll-call of the standing party-army'.[14] The tide of organized party domination in the electoral arena naturally spills over into parliament, which becomes a prime target for tightly disciplined party machines battling for newly enfranchised electorates.[15] The scope for independent deliber-ation and the rational balancing of opinions among members of parliament is destroyed. In a context in which combatants have already decided their bargaining positions before discussion begins, government by open debate becomes simply impossible.

Parliament becomes cluttered with party manoeuvrings and purposeless and banal discussion. It is choked by the obstructive tactics and misuse of parliamentary privilege by its radical (class) opponents, whose first aim is to manipulate parliament for their own particular economic and party-political ends. This threatens the equilibrating function of parliament. In Schmitt's eyes, nineteenth-century liberal parliaments, which normally defended their existing constitutions, were threatened by executive domination. By contrast, twentieth-century parliaments, dominated as they are by self-paralysing party politics, threaten the constitutional order and unity of the state. As parliament falls into decline, the state tends to degenerate into an 'unstable coalition *Parteienstaat*'.[16]

The corrosive effects of democracy by no means spare parliament's guiding principles of openness and discussion. According to Schmitt's idiosyncratic interpretation, the hybrid term 'parliamentary democracy' is self-contradictory and self-paralysing, since the essential principles of liberal parliamentarism and democracy are fundamentally at odds with each other.

This contradiction between parliament and democracy went unnoticed during the heyday of liberalism, when the two phenomena gained ground simultaneously. With the growing victories of democracy, however, it becomes evident that democratic principles are antithetical to limited government by unrestricted discussion. Democracy rests upon a principle of exclusion (here Schmitt draws upon an aspect of Aristotle's definition of democracy[17]). It specifies that even though all persons may be equal, some are certainly more equal than others; that is, that only equals, and not unequals, are worthy of being treated equally. The practice of universal and equal suffrage among citizens is based upon this democratic principle. So also are attempts – evident in Bolshevism, fascism and other forms of dictatorship[18] – to exclude from the franchise unequals, whose admission to citizenship would ruin the spirit of equality and homogeneity so essential to democracy. 'A democracy demonstrates its political power by knowing how to eliminate or keep at bay something that is foreign and unequal and threatens its homogeneity.'[19]

The democratic principle of equality among equals also supposes that the citizens' will is sovereign, and that these citizens are capable of expressing a unanimous opinion – a general will – on matters of common political concern. Essential to democracy is the argument (here Schmitt draws upon Rousseau's *Du Contrat social*) that the real will of outvoted minorities is in fact identical with the general will, as and when it is expressed in the will of the majority.[20] In principle, democracy therefore supposes that political harmony will reign when authority comes from those over whom it is exercised, that is, when rights of control are fully entrusted to those who are to be controlled.

These democratic ideas concerning equality and unanimity have profoundly subversive implications for liberal parliamentarism – or so Schmitt argues. Obviously, the characteristic yearning of democracy for homogeneity and (restricted) equality contradicts the liberal, parliamentary emphasis upon the (initial) diversity of social interests, and therefore upon the probable controversy and disagreement among citizens and their representatives. Less obviously, democracy confronts parliament as an unnecessary and outmoded institution. (Schmitt particularly directed this point at the Weimar constitution which, in his view, contained a self-contradictory mixture of arguments for liberal and democratic principles, for the Reichstag and the Reichspräsident.) According to Schmitt, the democratic idea supposes that it is the assembly of citizens, and not parliamentary representatives, who enjoy the ultimate prerogative of deciding and altering laws. Democracy further supposes the possibility of an identity of the governed and the governing, of those who command and those who obey.[21] This supposition becomes especially evident in a crisis situation when, according to the democratic principle, the people's sovereign will should hold sway, regardless of the constitutional framework or the decisions of parliamentary representatives. It is a short step from this claim to an anti-parliamentary conclusion: Since the state can and should become identical with the popular will (through devices such as elections and referenda), the institutional separation of the state and civil society – as well as the equilibrating role of parliament – become redundant. Democracy views undivided state power as a natural and healthy consequence of the growth of active citizenship among equals. It destroys the anti-political hopes of classical parliamentary liberalism.

The Total State

The growing victories of democracy over parliamentary liberalism reinforce Schmitt's conviction that the age of parliament is coming to an end. Under pressure from the accelerating push for greater democracy, the state, in responding to social demands, begins to absorb civil society into its bureacratic structures. The classical liberal separation of the state and civil society is destroyed, and replaced by the total state.[22]

In several respects, this argument is less than convincing. Schmitt's claim that there is a symbiotic relationship between democratic principles and total state power is highly questionable.* His thesis that democratization – in the sense of popular power – stimulates the growth of the total state also fails to anticipate fully the ways in which democratization stimulates the *renewal* of the cleavage between the bureaucratic state and civil society.[23] He merely expresses concern that the growing influence of organized social powers within the state may destroy or weaken its capacity to govern.[24]

Faced with that threatening possibility, he emphasizes the exciting *political* implications of the loss of identity and independence of civil society. The collapse of civil society into the total state (potentially) destroys parliament in its classical liberal form. It becomes an 'empty apparatus' situated in the shadows of state power.[25] The merging of civil society into the total state also (potentially) dissolves the liberal illusion – here Schmitt attacks Otto von Gierke's theory of association, as well as Figgis, Laski

---

* Schmitt points insightfully to the Jacobinist potential of the doctrine of popular sovereignty (*Die geistesgeschichtliche Lage*, pp. 40-41). He argues that the nineteenth-century idea that all power derives from the people is an inverted, secularized form of the idea of divine right: the older theological belief that all authoritative power comes from God is brought to earth and replaced by the principle that the immanent source of power and authority is 'the sovereign people'. (Schmitt consistently adopted the view that 'all significant concepts of the modern theory of the state are secularized theological concepts' (*Political Theology*, p. 36).) The sovereign people may temporarily be incapable of recognizing that they are God, in which case – here Schmitt observes the Jacobin implications of the popular sovereignty doctrine – an enlightened minority can legitimately act as the 'temporary' bearer of the people's power and authority. This part of Schmitt's thesis is compelling. However, its extremely narrow definition of democracy – which owes most to Aristotle and Rousseau – is unconvincing. It takes no account of the considerable overlaps between liberal thought (in Schmitt's sense) and the much more influential tradition of *representative democracy* – the great invention of modernity, according to Hamilton and other authors of *The Federalist Papers*. In the view of a substantial number of late eighteenth and early nineteenth century thinkers such as Madison, Bentham, James Mill, Constant, J.S. Mill and Tocqueville, the whole of the people cannot themselves gather in large-scale polities to regularly decide on specific issues. They saw the vital importance of an elected committee of responsible (male, property-owning) citizens, from which in turn is drawn a government of representatives, which remains dependent upon the general body

and the English pluralists[26] – that the state, as the servant and guarantor of civil society, is merely one association among others. Thanks to the emergence of the total state, political power makes a comeback and, Schmitt hopes, this in turn will stimulate awareness of the essential principle of politics: the ability to distinguish between friend and enemy.

Summarized briefly, Schmitt's argument is that the political world is a pluriverse, a dangerous jungle of self-interested partnerships, shifting tactical alliances, open disagreements and outbreaks of violent conflict. These specifically political phenomena are a reflection of the fact that human beings are dynamic and dangerous creatures who are often driven, by force of circumstances, to commit devilish acts.[27] Those who rule through the state are consequently forced to recognize that, at home and abroad, they are always confronted by alien others, by strangers with whom extreme and violent conflicts are possible and indeed likely. In the sphere of politics, the liberal parliamentary attempt to sublimate political enemies into economic competitors and debating partners makes no sense at all. The openness and discussion principles of parliament cannot substitute for the friend–enemy principle of politics. In politics, only fools suppose that they can treat their enemies as honest debating partners,

---

of citizens through mechanisms such as periodic elections, freedom of public assembly, and unrestricted rights to publicly discuss and criticize those who govern. These representative-democratic themes clearly overlap with liberalism (as Schmitt understands it) in several decisive respects. Many representative-democratic and liberal thinkers feared the general loss of liberty that would result from undivided arbitrary government (essay 2). Consequently, they often doubted the principle of unbridled majority rule (of male property-owning citizens). Also, they viewed with suspicion the possibility of an identity between governors and governed. ('The chief merit of representative government', observed Alphonse de Lamartine in *Bien public*, 'is to make a country think.') Perceiving the dangers of undivided state power, many liberals and representative democrats of this period also valued parliament as the indispensable mediator between governed and governors, between civil society and the state. In short, parliament, openness and public discussion are seen by these thinkers as essential preconditions of democratic representative government – and not, as Schmitt claims (*Die geistesgeschichtliche Lage*, p. 42), as mere 'expedients' which have nothing at all to do with the essential principles of democracy. See, for example, Alexander Hamilton et al., *The Federalist Papers*, New York 1964, especially nos. 9, 14, 37; James Mill, *An Essay On Government*, Indianapolis 1955, chapters 1-6; J.S. Mill, 'Considerations on Representative Government', in *Essays on Politics and Society*, edited J.M. Robson, Toronto 1977, pp. 399-412; Alexis de Tocqueville, *De la démocratie en Amérique*, Paris 1981, part 2, ch. 7, pp. 343-60.

peaceful competitors or adversaries in need of tolerance, understanding and compassion.

Those who are politically wise bear in mind the constant possibility of deception, cunning and violent opposition from their
opponents. They know that armed conflict against pre-defined
enemies – the attempt to neutralize or eliminate them physically
– is the ultimate political event. They also know that the state
should be the sovereign entity – sovereign in the exact sense (here
Schmitt draws upon Bodin's classic definition) that those who
rule through the state are required, in an emergency or exceptional situation (*Ausnahmezustand*), to make decisions about what
is to be done, including what is to be done against the enemies of
the state. 'Sovereign is he [sic] who decides on the exception.'[28]
Concretely, this means that to those who rule politically belongs
the *jus belli*. They enjoy the unlimited right to define the domestic
or foreign enemy, as well as to fight and destroy that enemy with
all the available resources of state power. Political power confers
upon its holders an awful prerogative: the unrestricted power to
wage war and, hence, to 'publicly dispose of the lives of human
beings'.[29]

Under the umbrella of sovereign political power, Schmitt
observes, there remains room for the existence of independent
power groups, such as businesses, churches, trade unions and
parliaments.[30] Schmitt denies that the total state is totalitarian.
But he emphasizes that lesser, subordinate associations and institutions, including parliament, can exist legitimately within the
total state only on the condition that they do not endanger the
established political order. The total state should be considered
'the highest entity, not because it dictates omnipotently or subju-
gates all other entities, but because it decides, and hence within
itself can hinder all other antagonistic groupings ... Where it
exists, the social conflicts among individuals and social groups
can be decided in such a way that order – a normal situation –
prevails.'[31]

This conclusion makes clear that the liberal doctrine of parliamentary sovereignty has no place in the total state. According to
Schmitt, the ability to act effectively in an abnormal situation
declines as the number to be consulted increases. Since parliaments attempt to deliberate and decide by means of clumsy and
time-consuming group assembly and reasoned agreements
among conflicting partners, ultimate political power is best
invested in a single pair of agile hands.[32] In normal times, no
doubt, parliament can still legitimately debate and decide

matters of lesser political importance. In the luxury of quiet times, it may also function as a forum in which sociopolitical interests can be galvanized into a 'supra-party will', which in turn secures the unity of the state and its constitution. But Schmitt insists that when the political stability of normal times disappears, and push comes to shove, parliament – and all other subsidiary institutions – must render their obedience to those in charge of the state. In accordance with the Hobbesian 'protection-obedience axiom'[33], members of parliament and their constituents must recognize that the price of protection from enemies at home and abroad is unconditional obedience to the sovereign state authority.

First Principles of Parliament?

Even when summarized so briefly, Schmitt's criticism of parliament is impressive and challenging. It raises questions of fundamental importance to a democratic theory of civil society and the state. It challenges some basic postulates of the European parliamentary tradition. And its frank defence of the sovereignty of the political is – or should be – disquieting for anyone who values such parliamentary customs as open deliberation and non-violent agreement. Schmitt's impressive rejection of parliamentarism nevertheless remains unconvincing. It is crippled by three decisive weaknesses, which arguably derive from Schmitt's peculiar – metaphysical – method of analysing the origins, development and decline of parliament.

Schmitt's strategy for criticizing parliamentarism rests initially on an attempt to historicize parliamentary discourse – to view it as the product of liberal attempts to depoliticize the modern world. On that basis, Schmitt, the metaphysician, attempts to strip away the appearances surrounding parliament and, thus, to reveal and explain its essential nature. This unmasking of parliamentary phenomena is attempted by enquiring after its first principles. All important institutions, Schmitt says, rest upon certain characteristic or essential ideas – upon what Montesquieu called the principle of a governmental form.[34] These essential principles of an institution can be uncovered through careful and systematic reflection upon what has been said and written about it. Thus, Schmitt attempts to divine 'the ultimate core of the institution of modern parliament'[35] by carefully reflecting upon the writings of its staunchest defenders (Burke, Bentham, Guizot, J.S.

Mill) who lived through the golden age of parliament. These essential principles of parliament, discussed above, are not to be confused with 'practical' or expedient arguments in its favour. Nor are they necessarily identical with the actual day-to-day functioning of parliament; indeed, parliament can stray from its own specific principles, even to the extreme point of assuming a form which contradicts them and renders them passé.

Schmitt's metaphysical account of the essential principles of parliament is unusual, considering that the study of parliament – following Maitland's nineteenth-century defence of the 'pedestrian method of description' – has been conventionally pursued through narrowly empirical methods. It is nevertheless vulnerable to the simple, non-empiricist objection that its criteria of validity are not specified, but *assumed* by Schmitt to be true. That assumption, in turn, is vulnerable to the more consequential objection that Schmitt's method of grasping the essentials of parliament is in fact only one – necessarily limited and biased – method among possible others. Like all other approaches to the study of parliament, Schmitt's rigorous questioning of its 'essential principles' cannot claim to be either exhaustive or unprejudiced. It rather approximates a form of ideal-typical analysis (in the sense of Max Weber). In other words, it is better viewed as one particular account of parliament which rests upon simplifying conceptual abstractions, and which therefore selectively, that is, one-sidedly, scrutinizes and emphasizes only *some* of the characteristic features and predicaments of parliament.[36]

The (unacknowledged) one-sidedness of Schmitt's interpretation is evident in several ways: first, in its striking disregard of the pre-liberal history of parliament; in its failure, secondly, to spot the wide gulf between the liberal principles of openness and discussion and the actual functioning of nineteenth-century parliaments; and, finally, in its blind dismissal of the possibilities of democratically reforming parliament, of strengthening its power in opposition to the 'total state'. Since these three weaknesses in Schmitt's interpretation bear heavily on the issue of whether or not parliament has an important place in a contemporary theory of the state and civil society, they are worth examining in greater detail.

Pre-liberal Parliaments

Schmitt's neglect of pre-liberal parliaments is problematic, in view of their ubiquity, their rich history and – above all – their deep continuity with parliaments in the age of liberalism and beyond. Parliaments may be broadly defined as assemblies of decisionmakers who consider themselves formally equal to one another in status, and whose authority as members of parliament rests on their claim to represent a wider political community. Parliaments in this sense first developed in the field of high tension between the public power of feudal monarchs and the cluster of private interests represented by the estates of nobility, clergy, peasantry and burghers. The dualism between monarchs and estates – which developed nowhere else in the world, and was the forerunner of the polarity of state and civil society of the early modern era – is basic to understanding the origins of European parliamentary assemblies.[37]

So far from being absent in Europe before the era of modern liberalism – as Schmitt implies by his silence – parliamentary assemblies appeared at the end of the twelfth century, flourishing thereafter, at one time or another, throughout the British Isles and continental Europe west of Russia and the Balkans.* Parliaments superseded the traditional medieval assemblies (such as the German *Hoftage* or English *witanegemots*), which had functioned mainly as loosely organized, ad hoc consultative bodies summoned by the monarch for the purposes of seeking their counsel or opinion, or publicizing among the monarch's subjects special events, such as dynastic marriages, international treaties and new judicial and legislative measures.[38] In contrast to these medieval assemblies, parliaments such as the Spanish *cortes* and the French *parlament* (or *parlamentum*) met more frequently and regularly, and also functioned as both consultative and delib-

---

* Parliamentary assemblies of this kind first appeared, at the end of the twelfth century, in the Spanish kingdom of Léon. During the thirteenth century, they spread to Aragon, Castile, Catalonia and Valencia, to Sicily and Portugal, England and Ireland, and the states of the Empire, such as Austria and Brandenburg. During the next two centuries, parliaments developed in the large majority of German principalities, in Scotland, Denmark, Sweden, France, the Netherlands, Poland and Hungary. Nearly all of them survived until the seventeenth and early eighteenth centuries; despite the growth of absolutism, many continued to function until the French Revolution, and a few (the Swedish *Ridsdag* and the Hungarian *Diet*) lasted into the nineteenth century, while the powerful Estates of the Duchy of Mecklenburg survived intact until 1918. See H.M. Cam et al., eds, *Recent Works on the Origins and Development of Representative Assemblies*, Florence 1955. More recently, see H.G. Koenigsberger, *Estates and Revolutions: Essays in Early Modern European History*, London 1971, and A.R. Myers, *Parliaments and Estates in Europe to 1789*, London 1975.

erative bodies. Especially when the cohesion and influence of estates increased, and when at the same time government typically assumed the form of the *Ständestaat* – a monarchy ruling over a society dominated by orders – parliaments became a vital intermediary between monarchic rulers and the (elected or appointed) representatives of the most privileged estates, who sought to define and defend matters of concern to the whole 'realm'.

These early European parliaments were by no means weak or intermittent. Not only the English parliament – often assumed to be the unique example of a powerful representative assembly – but nearly all continental parliaments exercised considerable powers of granting taxes, participating in legislation and determining the justice of matters as diverse as succession and foreign policy. Throughout Europe, monarchs could rarely impose taxes without the consent of their parliaments, which also very often collected these taxes through their own agents and treasuries, and prescribed how they should be spent. Parliaments also exercised considerable powers of initiating legislation (for instance, in the form of bills that became statutes upon receiving royal assent). They investigated alleged injustices and illegal acts committed by monarchs or their officers, and enforced the principle that grants of supply be conditional upon the monarch's redress of these grievances within the realm. These parliamentary powers of taxation, legislation and litigation were reinforced, especially in times of crisis, by the exercise of other prerogatives, including the conduct of foreign policy, the settlement of succession to the throne, the guarantee of treaties, partitions and settlements, and the appointment of the monarch's advisers and ministers.

By ignoring the long and complex history of these pre-liberal parliaments, Schmitt's theory of the rise and decline of parliamentarism appears less plausible and less distinctive than at first sight. In spite of its unorthodox theoretical assumptions, it evidently stands within a hoary tendency among German political and legal thinkers of intellectually denigrating the history of parliamentary assemblies and (unwittingly) siding with the monarchs and state-builders who tried to suppress them.[39] It also overlooks the deep continuities between liberal parliaments and their medieval predecessors. Important differences no doubt divide them. The earliest parliaments convened less regularly, and often according to the whim or will of the monarch. Their proceedings – in contrast to those of their bourgeois-dominated counterparts of the liberal era – were most strongly influenced by the nobility and clergy (who claimed to represent the entire realm, including those interests unrepresented or unsummoned to the assembly). Moreover, the earliest parliaments rarely defended their positions through explicit political theories – such as those of the liberal variety analysed by Schmitt – instead basing their claims upon ancient customs and privileges, which they doggedly refused to modify. And the earliest parliaments were forged in the struggles between monarchs and estates in the era of the *Ständestaat*, whereas liberal parliaments, as Schmitt points out, operated as a bridge between a bourgeois civil society and a constitutional nation state.

Notwithstanding such important differences, medieval and liberal parliamentary assemblies are links in the same nearly unbroken historical chain. Parliament is not a specifically liberal–bourgeois invention; and pre-liberal parliaments are therefore not merely of antiquarian interest. It is virtually impossible to determine the point in time where the older parliaments pass over into their nineteenth-century counterparts. Contrary to the impression left by Schmitt, liberal parliaments by no means held a monopoly on the principles of openness and deliberation. Pre-liberal parliaments sought equally to transform arbitrary, arcane and violent political decisionmaking into negotiated policy agreements founded on open deliberation and peaceful conciliation among (potentially) conflicting interests.

Schmitt's claim that the suspicion of political power was a unique trait of liberal parliamentarism is also unfounded. By standing on ancient customs, rights and privileges – a tactic not unknown to nineteenth- and twentieth-century assemblies – pre-liberal parliaments raised commonly shared grievances about a wide range of matters, from the environmental damage caused by the monarch's animals to forcible military recruitment and the excessive labour performed by the peasantry. And especially during the period of absolutism, these older parliaments also attempted to resist the growing tendency of monarchical governments to decide arbitrarily and without regard for their subjects' wishes. In this way, they served more than the particular interests of the dominant estates. They also acted as a counterweight to petty tyranny and absolute government, thereby keeping alive the spirit of liberty and constitutional government commonly associated with nineteenth-century liberal parliamentarism.[40]

Parliamentary Government as Utopia

To emphasize the deep historical continuities of European parliaments is not to fall victim to a blindly Whiggish interpretation of parliamentary history.[41] The Whig image of mettlesome, refractory parliamentarians struggling in dark times to establish a parliamentary opposition, which subsequently undermined absolutist monarchies and set nineteenth-century nation states such as Britain and the Netherlands on the high road to full parliamentary democracy, is misleading in several respects. The field of vision of pre-liberal European parliaments was narrowed constantly by the self-interested demands of the estates which dominated their proceedings; well into the nineteenth century, as Ostrogorski remarked of Britain, parliamentary politics remained 'the pet hobby of a select group, the sport of an aristocracy'.[42] Looked at from the more cynical standpoint of monarchs and state-builders, these European parliaments also frequently served as a convenient, even ingenious political instrument for regularizing supply by consent, and for making laws more firmly binding upon those very same agents who were seeking to formulate these laws.[43]

The degree to which rational, independently spirited parliaments 'flowered' or 'came of age' during the heyday of nineteenth-century liberalism is also wildly exaggerated by the Whig view – to which Schmitt's account of liberal parliamentarism is surprisingly close. According to Schmitt, liberal parliaments were structured by the principles of openness and deliberation. Parliamentary deliberations consisted of the free exchange and competition of opinions among speakers and listeners bent on persuading each other of the truth of their respective views. There are two problems with this view.

In the first place, it defines liberal parliamentary principles too narrowly. As Hermann Heller originally pointed out against Schmitt, the intellectual basis of liberal parliamentarism is 'not the belief in public discussion as such, but belief in the existence of a common basis of discussion and *fair play* for an opponent, with whom one seeks to reach agreement under conditions that exclude naked force'.[44] Secondly, Schmitt's view substitutes the alleged 'essential principles' of liberal parliament for its actual (and rather different) patterns of operation. On that basis, it misunderstands the status of the principles of openness and discussion, which functioned less as 'essential principles' and more as a 'utopian' ideal at odds with the reality it claimed to defend.

Recent research has indicated that the conventional image of the freely deliberating parliamentarian – the private member of judicious temper who usually voted as he freely willed without incurring more than the momentary displeasure of his party leaders – is contradicted by the pro-government moderation, vested interests and patterns of sectional voting which actually dominated liberal parliamentary procedures and outcomes.[45] Certainly, between the 1832 and 1867 Reform Acts in Britain – the supposed golden age of *the* model parliament – the monarchy lost its unfettered ability to choose ministers. Government policy on various occasions was also overruled or amended by parliament; and the removal of ministers or even changes of government sometimes depended on the voting preferences of members of the House of Commons.[46]

Yet these trends do not prove beyond doubt that parliamentary proceedings approximated to Schmitt's essential principles. The geographic distribution of parliamentary constituencies remained highly skewed. Rotten boroughs had by no means been eliminated; the franchise remained highly restrictive; and the aristocracy continued to hold great political sway in parliament.[47]

The conventional image of the golden age of British parliament also exaggerates the degree to which parliamentarians (in the House of Commons) voted independently of civil society or their party. This image is sustained by focussing attention on rebellions of private members against their parties during the dramatic and highly emotional issues of that time – such as the extension of the suffrage and Irish Home Rule. When this highly selective emphasis is supplemented with consideration of the normal patterns of voting behaviour on the settled issues, on the more specific, humdrum questions which occupied most of parliament's time, a markedly different picture emerges.[48]

Throughout the nineteenth century, governments were rarely defeated on the floor of the House of Commons. Even during the stormiest decade (1851-60), when the House was most fragmented and minority government lasted almost three years, less than a handful of amendments to government legislation was carried each year against the government whips.[49] This suggests that a large majority of members of parliament acted not so much out of a reasoned independence, but on the basis of a shared consensus about the aims and methods of (parliamentary) government. The conventional view – expressed by Schmitt – of the mid-nineteenth-century independent parliamentarian mistakes moderation for independence. The genuinely independent parliamentarian was most often in a minority, and situated on the extreme wings of his own party. There was 'government by the moderate centre', rather than government by open deliberation or (as later) party government.[50] Finally, whenever intraparty disputes broke out, they typically assumed the form of *sectional* conflicts – an example is the ongoing struggles within the Liberal Party between radicals and moderates – while crossbench deviations from party rule were guided less by the promptings of oratory and conscience, and far more by the (threatened) sanctions brought to bear upon parliament by various outside social power groups. Organized or rumoured sanctions against parliament were facilitated by the small and restricted constituencies, the personal relationship which existed between the member and his electors and, increasingly, by the growth during this period of political clubs, registration societies and election funding.

All this suggests the existence of a wide gap between the reality of liberal parliamentarism and its utopian self-image as a public sphere of openness and free deliberation. Schmitt's account of the age of liberalism actively denies this gap by theorizing it away; the 'essential principles' of the liberal self-image are interpreted as identical with reality itself. Not surprisingly, the subsequent history of parliament is made to follow a fatal course of decline. A lost golden age of parliament becomes the standard for tracking its subsequent decline, and declaring parliament to be a thing of the past.

Reforming Parliament

The pseudo-tragic quality of Schmitt's observations on the decline of parliament provides a clue to a third negative consequence of its metaphysical search for 'essences': its failure to consider the chances of democratically reforming twentieth-century parliament, making it less a mouthpiece of arbitrary state executives and more capable of functioning as the guardian of the powerless within civil society and the state. Schmitt's argument a priori eliminates this possibility, as if parliament were destined to fulfil its historical fate by remaining a permanently crippled object of total state power.

Schmitt's diagnosis of the sources of paralysis of parliament – its colonization by organized party politics, for instance – certainly contains grains of truth. Since the early decades of this century, the task of radically reforming parliament has become more pressing – and certainly more difficult. The catalogue of complaints against parliament, although varying from one west European parliamentary system to another, has grown steadily. Parliament nowadays tends to be viewed increasingly as a rubber stamp on decisions reached elsewhere. This view often dovetails with complaints about parliament's gentlemanly pomp, ritualized debates and preoccupation with trifling details. There are also signs, strongly evident within social movements, of a growing conviction that democracy is not a matter for parliament alone, and that local-level commitments and social initiatives are preferable. These diffuse complaints against parliament are worth analysing more carefully, if only to clarify the magnitude of the task facing democratic reformers of parliament.

(a) Parliamentary proceedings are normally controlled by well-organized party machines, and especially by their parliamentary executives. Executive stranglehold over parliamentary proceedings originated in great crises, especially war,[51] and has for some time been reinforced by the compromise party system (essay 4). This trend towards a government-managed parliament is strongly evident in Britain, where the executive has virtually unfettered control over parliamentary proceedings. In matters of government expenditure, for example, parliament has no means of examining the amount or sources of government borrowing or the detail of spending estimates. It is procedurally impossible for parliament to propose increases in a department's estimate and proposals of reduction are always treated as issues of confidence. This kind of executive control is maintained by such practices as the use of royal prerogative in matters of war or signing treaties; the wide powers of prime ministerial patronage; and collective cabinet responsibility, which serves to shield the executive against criticism from any direction. Executive control is also maintained by informal executive pressures – from the friendly glass of whisky to offers of promotion – brought to bear against backbenchers, whose party loyalty and willingness to be pliable are increased by their relatively high chances of advancement due to the size of government. Consequent upon such practices, the House of Commons is reduced to a consultative body which registers the results of general elections and passes virtually all the legislation placed before it.

(b) Conventional parliamentary procedures or formal constitutional arrangements often reinforce the grip of strict party discipline and of executive domination.[52] These procedures range from heavy restrictions on backbenchers' rights to speak and the excessive use of closure and the guillotine to restrict debate, to the habit of spending too much time on discussing the inevitable, and far too little on the 'pre-legislative' and 'post-legislative' stages of legislation. The general decline of the control functions of the French parliament since the 1958 constitution provides one illustration of this broader trend. The 1958 constitution – certainly when compared with its 1946 predecessor – virtually gags parliament. The government indirectly fixes its agenda through the process for determining priority; it can also prevent parliament from organizing debates or passing bills without government assent. Furthermore, in matters of legislative and budgetary procedure, parliament is effectively bound and gagged. The well-known blocked vote procedure, for example, permits the government in legislative discussions to demand a single vote on the complete package of texts (including the amendments it has accepted), thereby squashing all discussion and all voting on its particular articles.

(c) The intervention of various media of mass communication between party-political leaders and the constituents of civil society has reduced the level of visibility of parliament in the realm of official politics. Heavy media coverage of the main party conferences and the privileging of leadership through television and radio interviews and addresses are contributing factors. So also are press reports based on the unattributed back-door leaks and briefings of the 'lobby system', and kite-flying – the unacknowledged spreading of rumours or disinformation by governments to test the waters of public opinion. All these factors have the combined effect of shifting the visual centre of official political debate from the parliamentary chamber to the extra-parliamentary realm. This process is accelerated by the proclivity of key government figures to regard parliament as a waste of time, and by their corresponding habit of withholding their opinions in the name of 'official secrets', 'parliamentary privilege' and other versions of the doctrine of *raison d'état*.

(d) The growing scope of state power has ensured that parliament is swamped with business, and surrounded by apparatuses whose business is scarcely known, let alone controlled by parliament. Schmitt's observation that parliament threatens the constitutional order and unity of the state consequently needs to be reversed. In contemporary west European democracies, parliament is besieged by the massive growth of unaccountable and invisible government.[53] The practice of state secrets, *Arcana rei publicae*, a central theme of political writing from the sixteenth century onwards, is again becoming a central ingredient in the operation of state power. A plethora of invisible and unaccountable sites of political decisionmaking – state-owned and state-subsidized industries and services, nuclear regulatory and processing bodies, quasi-governmental authorities, secret police and 'national security' organs conducting covert intelligence and military operations – outflank the parliamentary forum. There are even bizarre incidents, in which parts of the elected executive branch of the state systematically disinform parliament, snoop on their potential rivals (Watergate), or conduct secret junta-like operations (the Iran–Contra affair) behind the back of parliament.[54] All of these developments suggest that political decisionmaking operates increasingly in the shadowy, unelected zones of state power, and that the historic (if never completed) transformation of European absolutist states into constitutional parliamentary states is nowadays undergoing a reversal.

(e) During the second half of the twentieth century, there has been a considerable growth of supranational policymaking and administration. A considerable number of parliamentary choices are consequently either limited or foreclosed by a state's membership in military arrangements such as NATO and other intergovernmental organizations such as the UN, the IMF and the EEC, as well as by the investment decisions of transnational corporations. Especially in matters of foreign policy, these supranational trends shift decisionmaking power away from parliament. They increase the level of electoral unaccountability and secrecy of government operations. And, since supranationalization encourages particular governments to allege the necessity of political compromise with other governments, it leads governments to formulate 'flexible' negotiating positions rather than firm decisions, thereby discouraging parliament from 'interfering' in supranational negotiations.[55]

Each of these developments subjects parliament to threatening pressures. They also indicate that parliament would clearly benefit from some drastic repairs and radical innovations which go beyond tinkering with its committee systems, televising its proceedings or improving its cost-effectiveness and internal efficiency. Certainly, there are *ineradicable* limits upon parliament's ability to fully and effectively supervise the manifold operations of state institutions. Such limits are inherent in the division of labour between the law-making/supervisory functions of parliament and the state agencies which are supposed to interpret and implement its decisions. These limits are also inherent in the manifold opportunities for both social power groups and state administrators and workers to legitimately redefine, postpone, evade or even quash parliamentary directives. Limits on the 'sovereignty of parliament' are inherent in a system in which power is dispersed and divided democratically between the state and civil society. To suppose that the power of parliament could become, in the words of Edward Coke, 'so transcendent and absolute, as it cannot be confined either for causes or persons within any bounds'[56] is therefore to reach for something never fully attainable. The doctrine of parliamentary sovereignty is, and shall always remain, an elusive utopia.

Parliamentary reform is none the less a pressing and vital condition of the effective and open government so central to democratic politics. Several possible types of reform – corresponding to the developments threatening parliamentary power – can be mentioned here briefly.[57]

The excessive grip of party machines on parliament could be weakened by giving institutional recognition to the limits of political parties and by various other changes in the party system (outlined in essay 4). Executive domination of parliamentary proceedings might be curtailed by the regular election of ministers by the governing parliamentary party or coalition, by restricting the powers of prime ministerial patronage, loosening the practice of collective cabinet responsibility and (in the case of Britain) abolishing the use of royal prerogative to declare war, sign treaties or to reshape or dissolve parliament. Other improvements could include more convenient sitting hours, better office accommodation and research and assistance facilities. Changes in the timing and geography of parliamentary procedure – equalizing the speaking rights of parliamentarians, particularly on urgent and topical debates, and allowing backbenchers to concentrate on the pre-legislative and post-legislative stages of law-making – would also assist the process of strengthening parliamentary control of the state. These changes, in turn, would likely heighten the level of serious media coverage – and public recognition – of parliament. More open media coverage of parliament might also result from the lifting of governmental controls upon parliamentary procedures. Of special importance would be the abolition of the 'lobby system', various forms of which presently function to limit publicity surrounding potentially controversial developments in favour of selected journalists and government policies. The (further) development of independently-minded, publicly accessible standing committees – of the legislative, investigatory or advisory kind anticipated in the Bundestag and American Congress – could allow more effective scrutiny and regulation of both the executive and the 'invisible' branches of the state apparatus. Invisible state power might also be rendered more publicly visible by transforming the upper house (of bicameral systems) into a 'social parliament', an advisory chamber comprising the elected representatives of the functional interests of civil society.[58] Finally, the expanding economic, political and military power of supranational organizations might be subjected to greater parliamentary supervision through various mechanisms. These could include strengthened standing committees, closer co-operation among national legislatures and, in turn, their co-ordination with supranational parliaments – such as the European parliament – whose strengthening, contrary to some expressed doubts, might well contribute to the reviviscence of their national counterparts.

Dictatorship and Parliament

The viability of proposals for democratizing parliament and strengthening its role within the state clearly depends on factors such as the particular national and historical contexts of the parliament in question. It also depends on the inner coherence (and unanticipated side-effects) of the reform proposals themselves, and, above all, on the degree of support they enjoy within civil society, the party system and the state. The viability of radical reform proposals further depends upon the ability of their protagonists to successfully resolve the possible dilemma that radical parliamentary reforms may work, in the short run at least, in favour of anti-democratic parties and social forces.[59] Finally, their credibility depends on meeting Schmitt's fundamental challenge on the issue of political sovereignty. For if, as Schmitt claims, the ability of a limited number of individuals to find friends and deal swiftly with enemies in an abnormal situation is the essence of successful political leadership, then executive state power must ultimately override parliamentary deliberations, as well as whatever rights might be enjoyed by its constituents in civil society.

The crucial political issue, according to Schmitt, is who shall decide in the event of a state of emergency (*Ausnahmezustand*). He was in no doubt that such crisis situations could be resolved only by the decisions of shrewd, strong-willed and well-armed political leadership. Sovereignty resides neither in parliament nor the constitution and its laws, but with the individual (or small group) who decides under pressure. In emergency conditions, when time and events appear to be out of joint, and when political nervousness signifies weakness and emboldens opponents and subordinates, neither slow-moving deliberative assemblies nor anonymous constitutions are capable of deciding. Only political leaders can defend the state and its laws effectively – without delay and without appeal.[60]

Schmitt qualifies this point by distinguishing two fundamentally different forms of sovereign leadership.[61] 'Sovereign dictatorship' (of the kind evidenced in Marxism–Leninism, but traceable to eighteenth-century Enlightenment thinkers such as Mably and Sieyès) is driven by its antipathy to the status quo. It struggles to overthrow the old constitutional order, and to establish a new and more 'authentic' political-legal order. The ultimate aim of sovereign dictatorship is 'to create a condition which makes possible a constitution that it regards as a true constitution'.[62] It acts in the name of the principle of popular sovereignty and on behalf of its subjects, who are treated as little more than a 'formless *pouvoir constituant*'. Sovereign dicatorship is supposed to be a temporary affair, lasting only until such time as the popular will is capable of expressing itself freely or, in the Marxian version of socialism, until the transition to pure communist society is effected.

Distinct in principle from this first form of dictatorship is the 'commissarial dictatorship'. Unlike the sovereign dictatorship, it declares itself the friend of the established constitutional order, its aim being to combat a crisis and to re-establish normal conditions. While a commissarial dictatorship is only temporary – its tenure is limited to the duration of the crisis – this does not mean that its hands are tied, or that it is weak-willed or faint-hearted. The commissarial dictatorship must be as powerful as necessary. Although it is the defender of the *pouvoir constitué*, and hence cannot alter either the existing government or the laws or the constitution, it is entitled to invoke all measures deemed necessary for the restoration of order, including the suspension of parts of the constitution. When the crunch comes, the commissarial dictator must be intolerant of associations within civil society, regarding them as 'worms within the entrails' of the body politic (Hobbes). Sovereign power must be supreme. It must be granted the plenitude of power and cry, with Dante, that the *maxime unum* is the *maxime bonum*. But after completing its mission, the commissarial dictatorship is relieved of its post by the body – parliament, for instance – which governs in normal times. The dictatorship is absorbed back into the political–legal order, in effect ceasing to exist – until the next crisis appears.

Schmitt's careful distinction between two models of dictatorship is intended to distinguish between revolutionaries who seek to overthrow the existing order and constitutionalist proponents of the status quo. A nation state, he argues, can have 'either a sovereign dictatorship or a constitution; one excludes the other'.[63] In the circumstances of Weimar, this argument was directed against reactionary monarchists, revolutionary communists and others opposing the constitution, and in favour of the supporters of the Weimar republican constitution. But this argument also lent support to proposals for resolving political crises through commissarial dictatorship. Consistent with his chronic fear of political disorder and his preference for the established political and legal order, Schmitt insists that commissarial dictatorship, and not parliamentary decision, is necessary for resolving political crises. Under emergency conditions, citizens must confront the state in awe and fear; the presumption in resistance is always firmly against them. The price of protection from enemies at home and abroad is their unconditional, if temporary, obedience to the dictatorial powers of the sovereign political leadership.[64]

Schmitt's defence of commissarial dictatorship against parliament is elaborate, daring and crisply argued. Yet it provides no counter-argument against three serious doubts. Each bears on the problem of despotic power, and parliament's role in reducing its likelihood.

First, an emergency situation (whose existence, duration and termination are defined as such by the sovereign political executive!) usually aggravates the difficulties of government by parliament.[65] Schmitt's defence of commissarial dictatorship, resting as it does on a mixture of cynicism and stinging criticisms of the 'weakness' of parliament, is potentially a self-fulfilling claim. In theory, it is tautological, and therefore self-justifying. Schmitt himself recognized that his concept of sovereignty was structurally akin to the theological idea of a miracle. This admission is revealing. For since emergencies, like miracles, may take place in an infinite number, and since their recognition as such is always a hotly contested business, and therefore has to be actively authenticated by a particular power group, it follows, logically, that the decision that a particular context is in fact an emergency situation must be made by the very same sovereign power group which Schmitt supposes only *reacts* to emergency situations. Schmitt's defence of commissarial dictatorship necessarily traps itself within the chain of reasoning of Joseph de Maistre's *Du Pape* (1821): 'There can be no human society without government, no government without sovereignty, no sovereignty without infallibility.' In practice, Schmitt's defence of commissarial dictatorship also renders rule by decree ever more likely and necessary. The relegation of parliament to a subsidiary or negative role not only assures the domination of the executive and bureaucratic agencies of state power. It also accelerates the decline of parliament's influence on public opinion, and this, in turn, usually magnifies the attraction of anti-democratic propaganda and authoritarian parties and movements promising a political order without 'obstructive' or 'weak-minded' parliaments.

Secondly, Schmitt's assumption that the commissarial dictator will remain a *pouvoir neutre*, a non-partisan power standing temporarily over and above parliament and other conflicting social and political groups, is unconvincing. Schmitt indicates that the powers of the commissarial dictator can and ought to be limited to enacting measures (*Massnahmen*) of a factual kind.[66] The dictator is supposed to be the honest guardian of the status quo, and to have no legitimate powers of initiating legislation or administering justice.

In the face of the well-known temptations of executive power, such assurances are glib, even provocative. Schmitt himself noted the classical Roman cases of Caesar and Sulla, both of whom violated the existing constitutions and deviated from their roles as commissarial dictators.[67] Moreover, if, as Schmitt says, human beings are dynamic and dangerous creatures who are often driven, by force of circumstances, to commit devilish acts, then this 'rule' of human nature must also apply to commissarial dictators. The point is that the divide between commissarial and sovereign dictatorships – assumed by Schmitt to be fundamental – tends always to be paper-thin. Temporary dictatorships have a nasty habit of becoming permanent arrangements. Since they are always pressured by potential (real or imagined) opponents, as well as being tempted by weapons of power ranging from disinformation and demagogy to assassination, torture and imprisonment, they very often prepare the way for sovereign dictatorships. Commissarial dictatorships, to borrow a phrase from Bismarck, are often the 'early fruit' (*Vorfrucht*) or precursors of sovereign dictatorships. They greatly strengthen the military and police bases of state power; they accustom citizens to dictatorial conditions, encourage them to act in self-serving and toadyish ways; and they enable the sovereign dictatorship to justify itself by referring to its predecessors.[68]

Thirdly, Schmitt's insensitivity to the dangers of permanent dictatorship – his inability to foresee the rise of totalitarianism – is evident in his implied defence of already existing (and long-lasting) sovereign dictatorships. Following the Hobbesian equation that states ought to provide security in exchange for their subjects' obedience, Schmitt always regarded deference to a legally constituted state authority as a fundamental precept of political life.[69] Logically, this precept holds true even for regimes secured by a sovereign dictator. Schmitt's theory of political sovereignty takes its stand upon the beatification of order. It does not ask questions about the purposes for which order is maintained. It cannot conceive of the illegitimate – as distinct from illegal – conquest or deployment of state power. It thereby places itself at the disposal of the political group which happens, at any given historical moment, to control the state. Whoever rules through law is right or, as Schmitt liked to say: *Auctoritas, non veritas facit legem* (Authority, not virtue, makes the law). The 'essence' of a constitution, even that established by a sovereign dictatorship, is inviolable. This being so, constitutional amendments must be strictly limited – and wholesale constitutional changes, including those aimed at restoring a measure of social and political pluralism, rendered illegal.

Parliament and Socialism

Schmitt's blindness to the dangers of absolute power is emphasized here in order to suggest an answer to his fundamental challenge to all supporters of the kind of democratic parliament defended in this essay. Since the original principles of parliament are exhausted, Schmitt argues, new ones must be invented in its favour if it is to be considered a viable institution: 'whoever still believes in parliamentarism must at a minimum propose new arguments in its defence.'[70] The reply suggested by this discussion of parliament is old-fashioned, but thoroughly modern: Open, active parliaments are a sine qua non of the survival and flowering of principles as such – at least, a genuine plurality of them. In the absence of a civil society independent of the state, and their parliamentary defence and mediation in turn, a plurality of principled forms of life is impossible.

No doubt, parliament alone can never guarantee the survival of democracy in this sense. The strongest assembly cannot rise above a deeply hostile society or state. Moreover, the pluralizing functions of parliament can be supplemented by courts of law, the press, and trade unions and other independent social power groups. And it is also true – as Bagehot's classic essay pointed out[71] – that parliament can have a variety of functions. Nevertheless, two sometimes tensely interrelated functions of parliament are of special importance to democracy.

First, a democratic parliament is an indispensable means of aggregating, co-ordinating and representing diverse social interests. This integrative capacity of parliament has often been misunderstood – by the Marxist tradition especially – as a mechanism of bourgeois class rule. Parliament *may* become the political means of class domination – 'simply a machine for the suppression of one class by another'.[72] But a cursory familiarity with the long history of European parliamentary assemblies suggests that there is no *essential* relationship – or even 'elective affinity' – between parliament and bourgeois domination. The effects of parliamentary forms are not necessarily produced by the forms themselves. For this reason, the 'sovereignty of parliament' is a necessary – if tentative, and never attainable – utopian fiction within democratic systems.* For only when there is a supreme and *accountable* political body – a national parliament – can *final* decisions be taken which fairly and openly balance and transcend the particular, conflicting group relations of civil society. No 'natural' harmony among social groups can be

---

* Here I dissent from the recent tendency of some democratic socialists to abandon altogether the utopian, but politically fertile doctrine of parliamentary sovereignty, on the grounds of its lack of 'realism'. See, for example, Barry Hindess, *Parliamentary Democracy and Socialist Politics*, London, Boston, Melbourne and Henley 1983, chapter 2. The principle of parliamentary sovereignty is certainly 'unrealistic', in the sense of being out of step with political reality. And Hindess's emphasis on the importance of extra-parliamentary struggles in the development of democratic socialism is wholly convincing. But the alternative he

assumed. And there is never a 'natural' equilibrium between society and the state. There is a constant danger in a democratic system that party competition, freedom of association, the rule of law and other democratic procedures will be used to defeat democracy. Hence, parliament is an indispensable mechanism for anticipating and alleviating the constant pressure exerted by social groups upon each other, and upon the state itself. And, when faced with recalcitrant or power-hungry organizations in crisis situations, parliament becomes an indispensable mechanism for ordering the suppression of those groups committed explicitly to destroying pluralism.

The integrative function of a democratic parliament is not its only possible role. Parliament is also a vital means of checking the secretive or unaccountable operations of state power, and hence, of dampening the desires of would-be dictators – making it difficult or impossible for them to govern without open debate and organized opposition to state policies. The oppositional role of parliament is based on the (originally medieval) premise that there is no incompatibility between effective government and effective opposition. It is also based on the premise that opposition to state power can be effective only when the special privileges traditionally monopolized by those who rule – immunity from prosecution, rights to freely criticize and guaranteed pay and political status – are shared with their opponents.

Parliament's (potential) oppositional function is by no means obsolete, as Schmitt supposed. 'Constant experience shows us that every person invested with power is apt to abuse it, and to carry that power as far as it will go.'[73] This remark by Montesquieu remains as pertinent today as ever. Probably more so, considering the alarming growth during the twentieth century in the range and number of sophisticated and macabre weapons available to the power-hungry. Montesquieu's maxim certainly applies as strongly to democratic socialists as to their opponents. Socialists seek to radically alter the existing distribution of power

---

proposes – multiplying the centres of democratic authority within and outside the state – begs questions about their interrelationship, their likely conflicts, and therefore about the appropriate mechanisms of conflict resolution and suppression. The same difficulty surfaces in early twentieth-century pluralist and Guild Socialist theories, whose advocates normally assumed, naively, that peaceful equilibrium – and not a free for all – would result from the de-emphasis of parliamentary struggles and, ultimately, from the abolition of the state as we know it.

within and between the state and civil society. They are therefore certainly to be confronted with various acts of resistance and sabotage and, hence, with the temptation of overcoming such obstacles by accumulating ever more political power. The lust for power is polymorphously perverse. It knows no political affiliation. It can cripple and peacefully undermine its protagonists, in which case its subjects are lucky. But more often than not – the disastrous twentieth-century history of socialism in power reminds us – the lust for power easily blinds its protagonists. It often catapults them into ecstasy – and sometimes into the highest bloody rapture.

Actively functioning parliaments are a necessary condition of democratic regimes, precisely because of their capacity for provoking public debate, criticizing governments and resisting their monopoly and abuse of power. This point (emphasized by Rosa Luxemburg, Karl Kautsky and others against the Bolsheviks) is seriously neglected by the insurrectionary socialist tradition. Its condemnation of 'parliamentary cretinism' (Trotsky) has most often served as a ruse for exercising its (qualitatively worse) state variant. The same point is neglected in Lucio Colletti's well-known distinction, directed against 'the Stalinist mentality', between parliament (which could be eliminated by a future socialist state) and political and civil liberties, which are inviolable, and thus a necessary feature of socialism. 'Every socialist', says Colletti, 'must be reminded constantly that public liberties – the suffrage, freedom of expression, the right to strike – are not identical with parliament.'[74] This is undoubtedly true. The liberties of a democratic civil society encompass activities deeper and wider than parliament and its associated political freedoms. And yet Colletti's hint that civil and political liberties could be preserved and strengthened *without* parliament forgets their inner connection: the liberties of an active, self-organizing civil society cannot be defended without a central parliamentary assembly, which enables the particular interests of civil society to argue their case and to resolve their differences, openly, non-violently and without state repression.

There has never been a political regime which simultaneously nurtured democratic civil liberties and abolished parliament. Nor has there ever existed a political regime which simultaneously maintained a democratic parliament and abolished civil liberties. And, so far, there has never existed a political regime in which a post-capitalist civil society was twinned with deep political freedoms and an active and vigilant parliament. To build exactly that kind of regime might be said to be one of the historic challenges facing the contemporary democratic tradition.

Notes

1. Among the best known of this literature from the first quarter of the century is: M. Ostrogorski, *Democracy and the Organisation of Political Parties*, London 1902; Sidney Low, *The Governance of England*, London 1904, especially chapters 4-5; James Bryce, *Modern Democracies*, London 1921; Harold J. Laski, *The Foundations of Sovereignty and Other Essays*, London 1921.

2. This essay deals only with Schmitt's general claims concerning the twentieth-century crisis of parliament. For reasons of space and contemporary relevance, it does not trace the ways in which Schmitt's dismissal of parliament is driven by the specifically German events of his time: the collapse of the Wilhelmine order; war and military defeat; the panicked reaction to the Bolshevik Revolution; the worker–soldier councils; the Versailles Treaty; and the permanent instability of Weimar. Nor does this essay deal with questions surrounding his writings' contribution to the destabilization of the Weimar Republic; or the extent of his collaboration with the Nazis; or his ingenious – and insidious – capacity to act as an intellectual chameleon, who literally adjusted his writings to fit in with changing social and political circumstances. These issues are discussed in Alfons Söllner, 'Jenseits von Carl Schmitt', *Geschichte und Gesellschaft*, 12, 1986, pp. 502-29; 'Carl Schmitt in Gespräch mit Dieter Groh und Klaus Figge', in Piet Tommissen, ed., *Over en in Zake Carl Schmitt*, Brussels 1975; Hans Barion et al., *Epirrhosis: Festgabe für Carl Schmitt*, 2 vols, Berlin 1968; Joseph W. Bendersky, *Carl Schmitt: Theorist for the Reich*, Princeton 1983; George Schwab, *The Challenge of the Exception. An Introduction to the Political Ideas of Carl Schmitt between 1921 and 1936*, Berlin 1970; Jürgen Habermas, 'Sovereignty and the Führerdemokratie', *Times Literary Supplement*, 26 September 1986, pp. 1053-4.

3. See my 'Despotism and Democracy: The Late Eighteenth Century Origins of the Distinction Between Civil Society and the State', in *Civil Society and the State*, London and New York 1988, and the classic interpretation of C.B. Macpherson, *The Political Theory of Possessive Individualism*, Oxford 1962.

4. Carl Schmitt, *Der Begriff des Politischen*, München 1932, p. 58; cf. his *Die geistesgeschichtliche Lage des heutigen Parlamentarismus*, Berlin 1926, pp. 51-2; and Schmitt's interpretation of the definition (given by the Spanish conservative, Donoso Cortés) of the bourgeoisie as *una clasa discutidora* (a 'discussing class') in *Political Theology, Four Chapters on the Concept of Sovereignty*, trans. George Schwab, Cambridge, Mass. 1985, pp. 59 ff.

5. *Die geistesgeschichtliche Lage*, pp. 50-52.

6. *Political Theology*, p. 63.

7. *Die geistesgeschichtliche Lage*, p. 9.

8. Ibid, p. 12.

9. Ibid, pp. 43-4.

10. Ibid, pp. 63-77.

11. Ibid, pp. 6-7. See, for example, Max Weber, 'Parlament und Regierung im neugeordneten Deutschland', in Johannes Winckelmann, ed., *Max Weber. Gesammelte Politische Schriften*, Tübingen 1980, pp. 353ff.

12. *Die geistesgeschichtliche Lage*, p. 7; cf. ibid, p. 62.

13. Ibid, p. 30.

14. *Der Hüter der Verfassung*, Tübingen 1931, pp. 86-7.

15. *Die geistesgeschichtliche Lage*, p. 8.

16. *Der Hüter der Verfassung*, p. 88.

17. Aristotle, *Politicia*, in *The Basic Works of Artistotle*, ed. Richard McKeon, New York 1968, (1280a): 'In democracies ... justice is considered to mean equality ... It does mean equality – but equality for those who are equal, and not for all.'

18. *Die geistesgeschichtliche Lage*, pp. 22, 37, 41.

19. Ibid, p. 14. Schmitt explains this point with the example of the British Empire's exclusion of three-quarters of its subjects from citizenship: 'Does the British Empire rest on universal and equal voting rights for all its inhabitants? It could not survive for a week on this basis; with their monstrous majority, the coloureds would outvote the whites. In spite of that, the British Empire is a democracy' (pp. 15-16). This passage also reveals something of Schmitt's characteristic yearning for an ethnically pure and sovereign state based on the principle of *Führerdemokratie*; see Jürgen Habermas, 'Sovereignty and the *Führerdemokratie*'.

20. Or, as Schmitt would add, as it is expressed by the assumed bearers of the general will. He argues that since the democratic principle of unanimity cannot become palpable reality in large-scale polities, democracy tends to produce Jacobinist programmes of 'people's education', the aim of which is to rectify the citizenry, so that they can recognize their own authentic will in that of their leaders (*Die geistesgeschichtliche Lage*, pp. 36-7). This inner connection between democracy and Jacobinism explains Schmitt's peculiar (crypto-fascist) description of Bolshevism, fascism and other forms of dictatorship as democratic (ibid, pp. 22, 37, 41).

21. Compare Jean-Jacques Rousseau, *Du contrat social*, Book III, ch. xv, in Roger D. Masters, ed., *On the Social Contract*, New York 1978, p. 102: 'Sovereignty cannot be represented for the same reason it cannot be alienated. It consists essentially in the general will, and the will cannot be represented. Either it is itself or it is something else; there is no middle ground. The deputies of the people, therefore, are not nor can they be its representatives; they are merely its agents. They cannot conclude anything definitively. Any law that the people in person has not ratified is null; it is not a law.'

22. See *Der Begriff des Politischen*, pp. 11-13; and *Der Hüter der Verfassung*, pp. 78-9. According to Schmitt, the emergence of the total state is also hastened by the growing political energy of nationalism. Nationalism emphasizes the awareness of belonging to a *political* community with a common fate or identity which differs from other, potentially hostile nations. Schmitt estimated that it would prove to be of greater political importance in the twentieth century than class conflict; see *Die geistesgeschichtliche Lage*, p. 88. Viewed retrospectively from the late twentieth century, Schmitt's anticipation of the total state underestimated two antithetical trends: the rise of the totalitarian empire/state (of the kind analysed in essays 4 and 6) and, elsewhere, the decline of the sovereign nation state, due to a combination of economic, military and political forces operating both from above and below the state (see David Beetham's suggestive essay, 'The Future of the Nation-State', in Stuart Hall et. al., eds, *The Idea of the Modern State*, Milton Keynes, 1984, pp. 208-22).

23. This argument is elaborated in essays 1 and 4; the introduction to John Keane, ed., *The Rediscovery of Civil Society*; and *Public Life and Late Capitalism*, Cambridge and New York 1984, essays 1 and 7.

24. This trend was observed by one of Schmitt's contemporaries, James Bryce (*Modern Democracies*, New York and London 1921), according to whom representative assemblies are losing some of their influence to organized extra-parliamentary interests, which serve increasingly as forms of public discussion and decisionmaking in competition with parliament. Schmitt also noted this trend, but with differ-

ent motives. His concern about 'the onslaught against the political' surfaces in *Political Theology*, p. 65 and in *Die geistesgeschichtliche Lage*, p. 62, where he makes the sardonic observation that 'what representatives of the large capitalist interest groups agree to in the smallest committees is perhaps more important for the daily lives and fate of millions of people than any political decision'. The same theme surfaces strongly in *Römischer Katholizismus und Politische Form*, Hellerau 1925, p. 24, where both liberalism and socialism are indicted for reducing life to a 'process of production and consumption', whereby politics becomes a mere mechanism for safeguarding economic interests.

25. *Die geistesgeschichtliche Lage*, p. 30.

26. See Otto von Gierke, *Natural Law and the Theory of Society. 1500 to 1800*, translated Ernest Barker, Cambridge 1958; J.N. Figgis, *Churches in the Modern State*, London 1914; and Harold J. Laski, *The Foundations of Sovereignty and Other Essays*, London 1921.

27. Schmitt quotes with approval from Wilhelm Dilthey's *Gesammelte Schriften*, third edn, Berlin 1923, II, p. 31: 'Humanity according to Machiavelli is not by nature evil. Some passages seem to indicate this ... But what Machiavelli wants to express overall is that human beings, if not checked, have an irresistible inclination to slide from passion to evil: animality, drives, passions – and above all love and fear – are the kernels of human nature. Machiavelli is inexhaustible in his psychological observations of the play of passions ... From this principle feature of human nature he derives the fundamental law of all political life' (quoted in *Der Begriff des Politischen*, p. 47).

28. *Political Theology*, p. 5; cf. Jean Bodin, *De la république*, Book I, ch. 8: 'All the characteristics of sovereignty are contained in this, to have power to give laws to each and everyone of his subjects, and to receive none from them.'

29. *Der Begriff des Politischen*, p. 34.

30. Ibid, pp. 26-7, 35-6; cf. George Schwab, *The Challenge of the Exception*, pp. 146-8.

31. 'Staatsethik und pluralistischer Staat', in *Positionen und Begriffe im Kampf mit Weimar-Genf-Versaillen, 1929-1939*, Hamburg 1940, p. 141; cf. *Der Begriff des Politischen*, p. 31.

32. In the context of the ailing Weimar Republic, when the issue of the power of constitutional review became crucial, Schmitt argued this conclusion in support of the *Reichspräsident* as the most appropriate interpreter and defender of the constitution. See *Der Hüter der Verfassung* and Joseph Bendersky, *Carl Schmitt: Theorist for the Reich*, pp. 112 ff.

33. *Der Begriff des Politischen*, p. 40.

34. Montesquieu, *De l'esprit des lois*, Paris 1979, vol. 1, Book III, pp. 143-53.

35. *Die geistesgeschichtliche Lage*, p. 30; cf. ibid, p. 33: 'We are concerned here with the ultimate intellectual foundations of parliamentarism itself, not with expanding the power of parliament.' Schmitt rarely discusses the supporting assumptions of this approach. One example is to be found in his conversation with Joachim Schickel, *Guerillos, Partisanen, Theorie und Praxis*, München 1970, p. 11: 'I rely on a method that is unique to me: Let phenomena come to me, wait a while, and then, as it were, think from the matter itself, not from ready-made criteria.' According to Reinhart Koselleck (in a conversation in Bielefeld, West Germany, June 1987), Schmitt always considered himself a 'concrete' political and legal thinker.

36. See Max Weber, *The Methodology of the Social Sciences*, edited Edward A. Shils and Henry A. Finch, New York 1949, pp. 110, 173, 150, and my *Public Life and Late Capitalism*, Cambridge and New York 1984, pp. 30-69. Schmitt's one-sided account of parliamentary principles – his overemphasis of the 'literary

appearances of things' – is pointed out in a different way by Richard Thoma, 'Zur Ideologie des Parlamentarismus und der Diktatur', *Archiv für Sozialwissenschaft und Sozialpolitik*, 53, 1925, pp. 215-17.

37. See the classic essay by Otto Hintze, 'Weltgeschichtliche Bedingungen der Repräsentativverfassung (1931)', *Staat und Verfassung*, Göttingen 1970, pp. 140-85.

38. See Antonio Marongiu, *Medieval Parliaments. A Comparative Study*, trans. S.J. Woolf, London 1968, part 1; W. Ullmann, *Principles of Government and Politics in the Middle Ages*, Harmondsworth 1961.

39. This tradition is discussed in F.L. Carsten, *Princes and Parliaments in Germany*, Oxford 1959, p. 434; 'The German Estates in the Eighteenth Century', in *Recueils Société Jean Bodin*, vol. 25, 1965, pp. 227-38; and *Essays in German History*, London 1985; cf. the general remarks on the statism of nineteenth- and twentieth-century German historiography in Hans-Ulrich Wehler, 'Historiography in Germany Today', in Jürgen Habermas, ed. *Observations on 'The Spiritual Situation of the Age': Contemporary German Perspectives*, Cambridge, Mass., and London 1984, p. 222.

40. See Kurt von Raumer, 'Absoluter Staat, korporative Libertät, persönliche Freiheit', *Historische Zeitschrift*, vol. 183, 1957, pp. 55-96.

41. A classic and influential example is J.E. Neale, *The Elizabethan House of Commons*, London 1949; another is A.F. Pollard, *The Evolution of Parliament (1920)*, London 1964, p. 3: 'Parliamentary institutions have ... been incomparably the greatest gift of the English people to the civilization of the world.'

42. M. Ostrogorski, *Democracy and the Organization of Political Parties*, p. 15; cf. the remarks on the mismatch between Burke's conception of the freely judging member of parliament and the decadence of parliament during the first four decades of George III's reign in Harold J. Laski, *The Foundations of Sovereignty and Other Essays*, p. 36.

43. See G.R. Elton, *The Parliament of England 1559-1581*, Cambridge 1986.

44. Hermann Heller, 'Politische Demokratie und soziale Homogenität (1928)', in H. Heller, *Gesammelte Schriften*, edited Christoph Müller, Laden 1971, vol. 2, p. 427.

45. An early contribution to the 'golden age of parliament' thesis is evident in A. Lawrence Lowell, *The Government of England*, vol. 2, London 1924, pp. 76-8; a more recent version is defended by Philip Norton, *The Commons in Perspective*, Oxford 1981, pp. 14-15, 23.

46. John Mackintosh, 'Parliament Now and a Hundred Years Ago', in Richard L. Leonard and V. Herman, eds, *The Backbencher and Parliament: A Reader*, London and Basingstoke 1972, pp. 246-67.

47. According to D.G. Wright (*Democracy and Reform 1815-1885*, London 1970, p. 51), in 1841 more than half of the members of the British House of Commons were sons of peers, baronets, or near relatives of peers.

48. See Hugh Berrington, 'Partisanship and Dissidence in the Nineteenth-Century House of Commons', *Parliamentary Affairs*, vol. 21, 4, Autumn 1968, pp. 338-74.

49. Ibid, p. 360.

50. Cf. Walter Bagehot's 1867 description of the typical member of the British House of Commons as a lover of intellectual haze, moderation, practicality and other virtues appropriate to men of business, in *The English Constitution 1867*, introduction by R.H.S. Crossman, London 1963, pp. 159-60.

51. Bernard Crick, *The Reform of Parliament*, London 1964, p. 13.

52. Ibid, chapters 10, 11. On the French case discussed in this section, see Philip Williams, 'Parliament under the Fifth French Republic: Patterns of Execu-

tive Domination', in Gerhard Loewenberg, ed., *Modern Parliaments: Change or Decline?*, Chicago and New York 1971, pp. 97-109.

53. Norberto Bobbio, 'Democracy and Invisible Government', *Telos*, 52, Summer 1982, pp. 41-55.

54. Theodore Draper, 'Reagan's Junta', *The New York Review of Books*, 29 January 1987, pp. 5-14.

55. See Karl Dietrich Bracher, 'Gegenwart und Zukunft der Parlamentsdemokratie in Europa', in Kurt Kluxen, ed., *Parlamentarismus*, Köln and Berlin 1969, pp. 70-87, especially p. 85; and Antonio Cassese, ed., *Parliamentary Control Over Foreign Policy*, Alphen aan den Rijn 1980.

56. Thomas Erskine May, *Treatise on the Law, Privileges, Proceedings and Usages of Parliament*, edited E. Fellowes and T.G.B. Cocks, London 1957, 16th edn, p. 28.

57. Some of the following proposals are discussed at greater length in Bernard Crick, *The Reform of Parliament*, second edn, London 1968; and H. Rausch, 'Parlamentsreform in der Bundesrepublik Deutschland. Die Diskussion im Überblick', in Kurt Kluxen, ed., *Parlamentarismus*. On the peculiarities of the American Congress and its reform, see Philip Brenner, *The Limits and Possibilities of Congress*, New York 1983.

58. The argument that parliament is based on overly simple assumptions of territorial representation, and that it therefore takes too little account of the complex functional interests of civil society, was especially prominent in Europe during the first several decades of this century. It certainly deserves to be revived. See, for example, G.D.H. Cole, *Social Theory*, London 1920; Harold Laski, 'Parliament and Revolution', *The New Republic*, 19 May 1920, pp. 383-4; S. Webb and B. Webb, *A Constitution for the Socialist Commonwealth of Great Britain*, London 1920; and Karl Renner, 'Demokratie und Rätesystem', *Der Kampf*, 14, 1921, pp. 54-67.

59. David Judge, 'Considerations on Reform', in David Judge, ed., *The Politics of Parliamentary Reform*, London and Exeter 1983, pp. 181-200.

60. Schmitt's dismissal of the liberal constitutional failure to deal with the question of emergency situations is developed in *Political Theology*, chapters 1-2, cf. *Der Wert des Staates und die Bedeutung des Einzelnen*, Tübingen 1914, p. 83: 'No law can execute itself; only human beings can be designated as the defenders of laws.'

61. See *Die Diktatur. Von den Anfangen des modernen Souveranitätsgedankens bis zum proletarischen Klassenkampf*, München and Leipzig 1928. The failure to recognize this distinction and its consequences weakens the vague attempt of Andrew Arato and Jean Cohen to criticize Schmitt in 'Social Movements, Civil Society, and the Problem of Sovereignty', *Praxis International*, vol. 4, 3, October 1984, pp. 266-83.

62. *Die Diktatur*, p. 137.

63. Ibid, p. 238.

64. Schmitt often referred to the provisions of article 48 of the Weimar constitution, which empowered the Reich president to declare a state of emergency and to enforce the constitution with the aid of the armed forces. (This article was invoked more than 250 times during the Weimar Republic.) In *Die Diktatur*, pp. 246-7, and in *Verfassungslehre*, pp. 358-9, Schmitt argued for the presidential power to dissolve an obstructionist Reichstag and call new elections. He repeated this argument, against the Prussian SPD government and in support of the Reich government of von Papen, in the fateful Supreme Court trial of October 1932, *Prussia vs. Reich*; see Joseph W. Bendersky, *Carl Schmitt*, chapter 8. In a state of emergency, according to Schmitt, a president has the authority to dissolve a state government and to institute a Reich commissar for the purpose of defending the state and its constitution. Schmitt's first act of collaboration with the Hitler government was consistent with this precept. In April 1933, Schmitt co-drafted legislation which the Nazis utilized to take over state governments, without elections, through the appointment of commissars responsible only to Hitler;

see *Carl Schmitt*, pp. 198-200.

65. On the anti-parliamentarian implications of Schmitt's enthusiastic support for the introduction of a presidential system (with Hindenburg's appointment of Chancellor Bruning), see Karl Dietrich Bracher, *The German Dictatorship: The Origins, Structure and Effects of National Socialism*, New York 1970, pp. 169-72; Joseph W. Bendersky, *Carl Schmitt*, chapter 3; David Abraham, *The Collapse of the Weimar Republic. Political Economy and Crisis*, Princeton 1981, pp. 296-7. Compare also Hans Kelsen's charge that Schmitt's defence of extensive presidential powers in effect sought the revival of constitutional monarchy; *Wer soll der Hüter der Verfassung sein?*, Berlin 1931, pp. 8-10, 41-7, 53-6.

66. *Die Diktatur*, pp. 201-2.

67. Ibid, pp. 2-4, 25-7, 105.

68. Cf. George Schwab, *The Challenge of the Exception*, p. 50: 'What happens to the [commissarial] sovereign in normal times? From Schmitt's discussion it may be concluded that in normal times the sovereign is, so to speak, slumbering, and he is suddenly awakened at a crucial moment: namely, at the borderline between normalcy and the state of exception.' The commissarial dictator may well be likened to a slumbering giant, who has been awakened by the noise, smoke and fire of a political crisis. But this simile begs the fundamental questions: On the (realistic) assumption that the political giant will not voluntarily return to its bed after its public appearance, shouldn't it be prevented from the outset from leaving its bed? Or better: Shouldn't political animals be deprived from the outset of their aspirations to become political giants?

69. Schmitt's constitutional conservatism is evident in *Verfassungslehre*, where he states repeatedly that the (Weimar) constitution is essentially inviolable, that constitutional revision should not become constitutional abrogation, and that a two-thirds parliamentary majority did not have the authority to alter the constitution fundamentally into, say, a Soviet-type state or an absolute monarchy; see especially part 3. According to Bendersky (*Carl Schmitt*, p. 97), Schmitt's constitutionalism rests on the principle that only 'the people as a whole', the *pouvoir constituant*, can legitimately authorize basic constitutional changes. This overlooks the *paramount* importance of Schmitt's deep-seated fear of drastic constitutional changes (lest they destabilize the state, thereby making it prey to its enemies), and also gives the impression that Schmitt believed in popular sovereignty as an ultimate principle, which he most certainly did not.

70. *Die geistesgeschichtliche Lage*, p. 12. Underpinning this belief that the essential principles of parliament are exhausted, and irreversibly so, is Schmitt's unexplained assumption that the essential principles of different forms of state grow, mature and decline, as if the political and legal history of the human species followed an evolutionary course, which is however 'blind' and without a *telos* (conversation with Reinhart Koselleck, Bielefeld, West Germany, June 1987).

71. Walter Bagehot, *The English Constitution*, (1867) London 1963, chapter 4.

72. V.I. Lenin, 'The Proletarian Revolution and the Renegade Kautsky', *Collected Works*, London 1960, vol. 28, p. 369; cf. Max Adler, *Die Staatsauffassung des Marxismus. Ein Beitrag zur Unterscheidung von soziologischer und juristischer Methode*, Wien 1925, p. 125: '[Parliament] is a part of the class struggle. It is always the exercise of power, whereby one class, with its majority, seeks to force its laws onto the resisting class.' More recently, see Perry Anderson's attack on parliamentary representation as the 'principal ideological lynchpin of Western capitalism', and as a mechanism whose 'very existence deprives the working class of the idea of socialism as *a different type of State* ...', in 'The Antinomies of Antonio Gramsci', *New Left Review*, 100, November 1976—January 1977, p. 28. Aside from their neglect of the various arguments developed in this essay, these types of criticisms of 'bour-

geois parliaments' ignore the historical fact that the (admittedly uneven, always fragile) growth of socialist politics in the late nineteenth and early twentieth centuries was actually made possible by the existence of parliamentary forms. Other aspects of the problematic relationship between the Marxist tradition and parliamentary democracy are well analysed by Christopher Pierson, *Marxist Theory and Democratic Politics*, Cambridge 1986.

73. Montesquieu, *De l'esprit des lois*, vol. 1, Book XI, chapter 4, p. 293.

74. Lucio Colletti, *Politique et philosophie*, Paris 1975, pp. 48-9.

6

In the Heart of Europe

To be corrupted by totalitarianism one does not have to live
in a totalitarian country.

George Orwell

I've just returned from a visit to central Europe. Not for the first
time there, I spent a long evening drinking wine, sipping tea and
talking politics with friends around a bathroom table in their
basement.

Political discussion around a bathroom table? In a basement?
People who are familiar with life in the 'other half' of Europe will
know that such events are neither absurd nor exceptional. By any
standards, central Europe is full of astonishing surprises for sensitive western visitors. They find a world in which centralized state
planning is a euphemism for shortages, inefficiencies and
bureaucratic bedlam. They learn, to their surprise, that devout
Catholics despise the word socialism, live the spirit of the French
Revolution and, in opposition to state tyranny, favour social
ownership and control of property. They discover that a window-
cleaner is a university graduate or a playwright, a factory worker
a minister of religion.

Sensitive western visitors also learn that in this topsy-turvy
world the state authorities tightly monitor and restrict all genuine
public activity – forcing it underground into the relative safety
and privacy of unbugged pubs, subways, kitchens and basement
bathrooms. Whenever I leave these underground refuges and

return to the safety of my bathroom and chatty local pub, I always feel as though I've surfaced into a political vacuum. And, strange though it may seem, this numbness is nearly always reinforced by the reaction I get from my socialist friends when telling them about my latest trip. I've noted how their response, usually polite and interested at first, soon trails off into glazed eyes, furrowed brows, suppressed yawns, strained silence and, at last, a return to normal everyday conversation – to the weather, problems at home and work, children and football, local political gossip and a joke or two at the expense of the Tories.

I've never properly understood this reticence. Quite by chance, my last visit forced me – for the first time in fact – to think deeply about its causes. Perched that evening around the small bathroom table, my two Czech friends, Eva and Petr, asked me casually about the level of interest in central Europe among British socialists. If I remember correctly, the long conversation prompted by this one question ran along the following lines.

I began cautiously, relating to them the well-known insularity of the British, their general lack of enthusiasm for Europe. 'Britain is one of those European countries – Russia is another – whose citizens and governments often speak of Europe as a foreign territory. For large numbers of Britons, Europe is a faraway place. It is a part of the earth which is nice to visit occasionally to see friends, shop, drink cheap booze or simply to warm up and turn brown – a place in which to holiday, but not to make serious politics. In contrast, say, to the citizens of the Federal Republic of Germany, who accept that they are within Europe with relative ease, the British become tongue-tied and embarrassed when the subject of Europe is raised.'

'Does this disinterest in Europe extend into the ranks of the socialist tradition in your country?' asked Eva.

'It certainly does. It's a constant source of frustration for any British socialist convinced of the political importance of Europe. If anything, reticence towards Europe as a whole is strongest within the socialist tradition. For instance, significant numbers of Labour Party activists and members of parliament are still opposed to our membership of the European Economic Community and, by extension, they are deeply suspicious of everything European.'

I went on to suggest that this indifference to Europe sometimes has negative consequences. I mentioned the case of British socialists' virtual disinterest in the recent crop of avowedly socialist governments in Portugal, Spain, France, Norway and

Greece. But I thought it worth emphasizing that this patriotism isn't entirely bad. 'A healthy measure of patriotism can be productive. And it isn't incompatible with internationalism. A deep sensitivity to the historical traditions of Britain is indispensable for the success of socialist politics. George Orwell pointed that out forcefully in *The Lion and the Unicorn*. It urged the uselessness of any version of socialism that didn't take account of English history and character. Orwell's point remains relevant – especially given attempts by successive Thatcher governments to resurrect from the dead certain undemocratic traditions, notably those to do with the Nation and the so-called enterprise culture. These days in Britain,' I said, 'the living are engaged in a political battle for the souls of the dead ...'

My friends seemed lukewarm about pursuing this point to do with patriotism and internationalism. They were much more concerned to explore the reasons for the western socialist reticence about their half of Europe. 'Orwell's observations about the importance of patriotism are of great concern to us. With the exception of Yugoslavia, citizens in central Europe know that their states aren't sovereign. They constantly feel that they aren't at home within their own countries,' said Eva. 'But I'm quite puzzled about British socialists' unconcern about our "socialist" half of Europe. To what extent is some of this indifference specific to your country's socialist tradition?'

'I don't think I follow your question.'

My friends' eyes twinged with a second's impatience. Eva rephrased her question. 'Despite everything that's happened in our half of Europe during the post-war period, I still consider myself a socialist. But I feel undermined constantly by what I perceive to be western socialists' careless ignorance about central Europe. The symptoms of this ignorance are so obvious to me. But why is it so? I find it completely baffling – and demoralizing.'

Eva then switched to some questions which were hard to take. They prompted soul-searching questions. 'Let's take some examples. Why did the socialist parties in western Europe react so unenthusiastically to the Polish events of 1980-81? They almost breathed a sigh of relief when martial law was declared. Why will Mitterrand be remembered by posterity as the first head of state outside our bloc to meet officially with Jaruzelski? Why is it that west European socialist governments seem to get along best with our communist governments? Why do socialist politicians like Papandreou and Schmidt usually meet our government officials without ever asking at the same time to see us. That would be a simple gesture of solidarity which would provide us with the opportunity of publicly questioning our authorities' assumption that we are their property.

'Forgive me if I exaggerate – our circumstances often make us ignorant of the outside world – but why does the present leadership of the Labour Party appear to have no thought-out policy on the Soviet Union and its client states in central Europe? Why does the Labour Party turn a blind eye to the hundreds of thousands of democrats – I'm not exaggerating the numbers – who are systematically prevented from organizing publicly in our half of Europe? Why doesn't the Labour Party, given its prominence within the Socialist International, press for support for our democratic initiatives? . . . We're constantly lacking moral – never mind material – support for our initiatives. The Labour Party's silence is for us thoroughly demoralizing . . . especially when we consider the huge subsidies conservative organizations and parties channel into central Europe.'

I must confess to having felt a rush of embarrassment upon hearing these questions. Eva's questions – her bitter puzzlement – seemed to undermine much of what I stand for politically. For half my life I've considered myself a socialist of one sort or another. But here, squeezed between a bathtub and a table in a 'socialist' country, it all seemed ridiculously under siege.

Pursing my lips, I began to mumble. I remained unsure of how I could answer her questions. 'Well . . . There are British socialists . . . Bernard Crick, Eric Heffer and Mary Kaldor . . . er, are among the best known, who are deeply interested in central Europe and highly critical of your regimes . . .'

I began again. 'But they are definitely in the minority. For some time now, probably since the uncertain and confused reaction of the Left to the Hungarian events of 1956, the majority of British socialists have been repelled by the whole issue of "Eastern Europe", as they call it. They link it with the fake libertarianism of the conservative right. The right excels at publicly denouncing Soviet totalitarianism in the name of liberty and the rule of law. Look at Reagan's or Thatcher's melodramatic speeches on the Berlin Wall. At the same time, they actively support political repression in countries such as El Salvador, South Africa and Turkey. This hypocrisy of the right makes many socialists deeply suspicious of anyone who speaks openly against your "socialist" regimes. The handy rule-of-thumb for many socialists in foreign policy matters is that if Thatcher or Reagan are for something, then socialists must be against it.

When Thatcher says – as she did in a recent television interview
– that her party, the Conservatives, have shown that socialism is
not for Britain, and Britain is not for socialism, because socialists
would take us down the road to "Eastern Europe", many socialists get hot under the collar. Their reaction is automatic. They
aren't inclined to explain their stiff and angry response. So there
develops a strong impression among socialists that opposition to
your regimes is all a reactionary issue – something like a natural
ally of editorials in right-wing newspapers such as the *Evening
Standard* or *Sun*, or of columns in *The Times* or *Encounter* written
by Roger Scruton and other neo-conservative intellectuals.'

'With respect,' said Petr, 'this reaction strikes me as strange
and unjustified. And highly dangerous.'

'Why?'

'For a start, it's a very strange way of thinking. If British
conservatives contradict their own rhetoric of liberty and the rule
of law, that is their problem. That doesn't mean that political
conditions in central European countries such as Czechoslovakia
are less repressive than, say, in South Africa or Turkey. Even if
they were, surely the destruction of democratic liberties in one
country represents a blow against the democratic liberties of citizens everywhere?'

'The strange socialist reaction you describe is also unjustified
because most "dissidents" – as you call us – are not Thatcherites
or Reaganites dressed up in human rights clothing. What we are
for has nothing to do with the restoration of big business capitalism which, incidentally, could be done only through draconian
state measures in our part of the world, since almost nobody is
explicitly in favour of it. The principle we are struggling to defend
is that citizens are not the property of their states. I don't see how
this principle – and the corresponding civil and political liberties
we yearn for – can be labelled or dismissed as "reactionary" or
"right-wing" ...'

'Why do you say that the western socialist fear of being
labelled an anti-communist is politically dangerous?'

'It's always a basic and fatal political mistake to let governments of whatever kind decide one's position on anything. It is
plain foolishness. The widely respected Czech humorist, Jan
Werich, once observed that the struggle against stupidity is the
only human struggle that is always in vain, but can never be
relinquished. No democrats are exempt from the permanent
dangers of foolishness. Citizens should never be hostages to their
government's policy. In effect, this is what happens when western

socialists, fearing the anti-communist label, allow their anti-communist opponents to decide for them what to think.'

Eva nodded in agreement and poured more wine. 'I'm curious to know, are there other reasons why British socialists are so indifferent to our situation?'

Eva's question revived my own uncertainty and embarrassment. I continued to feel as though I was grasping at slim straws. 'Well, quite a number of socialists in Britain assume that the Soviet-type regimes of countries such as Poland, Czechoslovakia, East Germany and Hungary, have simply nothing to do with socialism. A few months ago I read *Socialism with a Human Face*, a book written by a prominent Labour politician, Michael Meacher, who insisted, quite typically, that people who identify socialism with "East European type bureaucratic centralism" are guilty of "lurid image-mongering, an identification sedulously fostered by the enemies of socialism".' I also recalled a recent television interview with Raymond Williams, a leading socialist writer. Pressed to speak about the threatening implications of the Soviet model of socialism for the western socialist tradition, Williams argued that the ideals of socialism are part of Britain's native traditions and, as such, unaffected by the disastrous outcomes of the Bolshevik Revolution and Stalinism.

'These responses typify the tradition of native British socialism. This tradition has a bewildering variety of origins. It stretches from Robert Owen's principles of co-operation, Methodist morality, and the militant political democracy of Chartism to the communism of William Morris, the playful aesthetics of Oscar Wilde, and revisionist Marxism. But those who currently identify with this old tradition more or less agree on what it means to be a socialist. The word socialism means, as it meant for the Owenites of the 1820s and 1830s, the collective regulation of human affairs on a co-operative basis. Freedom, happiness and the welfare of all are its goals. To be a socialist is to stress the fundamental importance of production and the need to redistribute social wealth. To be a socialist is to recognize the need to strengthen "socializing" influences in the lifelong education of citizens through co-operative, as against competitive and selfish activities. From this ethical standpoint, many British socialists see no reason whatsoever to be threatened by the avowedly socialist regimes of central Europe. These regimes are dismissed, with a sigh and a shrug of the shoulders, as anti-socialist, as "degenerate workers' states", as throwbacks or hangovers from "Asiatic" times, or as state capitalist regimes. And Neil

Kinnock, leader of the Labour Party, likes to describe your regimes as "downright objectionable".'

My friends looked quite bewildered, almost as if I had switched to speaking another language in mid-sentence. Eva remarked, with the intense and polite seriousness for which central Europeans are well-known, that this ostrich-like posture represents a profound retreat from the internationalist spirit of nineteenth-century European socialism, and at a time when the very idea of socialism is suffering a deep crisis of legitimacy. 'One of the surest ways of guaranteeing that the socialist idea comes to grief is to ignore the absurdity and barbarity committed in its name. I'd put it like this: In our part of the world, the arrows of socialism, like those of Nimrod, have been hurled at the sky, and have already fallen back to earth stained with infamy and blood.'

'So, is your objection to – what shall we call it? – ostrich socialism that it turns a blind eye to the possible moral and political extinction of the socialist idea in your half of Europe?'

'Well, that's only the most obvious objection, but it's important and worth elaborating. Everyone knows in our countries that socialism is a keyword of the Party-dominated state. This state seeks to entomb us, its subjects, within a pyramid of fictitious ideological clichés designed to silence everybody and to ensure their conformity to the state. Every day our state television, radio, and newspapers tell us a hundred times that our socialist system is young, improving and dynamic. It emphasizes that our system is testing in its stride ways of efficiently organizing and controlling social development. I could go on ...'

'What effect does this have on the population?'

'This hyperbole makes us claustrophobic. It gives us the feeling that we are living in one large prison, from which there's no escape. And it generates a widespread cynicism towards "socialism" – indeed, to all "isms". It also greatly strengthens the hand of nationalists, conservatives and market liberals within the ranks of our democratic opposition. Frankly, the political triumph of socialism in our part of the world is a Pyrrhic victory. Our socialist systems are proving to be the gravedigger of the idea of socialism.

'Petr and I personally continue to think of ourselves as socialists. But this label is of absolutely no interest to the vast majority of the population. None! For them, the word socialism is irrelevant, boring or frightening. A few days ago, a woman workmate told me a popular joke which illustrates this development. "What is socialism? Socialism is the dialectical synthesis of the various stages in the history of humankind. From pre-history it takes the method. From antiquity, slavery. From feudalism, serfdom. From capitalism, exploitation. And from socialism, the name."'

Muffled laughs sprang from all sides of the table. Petr poured more wine. I couldn't help feeling a deep unease about the subversive implications of my own laughter, as if I was mocking the flimsy silence of my socialist friends at home.

Earnest faces returned quickly to the table. Eva continued. 'The problem with ostrich socialism as you describe it, is not only that it turns a blind eye to the possible elimination of the socialist tradition in our half of Europe. There's a more worrying point. Socialists who think that the "original" ideals of socialism and our systems of "real socialism" are two absolutely different things are quite mistaken. I've come to the disturbing conclusion that the original socialist vision contained some seeds of our Soviet-imposed systems ...'

'You mean to say that there's something fundamentally wrong with the original nineteenth-century vision of socialism?'

'I'm afraid so. I therefore think that it needs serious revision.' Eva chose her words carefully. 'From the time of its emergence as a movement in Europe in the first quarter of the nineteenth century, the word socialism has meant: living together sociably and harmoniously, within a system which is defined by the collective ownership of property, and which attempts to collectively plan and regulate the social environment within which free and equal human beings interact. Much of this broad definition I still go along with – especially its democratic vision of liberty, equality and solidarity among human beings. The trouble is that this vision also contained, from the outset, deeply anti-democratic ideas and implications. These contradict its emphasis on liberty, equality and solidarity. My hunch is that ostrich socialists are blind to these anti-democratic implications. Hence, they are insensitive to the complicity between the original socialist idea and our "real socialist" regimes.'

We soon fell to discussing the most obvious example: the traditional socialist obsession with property. Socialism has always embodied the desire for liberty, justice and – against the 'anarchy' of capitalist production – rationality. From this point of view, we agreed, private property in the means of production has been held directly responsible for the unfreedom, injustice and irrationality of the capitalist system. It has also been viewed as the source of the most disparate evils – from alcoholism and suicide to prostitution and war.

Petr took the discussion further. 'The orthodox socialist emphasis on private property was, and remains, a liberating insight ...'

I interrupted. 'Are you saying that the old issue of capitalism versus socialism is not entirely dead?'

'In a way. I disagree with a number of our fellow members of the democratic opposition – Václav Havel in Czechoslovakia is among them – who consider that the question of capitalism or socialism is an outdated nineteenth-century problematic. It isn't. In contrast to the European liberal and conservative traditions, socialists have argued correctly that liberty and justice cannot be maximized in any society unless its property system ceases to be *exclusively* in the hands of private capitalist firms. I think it's imperative to hold on to this principle. In our countries, there are signs of a growing fascination with capitalism. People talk about it as if it were a fairy-tale from a distant land.' Petr paused, sipping his wine. 'But ... the liberating socialist emphasis on the property question is a sharp two-edged sword.'

'Why?'

'Because whenever the property question is made *central* to the definition of socialism, the latter becomes apologetic – neglecting other, often more important, sources of unfreedom and injustice. We know from bitter experience in central Europe that central-ized state power – whose ultimate resource is its control over the physical means of violence – can become the dominant fact of life. We've also learned the hard way that when that happens it has disastrous social and political consequences. So, the property question remains important for us, but it has ceased to be central. In central Europe – in Hungary and Yugoslavia, no less than in the GDR, Poland and Czechoslovakia – we live under the shadow of totalitarian states. Even though some of these states – Czechoslovakia and Romania for instance – are more repressive than others, they all force their populations to suffer one thing in common – to live a life without basic civil liberties.'

I suddenly realized the fundamental point of this remark about the need for socialists to consider sources of exploitation in addition to property. It dawned on me that many western social-ists' preoccupation with questions of property, class power and class conflict reinforces their reticence about the subject of 'East-ern Europe'. Its socialist regimes are seen to be somehow 'ahead' of capitalist countries such as Britain. Despite their 'faults', these regimes are assumed to have taken a bold, twenty-league stride beyond the capitalist world by abolishing private ownership of the basic means of production. Thereby, it is thought that they have eliminated or downgraded class exploitation, competition and possessive individualism – three evils of capitalism.

Eva and Petr looked puzzled, then incredulous when I tried to explain and illustrate this point. I began by mentioning how often one encounters sickly sentimentalism in western socialist discussions about the Soviet model of socialism. 'Only a tiny minority of British socialists are explicitly pro-Soviet. And old-fashioned fellow-travelling has largely disappeared. It has been replaced by an embarrassed silence – of the type found in the pages of magazines such as *Marxism Today* – about the repressiveness of Soviet-type regimes. Nonetheless, the assumption that Left should speak to Left in comradeship (as Aneurin Bevin put it in the 1940s), and that "Russia is on the side of the workers" – an intuition that developed in Britain between the October Revolution and the Stalin–Hitler pact – hasn't been exhausted. It lives on. It appears in unexpected places throughout the length and breadth of the Labour movement. Sometimes it binds together individuals and groups who otherwise don't see eye to eye.'

I recalled a fringe meeting which I had attended at the Labour Party Conference in 1985. 'At this meeting, the exiled Russian socialist Piotr Egides, a former editor of the opposition journal *Poiski*, spoke about a question he had put to Michael Foot at the time he led the Labour Party: "Why do British socialists invite representatives from the USSR to the Labour Party Conference?" Foot replied: "Because the USSR, in spite of its errors and everything else, is socialist." Egides reported that Tony Benn had given him exactly the same answer.'

My friends frowned, but I persisted. Now I'd started I could hardly stop. 'This pro-Soviet attitude often appears in weird forms. For example, I sometimes hear friends say that socialists should not adopt an oppositional stance against your regimes. They say that poking our noses into the affairs of your legally constituted "socialist" governments only adds to global tensions. I know of more than one local Labour Party branch which voted to discontinue material support for Solidarity after the declaration of martial law in Poland . . .'

'A new socialist law!' quipped Petr sarcastically. 'Citizens of different countries have no rights to speak to each other. Only governments can speak for citizens! Should we also apply that law to South Africa? Or Turkey?'

'Pro-Sovietism among British socialists is reinforced by knee-jerk reactions to the evils of American imperialism – most socialists are deeply concerned about threats to the independence of Nicaragua, whereas the topic of war in Poland or Afghanistan leaves them fairly cold. In Afghanistan, the Russians have murdered a million civilians, and forced five million Afghan people into exile. They've systematically destroyed crops, chemically poisoned fertile river valleys and bombed urban areas to rubble. A whole generation of Afghan painters, poets, playwrights and writers has "disappeared" ... with little more than a whimper from the British left. This shows how many socialists' thinking follows the path of lesser evilism: the supposed lesser force for evil, the Soviet Union, is quietly defended as if it were a force for good. Quiet pro-Sovietism of this kind is to be found not only among many prominent leaders of the Labour movement. It is also widespread among rank-and-file socialists. Many British socialists simply don't ponder in any depth the roots of their trust in the Soviet model. Scratch these socialists, and you'll quickly find them expressing a naive outsider's yearning for the good things about the "socialist achievements" of the Soviet bloc: full employment, streets free of consumer advertisements, spotless and efficient undergrounds, the absence of graffiti and vandalism, a peaceful and well cared for population. And to this list of "socialist achievements" women friends of mine sometimes add: freedom from sexist advertising and street corner pornography, and decent childcare facilities linked with guaranteed job rights and opportunities for women.'

My friends' patience and civility snapped. 'Efficient and orderly socialism! Equality for women! These socialists should come and live here!' said Eva. 'They'd soon see just how distorted their picture is. They'd be disillusioned quickly by the heavy, absurd and depressing atmosphere. And by the male-domination as well. Every day the Party reminds us that our socialist system has emancipated women. I agree completely with that – except that so far we've not been allowed emancipation from husbands, childbearing, queueing, cooking, cleaning and low-paying "women's jobs", which are practically compulsory, since without them our families couldn't make ends meet.'

I assured my friends that I wasn't exaggerating. I explained that there were more sophisticated versions of this trust in the 'post-capitalist achievements' of the Soviet model, especially among writers and political activists influenced by Trotskyism. 'Socialists influenced by this tradition give priority to the property question. This allows them to say that, despite everything else, your "Eastern European" regimes have at least abolished the tyranny of private property.'

Some examples sprang to mind. 'In a recent essay on the future of the Labour Party, Mike Rustin, one of our most prominent and respected socialist writers, observed that the "cadre regimes" of Eastern Europe secure and defend the social ownership of the means of production, and therefore to some degree represent and protect working-class interests against those of other classes. His view isn't exceptional. It's more commonly associated with the thinly veiled Trotskyism of a significant wing of the editorial committees of such journals as *New Left Review* and *Labour Focus on Eastern Europe*. It's also an article of faith among hard-line Militant activists on the fringes of the Labour Party.

'Among contemporary Trotskyists, central European regimes are viewed as halfway houses between capitalism and socialism. They argue that the exploitation generated by market-based commodity production and exchange has been liquidated in favour of a system of centralized state planning. In this sense, central European regimes are viewed as a proto-socialist stage of history. Yet Trotskyists also say that your regimes are prevented from building on their anti-capitalist achievements – from making the final leap forward to socialism – by a number of international and domestic factors. Emphasis is usually given to factors such as American imperialist encirclement and, at home, to bureaucratic "distortions", which are said to reinforce the power of a ruling group of party-state apparatchiks, who live off the working class like parasites. Guided by this reasoning, British Trotskyists denounce the present *governments* of central Europe. What remains to be done, they say, is to organize the "working class" to *complete* the revolution against capitalist society. But they confidently deny that there's anything *inherently* unsocialist about your regimes. That's why they continue to believe that western capitalism is Enemy Number One, and why the traditional (Marxian) socialist goal of organizing the working class for a revolution against capitalism – through a tightly disciplined Party that always knows what's best for the working class, of course – is still fundamentally sound ...'

Suddenly, the doorbell rang upstairs. My friends stood up. Out of thin air, a sharp pang of anxiety whistled through me. Questions rushed through my head. What time is it? Could it be neighbours? At this late hour? Each second passed in awkward silence. I felt numbed. Then panicky.

Eva and Petr gestured me to remain silent and to close the

bathroom door.They slipped quietly upstairs with the wine bottle and glasses.

I latched the door, and tried to disguise our small table with a towel and a bucket. I managed somehow to place myself on the lavatory seat.

I felt self-conscious, and guilty – and afraid for my two friends. I tried in vain to make out the indistinct sounds from above. The seconds continued to pass in slow motion. I felt queasy with fear.

Silence. More muffled sounds. Then a burst of laughter, a round of light-hearted neighbourly goodbyes, the thud of the front door closing. My heart pounded, but I breathed more easily. This time, we were safe – and lucky.

Eva and Petr came back down a few minutes later, juggling a full pot of tea, brightly coloured cups and saucers. My heart still thumped. They neither smiled with relief nor explained the events of the past few minutes. For them, this had been an every-day event. They returned at once to the conversation.

'About Trotskyism ...' said Eva, pouring tea into our cups. 'We're quite familiar with the views you described, even though only a small handful of Trotskyists continue to be active within our opposition circles. I respect their courage and determination. But I can't accept their views. For me, they are based on double-think. In spite of their best intentions, they have an apologetic function. I agree with you that the basic message of Trotskyism is: The basic ideas of Marxian socialism remain essentially correct; organize and struggle for their implementation; work for the proletarian revolution in both halves of Europe ... If only things were so simple!'

'What's wrong with this view?' I asked.

'To believe in overthrowing the dictatorship of the Party by revolution is both unrealistic and dangerous,' said Eva. 'Not only that. The more the basic Trotskyist message is stated clearly, the more it's obviously based on a serious contradiction. In the same breath, the "working class" – a term I no longer use in its Marxian sense – is said to be powerless, even though our regimes, by virtue of having basically "socialist" relations of production, are said to be workers' states. How can this be?'

'British Trotskyists would say that the party-state bureaucracy, which they regard as the basic mechanism of your regimes, is both an achievement – a positive step *beyond* capitalist exploit-ation – as well as the basic source of inequality and unfreedom.'

'Exactly!' snapped Petr . 'That's the problem with the Trotsk-yist view! As you say, it supposes that the decisive historical

achievement of our regimes – the replacement of capitalism by a
bureaucratic state – is at the same time their basic source of
unfreedom and injustice. That's double-think! ...'

'But if you reject the Trotskyist view that you're living under
proto-socialist conditions, how would you describe your regimes?
What are they like?'

'In this part of the world,' said Eva, 'no one believes that we
are living in a "workers' state" travelling the highroad from
capitalism to socialism. Everybody knows that, in contrast to
your capitalist systems in Britain and elsewhere, it makes no
sense to speak of our workers as employees who earn a wage or
salary within an "economy" separate from the state. No such
independent economy exists – which is why, incidentally, it's
incorrect to speak about our workers as a class in the Marxian or
Trotskyist sense. A class analysis of our situation simply doesn't
work. It fails to describe what is different – and more disturbing –
about our lives.

'We are being suffocated by a new type of state with unprecedented power over the individual. I'm not altogether sure what to
call it, although most of our writers describe this state as totalitarian. If you want to understand what it means for our daily lives,
try to imagine living in a political system in which the governing
Party is at the same time the only employer. The Party exercises
total control over people's means of sustenance in the broadest
sense. Since it is the sole employer, the Party in effect subjects all
of us to permanent blackmail. Working is a *duty* of citizens – in
return for which the Party provides us with our means of sustenance. Whenever citizens resist this power of the employer state,
they are branded automatically as critics of "the leading role of
the Party". For this, they can be punished in any number of ways
by the Party. The punitive power of the Party, I emphasize, is *not*
secured primarily by the police and the army – as has been the
case in other dictatorships, such as Franco's or Pinochet's.'

'But dissenting citizens are still treated brutally or sentenced to
many years' imprisonment, aren't they?'

'That's true. Violent methods of this kind persist. But the
employer state has much, much subtler methods at its disposal.
The Party can expel dissenting citizens from the official trade
union. It can order a school principal not to accept their children
into a school. As the sole employer, the Party can order a doctor
to cancel their invalid pension. It can order the police to revoke
their driving licence, or a telephone exchange to confiscate their
telephone. Such orders aren't exceptional or rare. Quite the

contrary. They are the chief means by which the Party exerts a permanent and suffocating pressure on the whole population. This novel form of manipulation is the central historical invention of our "socialist" regimes. It's much more effective than using the police or army. And it means fewer corpses and political prisoners.'

'So one of the tragic ironies of life under socialism,' Petr added, 'is that in our systems not only workers' freedoms but *all* civil liberties are in danger of extinction. Our Party-dominated state treats all its citizens as potential dissidents. That's why citizens' attempts to defend civil liberties from below is an inherently dangerous undertaking – for which they are made to pay heavily by the state authorities ...'

'Quite a few British socialists would say that civil liberties are under threat in Britain, too. They'd point, for instance, to the treatment of Greenham Common women or black people, who suffer constant police harassment, threats of court action and imprisonment ...'

Eva reacted sharply. 'This is a fundamental misunderstanding of our situation. Forgive me for simplifying. But from what I know about your situation, all British workers and citizens still enjoy a basic minimum of civil liberties – like the right to publish their own literature. We don't enjoy such basic liberties. That's the decisive difference between our two halves of Europe!'

'And this is why,' Petr added, 'we reject the old saying – repeated to us sometimes by visitors from western Europe – that the only difference between capitalism and socialism is that in the first man exploits man, whereas in the second it is just the opposite. I'm afraid that's false. Things are qualitatively *worse* in our half of Europe.'

'Does this mean that you also reject the view – associated with the writings of Edward Thompson, for example – that the Cold War inspires a political convergence between the two halves of Europe?'

'I'd take issue strongly with Thompson's view,' said Eva. 'I respect his courageous attempts to publicize the problem of a divided Europe squeezed between the superpowers. And the old-fashioned Whiggish love of liberty he sometimes displays appeals to me very much. But I simply can't accept that the Cold War is mainly responsible for the death of civil liberties in both halves of Europe.'

'In the most recent versions of his argument,' I continued, 'Thompson says that permanent military competition between

the two superpowers – the Cold War – infects the daily
operations of "peacetime states" such as Britain with an "emergency" mentality. He claims that a "permanent enemy hypothesis" is the animating spirit of contemporary state power. He says
that this hypothesis supplies authority to states in both halves of
Europe, just as the hypothesis of Satan supplied authority for the
medieval church. And he insists that this perverse dynamic works
with *equal* virulence on both sides of the Cold War divide. Just as
wrestlers with quite different backgrounds come to develop the
same muscles and facial expressions, so our formerly quite different systems come to resemble each other. As a consequence, he
argues, citizens in both halves of Europe become hostages to their
respective security states – which are unaccountable, and therefore punish any challenge to their authority with the stiffest
penalties ...'

'This is much too simple,' Eva replied. 'Actually, it's misleading. By implicitly treating the Russian and American superpowers
equally, it fails to understand the specific nature of totalitarian
systems. Everybody who lives in our half of Europe knows that
the Cold War is not the only, or main source of our subjugation.
To begin with, I'd remind you that Stalinist totalitarianism,
under whose shadow we still live, *predated* the Cold War. Indeed,
it was one of its major causes. Also, it shouldn't be forgotten that
totalitarianism was *imposed* on the peoples of central Europe forty
years ago by the armed forces of the Soviet Union, with the
approval of the western powers, in particular the United States
and Great Britain. The fate of millions in central Europe was
decided at Yalta by three old men: a bloodthirsty despot, a termi-
nally ill and poorly informed statesman, and a *Realpolitiker* of a
declining empire. The stability of our systems is still assured by
the Soviet Union's willingness – demonstrated several times
already – to reimpose these systems by military force.

'Thompson's observation that our two systems are becoming
alike is also mistaken. Of course, I don't underestimate the
profound threats to liberty in your country and throughout
western Europe – which is one reason why I'm not starry-eyed
about your political systems ... But the basic point is this: What
is at stake in our half of Europe is nothing less than the survival of
a democratic European culture. I don't go along with Milan
Kundera's nostalgic characterization of central Europe. Yet I –
and most of my friends – utterly agree with him that our half of
Europe is today under siege, that its spiritual identity is being
slowly strangled to death.'

'British socialists who are aware of your situation often say that things have become better in central Europe since the death of Stalin. Isn't that true?'

'Certainly, things have changed since those days,' Eva continued. 'At that time, no one – not even card-carrying Party members – were safe from the Party's delirious and brutal tactics. But especially since 1968, as I've explained already, the violence has become more economical, the manipulation more subtle and "civilized". This is one reason why it has become invisible to western eyes, which are anyway dazzled by our new media star, comrade Gorbachev. Nevertheless, despite these changes our regimes remain totalitarian. They're mobilized constantly to prevent the formation of a civil society independent of the Party-dominated political order.'

'There is a new phase of totalitarian state,' Petr added. 'Power is less delirious, more calculated and subtle – and perhaps harder to break. The Party no longer requires the population's fanatical devotion.'

'It's not interested in tearing human beings to pieces in order to put them back together again in new shapes, as Orwell says somewhere in *Nineteen Eighty-Four*?'

'Exactly. Our regimes now proceed much more cautiously. They recognize or insist upon mediocrity, respectability, self-censorship and moral flaccidity among our citizens. One of the most talented young Polish writers, Czeslaw Bielecki, has observed that True Soviet Man doesn't have to believe in order to practise. There's much truth in that. But it doesn't make life any more enjoyable. Our regimes are trying to break our democratic spirit and traditions. They're encouraging us to forget that the essence of freedom is the courage to resist arbitrary power. They're trying to bring into being decivilized nations who feel defeated. They aim, as Kundera says, to replace our popular memories with oblivion. They want the inhabitants of our countries to observe a few basic rules. Our regimes want us to accept that "socialism" stands or falls with the preservation intact of the Party-governed state. That there will ever be only one governing Party, to which everything, including truth and memory, belongs. They want us to concede that the world is divided into enemies and friends of the Party and, accordingly, that compliance with the Party's policies is rewarded, dissent penalized. Finally, they want us to acknowledge that the Party no longer requires the complete devotion of its citizens, only our passive, ritualized acceptance of its "socialist" dictates.'

Eva and Petr's description of life under late socialism cast serious doubts not only on Thompson's theory and on class-based definitions of socialism, such as Trotskyism. I tried to explain how their description also challenged another common-place among British socialists – the view that central European systems have overcome the 'anarchy' and irrationality of capital-ist market economies, and must therefore be considered an improvement since, at the very least, they *plan* the production and distribution of the basic necessities of life.

'The belief that centralized state planning has decided advan-tages over capitalist markets – guaranteeing everybody a right to a job, ensuring that old people don't die from hypothermia, that transportation methods are cheap and efficient – has a long history within the British socialist tradition ...'

Petr interjected. 'I don't quite understand. Are you saying that this belief in centralized state planning presently functions as another reservoir of sympathy for our regimes among British socialists?'

'Yes. It blinds them to the realities you've been describing. Just as it did for Stalin's Russia four or five decades ago. At that time, during the 1930s for instance, many socialists already accepted G.D.H. Cole's well-known thesis, developed in his *Principles of Economic Planning*, that it's natural ... to look to the experience of Russia, as the one country which has hitherto attempted to introduce a comprehensive national plan.'

I went on to explain how the idea that socialists could learn from the positive achievements of the Soviet model of comprehen-sive state planning was bolstered by the initiatives of the post-war Labour governments in matters of state intervention in the economy, selective nationalization and the establishment of public agencies such as the National Health Service. 'In the immediate post-war years, few British socialists would have disagreed with Prime Minister Attlee's famous remark that "in matters of planning we agree with Soviet Russia". Socialists much admired Tito's Five Year Plan of 1947. Very few would've disputed E.H. Carr's candid observation that "we're all planners now", and that, as he put it, this belief in the efficacy of state planning was "largely the result, conscious or unconscious, of the impact of Soviet practice and achievement".'

'It seems extraordinary to us,' said Petr, 'that the spell of this old "socialism equals planning" formula hasn't worn off ...'

'You must understand that the early post-war period still appears to many as something of a "golden age" of British socialism. Under pressure from the Thatcherites' present love affair with privatization and "free markets", many socialists remain strongly tempted to identify socialism with centralized state planning – despite warnings from Robin Murray, Alec Nove, Hilary Wainwright and others that the whole issue of socialism, markets and planning is urgently in need of rethinking.'

My friends expressed an interest in knowing more about this work, and I've since sent them a copy of Nove's *Feasible Socialism*. But they remained incredulous at my stories of the planning mentality of many western socialists.

Eva pointed to a disturbing irony in this fetish of planning (as she put it). 'For me what's interesting is that during the nineteenth and early twentieth centuries, socialists typically condemned the "anarchy" and dehumanizing effects of capitalist markets. They looked forward to a harmonious and decent socialist society based on rational planning. Today, after nearly seven decades of Soviet-style socialism, it's obvious to us that this equation must be reversed. Hungarian economists such as Kornai and Liska have pointed this out very effectively. Centralized state planning produces anarchy, shortages and dehumanization. Whereas, relatively speaking, the introduction of market mechanisms into our part of the world would have rational and humanizing effects; they would help weaken the grip of the totalitarian state, as well as enhance producers' and consumers' choices. I'd liken our "state planned" systems to that mythical empire whose emperor, wishing to produce a perfectly accurate map of his empire, brings the whole empire to chaos and ruin by forcing the entire population to devote its energy to cartography.'

'If the attempt to subordinate production and consumption, indeed your whole way of life, to centralized state planning organized by the Party has proven so disastrous, what alternatives do you envisage?'

'On the basis of the central European experience,' said Eva, 'I'd reject all talk of the need for generalized state planning as ideological. It's a recipe for totalitarianism. In my view, a clear distinction must be drawn between the full *nationalization* of property – the legalizing of total state control over property, which thereby assumes a "public" status – and the *socialization* of property relations ...'

'Aren't these the same things? Haven't European socialists always talked about the "socialization" of the means of production through state control?'

'I mean something quite different. Socialization refers to the process of reducing the amount of *political* control of productive property. It's the process whereby various groups in civil society establish direct control over how they produce, what they produce, and how they exchange and consume their products. Of course, this couldn't be done without a measure of centralized state planning and control of macro-economic decisions. But the strategy of socializing production and consumption recognizes the need to limit the functions of state power by fostering a plurality of productive units. Unavoidably, this supposes what Marx called commodity production and exchange and, hence, some reliance upon market mechanisms. Market mechanisms – contrary to Marx – aren't simply "bourgeois". I'm convinced that the idea of abolishing markets through comprehensive nationalization, although still today associated with socialism, must be rejected completely. As we know to our cost, it's a nightmarish formula. In my opinion, only the socialization of production could qualify as a genuine step in the direction of socialism.'

'But, then, socialism would mean something radically different than the grey, polluted and suffocating reality of regimes such as Poland and Czechoslovakia?'

'Yes. I disagree with those – the Russian novelist, Alexander Zinoviev, for example – who say that there can be no other kind of socialism than that of the Soviet type.'

'Would you also reject the view, conventionally associated in the west with social democracy, that socialism means the combination of bureaucratic state planning, selective nationalization and the partial control of markets?'

'I can't speak for western Europe. But in our part of the world, this view is meaningless. The earlier twentieth-century alternative between communist and social democratic reformism is dead. For me, socialism is a long-term project. It means attempting, from below, to re-establish and maintain – not to abolish, as Marx recommended – the division between the state and civil society. It also means attempting to make the state accountable to a pluralistic civil society by means of social initiatives whose aim is the expansion of civil liberties. Socialism means empowering citizens to publish freely, to assemble publicly, to produce their own culture. Socialism means empowering workers and consumers to determine the pace, quantity and direction of production. So understood, socialism for me would be synonymous with the goal of creating a genuinely democratic civil society guaranteed and supervised by accountable, strictly defined and limited state power ...'

It was already well after midnight. Discreet yawns had begun to appear around the table. Tomorrow I had to return home. My chair pressed impatiently into my back and legs. But I couldn't resist a closing comment on what I saw as the broader significance of Eva and Petr's revised way of talking about socialism.

'To speak, as you do, of socialism as a process of democratizing civil society and defending it through accountable state power is remarkably close to some new thinking in Britain. I shouldn't leave you with the impression that western socialists have only deaf ears for your situation. As I said at the outset, there are socialists in Britain who are deeply supportive of your work. Besides, there are some promising recent developments. Surely we must be heartened by the new flexibility and the new spaces for public dialogue which appear to be opening in the Soviet Union under Gorbachev. And, in the west, there are signs of new socialist thinking parallel to yours. It's evident, for instance, in the British Labour Party's *Charter on East–West Relations*. In recent years, similar thinking has also been very prominent in a number of Labour-controlled authorities, who have broken with the statist traditions of post-war social democracy. They've tried to view their local government power – what remains of it anyway – not as an end in itself, but as a resource to be shared and used in alliance with social groups and movements, so as to effect changes in civil society. Their new policy initiatives closely parallel your views.'

I was thoroughly surprised by the sharpness of my friends' reaction. I'd intended my observations to be conciliatory. I hadn't expected our lively conversation to suddenly turn sour.

Eva tried hard to hold back her anger. 'Undoubtedly, thinking in radically different ways about socialism is an urgent task at present. The parallels between our thinking are encouraging in this respect. I admit that we've a great deal to learn about your situation. But ... how can I say this? I'm very suspicious of easy agreements and talk of convergence between democrats and socialists in both halves of Europe. Everything you've told us about British socialism makes clear to us that the division between "East" and "West" is not only geographic, political and military. It is also a mental division.

'Your remark about Gorbachev is symptomatic of this. I have the impression that many people in the west think, or hope, that Gorbachev is something like a Russian Kennedy. That expectation is unrealistic – and disheartening for us. We're being presented with the Moscow version of the 1968 Prague Spring.

We're understandably bemused, asking ourselves what's in it for us. Are we witnessing the birth of civil society in the Soviet Union? Is *perestroika* in reality a Potemkin village, an elaborate set of counter-reforms designed to absorb its domestic opponents? To make the totalitarian system more efficient, and to give it a democratic façade? It's too early to tell.

'We don't necessarily believe that a totalitarian system is incapable of internal reform. But, frankly, most of us expect nothing. Nor do we intend to wait for changes, as if our rights of citizenship and self-determination needed sanctioning by the Kremlin. We're deeply circumspect – as our political experience has taught us to be. More than one party candidate to stand for election to the upper echelons of the Party: what a pathbreaking idea! Manufacturing quality goods: now there's a daring revolutionary proposal! Openness – for how long will it be tolerated this time? We'll see.

'I can't be sure that you or your friends understand our profound sense of caution and scepticism in these matters. Many western socialists either don't want to know about our situation, or they seem to be incapable of viewing our regimes except through western socialist eyes. They've simply not come to terms with our experience of totalitarian "socialism" – under which our people suffer greatly. What a catastrophe! Your friends' blindness and deafness is a fundamental blockage upon dialogue between democrats and socialists in both halves of Europe. It divides us by a wall of silent miscomprehension. It generates mutual suspicion. Consequently, we talk to each other as if we were strangers ...'

'*As if we were strangers* ...' These words – always upsetting when used among good friends – rang in my ears. They cluttered my head long after we'd packed up our chairs and left our basement refuge. That night, they followed me to bed, and interrupted my dreams. They still do.

7

Democracy, Ideology, Relativism

Anarchy is not the worst thing the democratic countries
must fear, but the least.

Alexis de Tocqueville

Civil Society and Ideology

The concept of ideology is today enjoying an important renaissance. References to the 'ideology' of capitalism, socialism, patri-
archy, nationalism or industrialism have become commonplace
within public debate. Unfortunately, the popularity of the term is
not matched by greater precision in its meaning. Serious reflection upon its origins, development and possible confusions and
weaknesses remains scarce. It is assumed that repeated use of the
term requires no further justification. There are several reasons
why this assumption should be questioned. More obviously, the
renaissance of the term ideology has multiplied its various
meanings, the (potential) confusions among which can be clarified and resolved only through serious theoretical reflection. But
there are other – less obvious and more compelling – reasons for
considering the term more closely. There is a special affinity
between the theory of ideology and the subject of civil society and
the state. Not only are the late eighteenth century origins of the
concept of ideology coterminous with the distinction between civil
society and the state. The theory of ideology also generates some
basic philosophical problems – concerning language, science,

relativism and its sociopolitical implications – whose resolution is of central importance to my attempt to 'democratize' the idea of socialism through the prism of the old state–civil society distinction.

The intimate relationship between the subjects of ideology, civil society and the state is first suggested in the writings of Marx. Marx was the first to seize the concept of ideology from its inventors – the late eighteenth century *idéologues* such as de Tracy – for the purpose of unmasking the power claims of the bourgeoisie. In consequence, the theory of ideology largely ceased to be identified with the *idéologues'* concern to destroy traditional prejudice and privilege and to develop *civisme* among the population through state policies guided by empirical-analytic knowledge (developed along the lines of chemistry and physics) of the laws governing the human psyche.[1] Marx also ensured that the term ideology ceased to be synonymous with the quixotic meddling of intellectuals intoxicated with abstractions, *esprit de système* and a naive faith in human perfectibility (the pejorative meaning ascribed to the term by Napoleon Bonaparte, who denounced the *idéologues* after Malet's abortive conspiracy of December 1812).

Marx gave a wholly new twist to its meaning: ideology is the collectively expressed ideas of the bourgeoisie – which rules civil society and therefore controls the state. Marx recognized that not all ideas are ideologies in this sense. An ideology is a special formation of ideas. It comprises dominant and dominating ideas, which function – though never fully successfully – to render the power relations of civil society invisible and, thus, to insulate them from public questioning and social and political action. Bourgeois ideology serves to conceal and to 'freeze' social divisions. It functions as a condition of false compromise and unity among potentially conflicting social groups, principally, the classes of wage labour and capital. It performs this legitimating function, paradoxically, by portraying the dominant private interests of civil society in grandiose formulations which make them appear, falsely, as detached and universal interests. Ruling ideas which claim to be universal are always those of a particular ruling class. For example, according to Marx the class relationships of civil society are held by bourgeois ideologists to epitomize universal justice and liberty, and to guarantee individuality and the rights of man. Yet bourgeois theories of universal liberty and individualism are ideological, for they conceal the property-based interests of civil society. Despite its 'appearance' of guaranteeing individual freedom, civil society actually guarantees merely the freedom of private property's interests to carry on a running battle to extract surplus-value from the mass of waged labourers.

Behind the litany and *maquillage* of universal liberty, there stands, in Marx's view, the harsh reality of civil society – its new form of 'slavery' and 'inhumanity' based on the dominion of private capital. In this way, Marx explains bourgeois ideology by way of a 'genetic method of critique'.[2] The illusory disinterestedness and universalism of ideologies is unmasked by confronting them with their actual social basis. Ideologies are accused of misrecognizing their own social conditions of production and, thereby, of trapping themselves within systems of ideas that apologize for the exploitation inherent within civil society.

New Doubts, New Problems

Sketched in this way, the classical Marxian theory of ideology seems to share several points of agreement with the theory of socialist civil society developed in previous essays. Both are critical of bourgeois domination of civil society and, by extension, the ability of private capital to manipulate and structure the outcomes of state policymaking and administration. The two approaches also share a deep reservation about universalist political claims. They suspect that such claims are often in practice a mask for particular interests, and that, as Marx and Engels observed, ruling power groups typically represent their own conditions of life as 'eternal laws of nature and of reason'.[3] Such affinities between the two theories are evident; nevertheless, there remain serious doubts about their compatibility and whether, in particular, the Marxian theory of ideology remains plausible. During the past several decades, this theory has suffered a marked loss of confidence. Numerous writers have sought to expose its fallacious nineteenth-century premises, arguing that those who follow in the footsteps of Marx's attempt at unmasking and abolishing ideological deception are themselves deceived. The arguments are by no means simple or consistent. And yet three reasons in particular explain why a controversy over ideology and its unmasking has broken out. Since these reasons bear crucially on the philosophical assumptions of the revised theory of democracy presented in this book, each merits detailed consideration.

The End of Ideology

First, in Europe and elsewhere it has been argued that twentieth-century developments have depleted old nineteenth-century ideologies – neutralizing the Marxian critique of ideology as a consequence. Perhaps the most famous version of this 'end of ideology' thesis was presented by Daniel Bell. He argued that calamities such as the Moscow trials, labour camps, the Hitler–Stalin pact and the brutal suppression of the Hungarian revolution have destroyed the credibility and popularity of Marxism and, indeed, of all chiliastic hopes and apocalyptic forms of thinking. Also, the critical optimism of early modern bourgeois ideologies has been sapped. Whereas they were universalist, 'humanist' and fashioned by controversies among intellectuals, the dominant contemporary forms of west European belief are modest, consensual and lacking in utopian content. The old terms of ideological debate between 'left' and 'right' no longer arouse passions. Consequently, the project of 'unmasking' ideology (in the precise Marxian sense of revealing the 'objective' interests lurking behind a protective mantle of grandiloquent ideas) is jeopardized. There is simply no longer a gap between reality and the claims made on its behalf. Both reality and its legitimating ideas become wholly consensual, even cynical. 'In the Western world', Bell concluded, 'there is today a rough consensus among intellectuals on political issues: the acceptance of a Welfare State; the desirability of decentralized power; a system of mixed economy and of political pluralism.'[4]

The degradation of ideological discourse and the emergence of a cynical, pseudo-moral reality is also a prominent theme of debate about the exhausted democratic potential of Marxism within the late socialist regimes of central-eastern Europe. Numerous writers – Václav Havel is among the more prominent[5] – emphasize that the official language of Marxism has degenerated into a sterile (though politically indispensable) ritual performed each day by the Party-dominated state. Ideology becomes, through a perverted form of idealism, the substance of political life: ideology *is* reality. The official ideology is actually a pseudo-ideology for, in offering one type of morality to its subjects, it encourages them to *part* with morality. It encourages their own trivialization, thereby ensuring their conformity to the status quo, as both victims and accomplices, under the 'diktat of the empty phrase'. The slogans of this pseudo-ideology ('proletarian internationalism', etc.) have one central function: to silence all public discussion independent of the Party-dominated state. This pantomime of pseudo-ideology is not designed to convince anybody. It seeks only to remind everybody of their political imprisonment. To the extent that this pseudo-ideology covers all and sundry, 'individuals confirm the system, fulfil the system, make the system, *are* the system'.[6] And since there are no independent civil checks upon state power, there is nothing to prevent the official pseudo-ideology from becoming wholly artificial and mendacious. While pretending to pretend nothing, it becomes an all-englobing excuse, a pure lie – a canopy of appearances designed to extinguish reality and to ensure total conformity to its hodge-podge of mendacious claims.

Variants of the end of ideology thesis have also made their way into the west European socialist tradition. It has been argued that the concept of ideology is becoming ever less relevant for analysing late capitalist systems. Both the theory and phenomenon of ideology – and its radical potential – have been victimized by the growth of manipulative forms of bureaucratic control. Ideology *strictu sensu* is said to be a type of vindicative discourse that emerges out of social conditions which have become problematic for the dominant class, and therefore require a defence through *justificatory* arguments – such as the early modern bourgeois ideologies of individualism and liberty. These classical ideologies sustained 'utopian' impulses. They functioned 'to justify and to mobilize public projects of social reconstruction'.[7] Under late capitalist conditions, according to Adorno, matters are worse. Old bourgeois ideologies, which emerged under conditions of intense sociopolitical conflict, are replaced by forms of false consciousness decreed from above by the culture industry. This administered consciousness is not susceptible of immanent criticism; it contains no transcendent, self-critical dimension. The culture industry produces total conformity. It successfully preaches the cynical injunction: 'Become that which thou art.' Reality and consciousness consequently merge. Late bourgeois ideology is not a specious veil masking a harsh reality. It is instead the 'threatening face of the world'.[8]

An influential version of this thesis was later developed by Habermas.[9] Under late capitalist conditions, Habermas explains, the official justifications of power are 'less ideological' than classical bourgeois discourses. Old bourgeois ideologies (of formal law, market competition and a free publc sphere) portrayed modern civil societies and states as a product of the choices of free and equal individuals and, thus, as emancipated from despotic power. Bourgeois ideologies typically criticized the past in the name of their own scientific and universally valid claims. In this way, they radically weakened the legitimacy of pre-modern metaphysics, myths and traditions. They also greatly strengthened the grip of the bourgeoisie upon civil society and the state. Representing its own particular interests as universal or *pro bono publico*, the bourgeoisie attempted to rule without appearing to rule.

Habermas observes that the bourgeois attempt to conceal its power was thwarted constantly by the fact that its ideologies displayed an 'evident contradiction between idea and reality'.[10] This contradiction endowed bourgeois ideologies with 'utopian' or 'illusory' qualities, which ensured their functioning as a source of wish fulfilment and substitute gratification among the powerless (as Marx observed of Christianity in his polemic against Feuerbach). Early modern ideologies were not simply 'false consciousness' (Engels). They 'are not defined exclusively as a necessary social consciousness which is purely false ... [They] also display a moment of truth, a utopian impulse which points beyond the present by questioning its justification.'[11] This utopian impulse also ensured that bourgeois ideologies were plagued by self-contradictions and, hence, subject to public controversies. Bourgeois ideologies invited radical criticisms of ideology (such as those of Marx) addressed to the powerless victims of civil society. Ideologies are coeval with the critique of ideology.

This instability of early bourgeois ideologies contrasts with the durability of the dominant ideas of late capitalist systems. According to Habermas, a 'glassy background ideology which idolizes and fetishizes science'[12] drives classical ideologies from the stage of public awareness. Whereas the latter spawned ethical argument and projected elaborate visions of 'the good life', the newer justifications of power speak only of scientific facts and technical and social imperatives. In the era of welfare state capitalism, scientific reseach and development becomes more than a crucial productive force. It also plays the role of a deep background ideology which legitimates the regulation of civil society by state power *and* suppresses public discussion as such. This technocratic consciousness is more irresistible, far-reaching and (from the point of view of the democratic tradition) politically dangerous. It obliterates the fundamental distinction between communication among speaking and acting subjects and manipulative, purposive-rational action. Technocratic consciousness aims to universalize the power of technical control (by extending it from nature to social life). It thereby justifies not merely the particular interests of a dominant social and political class (in the manner of classical ideologies), but jeopardizes the human capacity for publicly organizing and choosing political norms. Technocratic consciousness is the cunning and cynical enemy of democracy. It contains no utopian impulses. It suppresses consideration of the goals for which individuals, groups and whole systems could strive. And since technocratic consciousness is hostile to normative considerations, it outflanks and renders obsolete theoretical and practical strategies of challenging ideology immanently. The justification of democracy, Habermas concludes, must today fall back upon an ontological approach, founded on enquiries into the universal postulates of publicly expressed normative discourse.[13]

Science and Ideology

Some possible responses to this first challenge to the classical Marxian theory of ideology can be postponed momentarily, in order to introduce for discussion a second type of objection. This concerns Marx's reluctance to label the natural sciences as ideological. According to many critics, the philosophical status of the Marxian theory of ideology and that of the positivist natural sciences are inadequately distinguished. Marx's conviction that 'the material transformation of the economic conditions of production ... can be determined with the precision of natural science'[14] falsely assimilates the theory of ideology to the assumptions, empirical-analytic methods and instrumental aims of a nineteenth-century conception of natural science.[15] Marx embraced the Comtean positivist assumption that absolute knowledge of modern civil society and the state could be developed by adhering to the rules of observation, conceptual precision and methodological exactness. He supposed that this universal knowledge could be used to calculate, predict and control reality. The critique of ideology is construed as a species of technical knowledge.

Several negative consequences are said to flow from this positivist self-understanding of the critique of ideology. By contrasting the misrecognition fostered by ideology with the certain knowledge of natural science, the Marxian theory wedded itself, indirectly, to an optimistic bourgeois Victorian conception of scientific-technical progress, which in the meantime has become highly questionable. Marx assumes that neither the natural sciences nor the allied processes of technological development are (or could ever become) ideological.[16] The positivist bias of the Marxian theory also reinforced its simplistic accounts (or cavalier disregard) of certain forms of life – old peasant traditions, patriarchal households and disciplinary institutions are well-known examples – that did not conform to its general theory of the dynamics of modern civil society and the state. Precisely because it was convinced of its 'scientific' status, the theory of ideology underestimated the democratic – or undemocratic – potential of spheres of civil and political life and struggle beyond the realm of commodity production and exchange (see essay 2).

Perhaps the most serious objection to the latent positivism of Marx's theory of ideology is that it falls victim to the assumption, common to all scientism, that it is true knowledge capable of technical implementation. Marx's assumption that the theory of ideology generates scientific insights into the laws of motion of 'reality' has aroused the suspicion – expressed by Bauman among others[17] – that from the beginning the theory of ideology was an ally of manipulative power. In the name of the struggle of enlightened scientific reason against arrogant superstition, of true interests against false interests, it *preserved* rather than terminated the intellectualist bid for power and authority evident in the original 'civilizing' mission of the *idéologues*. Symptomatic of this is Marx's failure to consider whether his own theory of ideology might itself function as an ideology. A *tu quoque* question of this kind is surely legitimate, even within the terms of Marx's own discourse. If ideas are ideological because they justify inequalities of social power by misrepresenting, in grandiose universal claims, the real nature of civil society and the state, didn't Marx's ideas themselves (potentially) function in this way? And since, as Marx observed of classical political economy, truthful ideas could become ideological due to changes in the class structure of civil society, didn't this possibility apply equally to Marx's thought itself? These questions are suppressed by the original Marxian theory. As Mannheim observed, the Marxian theses on the relationship between structures of thought and the conditions of social existence are applied sparingly – to the opponents of Marxism and never to the Marxian structures of thought.[18] They lay claim to correct and politically useful knowledge of the modern state and civil society, which are conceived as a totality governed by a single determining principle of organization – changes in the forces and relations of production. In this way,

Marx's critics say, the science of historical materialism overrides its insistence that only the proletariat can emancipate the proletariat. It tends to adopt an instrumental relationship to its proletarian addressees. Their 'real historical interests' are known in advance. The Marxian theory plays the tune to which the 'dangerous class' is expected to dance.

The Problem of Signification

A third reason for the recent loss of credibility of the classical Marxian critique of ideology has to do with its neglect of questions concerning spoken language and other (non-verbal) forms of signification. This complaint should be expressed with care for, as Márkus has indicated, Marx recognized the decisive sociopolitical importance of language and linguistically inherited culture.[19] Moreover, it is false to suppose – as Gramsci reminded his contemporaries[20] – that Marx simply conceived ideology as pure appearance, as an artificial substance draped like a veil over an underlying reality. Social reality for Marx consists of interacting individuals, groups and classes who produce, by means of language, appearances which are something more and other than a veil of errors or lies. These ideological appearances are the distorted mode in which social activities manifest themselves in consciousness. As such, they have a material reality for social actors and (under conditions of a class-divided civil society and state, at least) this reality generates and presupposes appearances.

Many recent critics (most of them indebted to Althusser's influential essay on ideology)[21], acknowledge these caveats. They argue nevertheless that the classical Marxian theory of ideology rests upon the untenable distinction between the ideological forms in which 'reality' appears and a *prior* domain of 'reality', consisting of 'material' activity uncluttered by processes of signification. Consequently, ideology is understood as a posthumous misrepresentation of an underlying reality – the material life processes of civil society – which function as the pre-symbolic point of origin of ideology. This subterranean reality not only operates 'behind the back' of ideology. It also serves as a foundation which contradicts, as well as explains, the dissimulations of ideology.

Numerous attempts to solve the riddles of ideology by distinguishing a 'surface' or 'superstructure' of ideological representations from a subterranean 'base' of material life activity are scattered throughout Marx's writings. A characteristic example is

Marx's use of the Roman myth of Cacus (in the third part of *Theories of Surplus Value*) to identify and explain the material origins of ideology. Just as Cacus concealed his cattle-rustling activities by herding his prey backwards into his cave, so that it appeared that they had already departed, the bourgeoisie, Marx explains, conceals its parasitic role within the production process of civil society by picturing itself, falsely (and in contrast to Cacus, unconsciously), as the source of all wealth, which in reality is produced by the sweat and toil of the working class.[22]

The distinction between material practice and its ideological misrepresentation is also strongly evident throughout *Das Kapital*. For instance, certain 'imaginary' categories of bourgeois political economy (such as the 'value and price of labour'; 'wages'; 'the *fictio juris* of contracts'; the 'commodity') are seen by Marx to originate from capitalist relations of production. Contrary to the self-understanding of political economy, these concepts are neither timeless nor true. They are historically specific and function as mystifying 'categories for the phenomenal forms of essential relations'. These ideological categories depict complex relations (or relations among relations, such as the wages–money–value–commodity relationship) as self-evident relations, or simply as properties of things. According to Marx, these mystifying categories (which he also calls illusions, forms of manifestation, hieroglyphics, semblances, estranged outward appearances) must be distinguished carefully from – and explained and criticized with reference to – 'real relations', or what he also calls inner connections, essences, real nature, actual relations, or the hidden or secret substratum.[23]

The same 'genetic' treatment of ideology is evident in the earliest writings of Marx (and Engels). A fundamental contrast is drawn between the 'actual existing world' and what human beings imagine or say about the world.[24] The inverted illusions of the bourgeois epoch are said to be sublimations of the 'material life-process' of social labour, private property and class struggle: 'Ideologists turn everything upside down.'[25] Thus, for example, believers of religion are accused of failing to realize that 'man makes religion, religion does not make man'.[26] Marx emphasizes that religion is a form of illusory happiness. Therefore, the critique of religious ideology is at the same time a demand to abolish social conditions that require illusions: 'The criticism of religion is ... the germ of the criticism of the valley of tears whose halo is religion.'[27]

In such analyses, Marx (and Engels) emphasize that ideologies have no independent logic of development. Their birth, rise to dominance and decay is always determined by the logic of development of the social labour process. It follows that the grip of ideologies on the minds and lips of the powerless can be broken only through revolutionary changes of the 'actual existing world'. Life is not determined by consciousness; rather, consciousness is determined by life. Emancipation is not a matter of thinking and speaking differently. It is a 'practical' act, a matter of abolishing the material conditions of civil society.

These formulations have prompted certain objections. The Marxian theory of ideology, resting as it does on the fundamental distinction between material activity and its apparent forms, fails to acknowledge that *all* social and political life – including the forces and relations of production in both their objective and subjective dimensions – is structured through codes of signification.[28] The 'material life processes' of civil society do not comprise 'naked' productive activity. Signs (whether in spoken, written or visual form) are not cognate to deeds, since deeds are themselves always 'saturated' by signs. Social and political life, to put the point differently, is coextensive with symbolically mediated activity. The latter is not a level or dimension of civil society and the state. There is nothing specifically social or political – not even the labour process – which is constituted from an Archimedean point 'outside' or 'below' signifying practices.

Marx's failure to recognize this essential point, his critics argue, produced a number of undesirable consequences. The theory of ideology cannot provide a convincing explanation of how traditions (e.g. of political thought, music or sexual customs) exert a profound influence far beyond their time and place of origin. It also neglects the point – underlying these essays – that the periodic renewal of certain traditions is indispensable for the advance of democratic politics. Symptomatic of this blindspot is Marx's inability to come to terms with his own recognition that certain types of aesthetic creations (for example, Greek art and epics) have been endowed with 'eternal' significance, at least for European civilizations.[29]

Linked with this problem of understanding traditions is Marx's inadequate explanation of the relationship between material production and spiritual (*geistig*) production of poetry and music, and of the possibility (noted by Marx) that 'free spiritual production' within civil society may, and often does, conflict with politics, law, religion, morality and other 'ideological component parts of the ruling class'.[30] Finally, Marx's thesis that ideologies can be explained genetically, by referring to the prevailing forces and relations of production 'underlying' the surface forms of ideology, implies that ideology can be abolished. The elimination of commodity production and exchange (and hence the abolition of civil society and the state) would rid the world of illusions. Ideology would wither away. Forms of thought would become attuned to the 'real material conditions' of communist society. Processes of signification would become mere instruments of communication among free and equal subjects. According to Marx's critics, this communist dream of abolishing ideology is better described as a totalitarian reverie – as a dangerous fantasy of building a future society whose subjects, fully transparent to one another, would be burdened no longer by problems of misrecognition, misunderstanding, rhetoric and other ambiguities of communication.*

Reconstructing the Concept of Ideology

The Marxian theory of ideology is sometimes criticized for its conceptual imprecision, ambiguity and incompleteness.[31] These weaknesses are important, but they pale before the three challenges summarized above. At a minimum, these challenges – concerning the disappearance of classical bourgeois ideology, the positivist bias of the theory of ideology and its reductionist treatment of signifying practices – pose some basic questions about the overall plausibility of the Marxian approach. Of central importance is the issue of whether the concept of ideology continues to have a legitimate place in a revised, more fully democratic theory of civil society and the state. I believe it does. But I shall argue that the retention of the critical concept of ideology requires its fundamental *reconstruction* – its dismantling and reassembly in a new form, so as to realize its original democratic

---

* Compare the satirical treatment of this Marxian fantasy in one of the best-known plays of Václav Havel, *The Memorandum*, London 1967. Office workers are expected to learn a new 'strictly scientific' language, Ptydepe, which is said officially to banish the confusions of natural, unscientific language. It aims to maximize precision in communication by maximizing the difference between words, so that no word can be mistaken for another, the length of the word being proportional to its frequency of use (the word for wombat has 319 letters). In fact, Ptydepe baffles everybody who tries to learn it, producing a condition of administrative paralysis and absurdity.

potential. In turn, this reconstruction necessitates reflection upon each challenge to the original Marxian project of ideology criticism.

The Return of Ideology

Let us begin with the charge that the Marxian critique of ideology has been sterilized by the disappearance of classical bourgeois ideology. Sociological generalizations of this kind are always hazardous, and should be treated with caution. Nevertheless, it is indisputable that since the early modern era the dominant modes of legitimating power have changed considerably in Europe. This change is most evident in central-eastern Europe, where various species of Marxism–Leninism (most recently, *glasnost*) hold sway as the official source of legitimacy of the Party-dominated state. The collusion of key Marxist themes with the totalitarian order has slowly destroyed the credibility and popularity of Marxism, jeopardized all remaining forms of socialist discourse, and seriously cast doubt on utopian thinking in general.[32] It is also clear that since the Bolshevik Revolution the prevailing 'socialist' discourse has become more defensive, cynical and aseptic. Strict ideological control has been limited, grudgingly, in certain spheres (such as the natural sciences). And the ruling pseudo-ideology itself has been reduced to an eclectic web of slogans which nobody believes. 'Full of contradictions, the state ideology persists in the form of a diffused, shapeless collection of adages of various origins: a few remnants of Marxist vocabulary, seemingly ambiguous yet well-understood hints of nationalism and racism, vague humanist generalities, obvious lies, useless truisms, and meaningless absurdities.'[33] This hodge-podge pseudo-ideology functions as noise, designed to prevent the formation of an articulate civil society and to remind the population daily that the ruling power is strong.

These trends are strongly evident in the late socialist regimes of central-eastern Europe. Yet they do not warrant the conclusion that the concept of ideology is no longer sociologically relevant in analysing their structures of power. The *glasnost* doctrine – which emphasizes themes such as renewal, efficiency, production and democracy – indicates that the pseudo-ideology of late socialism is subject periodically to reanimation from within. This 'rejuvenated' ideological discourse may produce deep tensions within the ruling apparatus. It may also be used by the democratic opponents of the Party-dominated state – in the manner of the opponents of classical bourgeois ideologies – to embarrass and expose the dominant power group and to legitimate attempts to establish and expand civil liberties.

The 'return of ideology' within the ranks of the state's opponents must also not be discounted. The democratic opponents of totalitarianism share one overarching concern: the self-liberation of civil society from the yoke of the Party-dominated state and, ultimately, the creation of a measure of political pluralism (see essays 4, 6). Paradoxically, this concern for creating and tolerating a wide variety of social and political differences facilitates the rebirth of ideologies – justificatory discourses which defend particular interests in the name of a universal cause. A troubling example is the steady growth of a species of neo-conservatism which is hostile both to the totalitarian state *and* to the idea of a democratic civil society. It favours the formation of a powerful and respected state based on the rule of law and a nationalist consensus. It supposes that the humiliated nations of central-eastern Europe can only recover their identity by reasserting central European traditions, in particular those which emphasize 'the maintenance of common values'.[34] This brand of neo-conservatism may assert the primacy of 'common values', but in reality it also relentlessly selects and privileges some common values (especially nationalism) at the expense of others (workers' self-government, for example). It thereby traps itself within the same type of performative contradiction that plagued early modern ideologies. It opposes totalized state control in the name of universal (or 'common') values, while at the same time pursuing a course which entails, in practice, the suppression of other forms of activity which do not conform to its own particular values.

In the late capitalist systems of western Europe, the language of the dominant powers has also changed since the early modern period. Generalizations are again risky, but it seems safe to say that the influence of certain Enlightenment ideals (such as liberty of the individual and the rule of law) has tended to become less visible and more dispersed. These ideals have been supplemented or partially replaced, as Habermas and others argue, by professionalism, scientific expertise and other new discourses for justifying claims upon power. Yet there are three reasons why such developments do not render sociologically irrelevant the Marxian concept of ideology.

First, the 'end of ideology' thesis underestimated the empirical importance of a heterogeneous multitude of social and political traditions of solidarity and resistance (feminism and black culture are key examples) which survived – and continue to hinder and defy – the advance of the official 'post-ideologies'. End of ideology theorists (including Althusser, who speaks of the capacity of 'ideological state apparatuses' to 'interpellate' and reproduce subjects with self-conceptions appropriate to their place as 'agents' of an exploitative social division of labour) overstated the capacity of official ideologies to mobilize public support, to ensure consensus, and to silence alternative forms of life within and between civil society and the state.[35]

Secondly, Habermas and other neo-Kantian theorists of the new 'glassy background which idolizes and fetishizes science' typically emphasized its 'outer limits' – its incapacity to pose *non-technical* or *ethical* questions. This approach assumed that the endogenous capacity of technocratic discourse to enhance its powers of administrative control liberated it from 'inner limits'. Strangely, this assumption ignored the self-contradictory nature of technocratic discourse and, hence, overstated its capacity to remain a 'background ideology' capable of silencing dissent. As I explained at length in *Public Life and Late Capitalism*, state and corporate organizations seeking to administer their environments by means of scientific-technical rules are obliged continually to solicit the active participation of their members and clients, whose initiative and autonomy these organizations must nevertheless forbid. This self-contradiction of technocratic discourse is compounded by the fact that complex, highly mechanized and scientifically planned organizations are high-risk systems and cannot operate cybernetically, that is, without constant human input. Collective and individual judgements and improvisations are required to control and resolve the unstructured and open-ended problems which they generate, as well as to prevent them from regularly malfunctioning in unexpected and dangerous ways (as at the nuclear power plants in Chernobyl and Three-Mile Island).[36] For these reasons, technocratic discourse cannot suppress demands for democratization. On the contrary, like all ideologies it fails to live up to its own grandiloquent claims, and thus stimulates *from within* public criticisms of its self-contradictory logic.

Finally, doubts must be raised about the degree to which the 'ruling ideas' of late capitalist systems have become cynical, and therefore incapable of serving as a reference point from which alternative insights and initiatives can be derived immanently.[37] This end of ideology thesis is evidently contradicted by the intense controversies over the limits of state action and the future of state-administered socialism. These controversies indicate a *renewal* of ideological forms of discourse. They signal the return of types of vindicative discourse within social conditions which have become problematic for the dominant power groups, who defend themselves through justificatory arguments. These controversies also signal the renewed possibility of immanently criticizing the dominant ideologies – as the theory of socialist civil society indicates – thereby contributing to the social and political task of creating 'the new world through criticism of the old' (Marx).

From Science to Relativism

In arguing against the end of ideology thesis and for the continuing sociological relevance of the (Marxian) concept of ideology, the preceding section to some extent has simplified its complex meanings. In addition, the traditional links between the concept of ideology and the subject of civil society and the state have been de-emphasized. The term 'ideology' has been used, loosely, to indicate the persistence, throughout Europe at least, of collectively expressed ideas of power groups, whose particular interests are justified publicly in grandiose formulations which make them appear, falsely, as universal interests. This imprecise formulation remains unsatisfactory. It still begs the salient questions raised by the second and third criticisms of the concept of ideology.

The second objection to the Marxian theory of ideology criticism is arguably the most serious, since it raises the question whether the theory of ideology can be rescued from its arrogant positivist assumption that science and ideology are diametrically opposed entities. More precisely, the issue is whether a revised theory of ideology can remain *critical* whilst breaking with its positivist heritage, restraining itself from making absolute truth claims, and acknowledging its historicity, its embeddedness within a contingent sociopolitical context. Can the accounts of social and political life provided by a critical theory of ideology understand themselves as *interpretations* (in the sense of contemporary hermeneutics), as therefore subject to self-contradiction, unforeseen social and political developments, drastic revision or even open rejection by its public addressees, without at the same time being reduced to bland and apologetic propositions which kowtow to the status quo?

Such theoretical questions concerning the possibility of a

'post-scientific' critique of ideology – a socially and politically engaged critique of ideology which abandons its traditional fetishism of empirical-analytic science – are topical, and of great social and political importance. During the past decade, the epistemological self-confidence of the Marxian theory of ideology has dissolved. In its place there has developed a strong revival of the tradition of cognitive and ethical relativism, whose essence is captured eloquently in Pascal's maxim: 'What is truth on one side of the Pyrenees is error on the other.' 'No privileged truths, only interpretations! Down with the vanguardism of reason!' might be said to be the watchword of those currently disillusioned with the critical theory of ideology. According to Marx's critics, the struggle to unmask ideological illusions fails to examine its *own* authority. The critique of ideology clings dogmatically to its own misguided belief in the superior innocence of its own premises. In the view of these critics, the (Marxian) search for truth free of illusions must be called off. Theoretical enquiry must relinquish its traditional claim to absolute knowledge – instead embracing the logic of particularity and context-dependent polytheism. The real world is only a fable and a struggle among competing fables. Religion, science, democracy, socialism, liberalism are so many diverse interpretations of the world or, rather, so many variants of different fables which must be taken at face value, since they have no ultimate reference point or standard of truth outside themselves.

Does this relativist challenge to the critical theory of ideology constitute a welcome liberation from traditional sociopolitical and philosophical prejudices, particularly of a positivist kind? Or is it better seen as a scurrilous attack upon the democratic potential of the classical theory of ideology?

A straightforward response to these awkward questions cannot be summarized easily, although one proposal deserves a mention at the outset. Beginning with Hans Barth's *Wahrheit und Ideologie*[38], it has been argued that relativism jeopardizes the project of emancipation from ideologies and that, consequently, a contemporary theory of ideology must attempt to distinguish between false (ideological) and true descriptive and normative claims. According to Barth, a basic condition of human association is agreement, and the essence of agreement, whether in scientific investigation or daily life, is the idea of truth. Thompson's recent defence of a model of rational argumentation stands within the tradition initiated by Barth.[39] Thompson's thesis is that a theory of ideology must account for the ways in which processes of signification serve to induce and sustain the servile dependency of speaking actors upon each other. He sketches a model for the 'depth interpretation' of ideological domination. This model evidently raises questions about the specific institutions and procedures through which conflicting interpretations can be adjudicated openly and fairly within social and political life (a problem left unaddressed by Thompson). It also prompts questions about the truth status of depth interpretation: 'If "ideology" is an evaluative term, if its very use conveys a critical note and calls for a process of critique, then how are we to justify the characterization of some discourse as ideological? How can we pretend to stand above the fray, aloofly assessing the discourse of others, when our interpretation is but another interpretation, no different in principle from the interpretations of those whose discourse we seek to assess?'[40]

In response to such questions, Thompson resorts neither to a positivist appeal to 'science' (as the saviour of truth against the appeals of ideology) nor to relativist conclusions. He instead defends a version of the justificatory analysis of truth. This theory of truth is guided by the principles of self-reflection, rational debate and consensus formation among subjects interacting freely within independent public spheres. In Thompson's view, ideology is a form of signification which serves to sustain relations of domination among speaking and acting subjects who are situated within a social and political framework of asymmetrical power relations, which would be recognized as such if these subjects could freely discuss their conditions of existence, and thus vindicate the *interpretation* of ideological domination offered by its critics.

This view (as Thompson acknowledges) draws upon a modified version of Habermas's theory of universal pragmatics, and it is therefore doubtful whether it can escape unscathed from the latter's unresolved difficulties. Particularly important is the failure of the theory of universal pragmatics to address directly the challenge of cognitive and ethical relativism. Habermas's communication theory underestimates the probability of subjects' refusal or inability to enter into action oriented to reaching understanding and agreement. This deficiency prevents the theory of universal pragmatics from generating a critical theory of ideology with democratic intentions. Recent versions of Habermas's theory suppose that a certain type of communicative action – 'consensual action' – is guided (implicitly or explicitly) by the common conviction that certain 'validity claims' are being honoured. It further supposes that such communicative action can be analysed as *the* fundamental form of communicative and strategic action.[41] In this way, the theory of communication theoretically privileges consensual action, that is, a particular type of language game in which speaking actors *already* co-operate on the basis of certain mutually acknowledged premises. Habermas's explication of the logic of communication thus sidesteps the problems raised by relativists. It presumes the existence of competently speaking and acting subjects who are (a) already in explicit agreement about the need to reach mutual understanding; (b) already capable of distinguishing between the performative and propositional aspects of their utterances; and (c) already share a tradition and, thus, a common perception of their social and political situation. The challenge mounted by relativism remains unaddressed.

An alternative and politically more fruitful way of dealing with the relativist challenge – and of redesigning a concept of ideology appropriate for a democratic theory of civil society and the state – is to 'radicalize' the relativist argument by asking after its unspoken premises and sociopolitical implications. This type of counterfactual enquiry requires careful reflection upon the institutional conditions necessary for the theoretical and sociopolitical actualization of relativist claims. Consider, for example, the influential essay on post-modernism by Jean-François Lyotard, *La Condition postmoderne*.[42] Of special interest to Lyotard is the problem of legitimacy, that is, the processes by which every particular language game seeks to authorize its 'truth', 'rightness' and (potential) efficacy – and therewith its superiority over other, rival language games – through utterances which specify, more or less explicitly to the agents of that language game, rules concerning such matters as the need for narration, internal consistency, experimental verification, and (in the case of Habermas) consensus obtained through discussion. These rules consist not only of guidelines concerning how to form denotative utterances (in which the true/false distinction is central). These rules pertain also to notions of *savoir-entendre*, *savoir-dire*, *savoir-vivre*, that is, to the ability to form and understand 'good' evaluative and prescriptive statements and, thereby, to speak and interact with others in a normative way. It is precisely consensus about these pragmatic rules, Lyotard argues, that permits the participants within a language game to identify each other as interlocutors, as well as to circumscribe their language game, distinguishing it from other, possibly incommensurate language games.

From this (neo-Wittgensteinian) perspective, Lyotard emphasizes that every utterance within a particular language game
should be understood as an activity, as a 'move' with or against
players of one's own or another language game. Utterances may
in addition be understood as moves in opposition to the most
formidable adversary of all: the prevailing language itself. This is
Lyotard's 'first principle': to perform speech acts involves jousting,
adopting agonistic or solidaristic postures toward other players or
language itself.[43] It follows from this principle that players within
language games are always embedded in relations of power – power
here understood as the capacity of actors to wilfully block or effect
changes in the speech activities of others within the already existing
framework of a language game, which itself always pre-structures
the speech activities of individuals and groups.

This point about power and language games also implies –
this is Lyotard's 'second principle' – that language games must
be considered as definite social practices. To perform rule-bound
or rule-breaking utterances is at the same time to participate in
the production, reproduction or transformation of forms of social
life.[44] Society can be understood neither as an organically
arranged functional whole (Parsons) nor as a totality subject to
fragmentation and simplification along class lines (Marx).
Rather, the social bond resembles a complex labyrinth of many
different, sometimes hostile, slipping and sliding language games,
which obey rules of an indeterminate variety and therefore
cannot be apprehended or synthesized under the authority of any
single meta-discourse. Lyotard quotes Wittgenstein (*Philosophical
Investigations*, section 18) to drive home this point concerning the
thousands of language games, trivial or not so trivial, that weave
the fabric of our societies: 'Our language can be seen as an
ancient city: a maze of little streets and squares, of old and new
houses, and of houses with additions from various periods; and
this surrounded by a multitude of new boroughs with straight
regular streets and uniform houses.'

The aim of post-modernism, in Lyotard's view, is to accentu-
ate this recognition of the infinite and splintered character of the
social. Practically speaking, this means that post-modernism is
committed to the task of dissolving the dominant language games
which have hitherto cemented together and 'naturalized' a particular – modern – form of social bonding. Contrary to the
Marxian theory of ideology, the multiplicity of language games
circulating in any society cannot be transcribed and evaluated in
any totalizing meta-discourse. Attempts to do precisely that must

therefore be countered by the practice of paralogism (*la paralogie*), that is, by attempts to defer consensus, to produce dissension and to permanently undermine the search for commensurability among non-identical language games. Lyotard's argument is at its finest and most insightful when interrogating and doubting the rules of various types of language games: the Platonic dialogue, with its patterns of argument oriented to reaching a consensus, a *homologia* between communicating partners; the popular narratives which define what may or may not be said and done in traditional societies; modern scientific discourse, which depends mainly upon post-narrative techniques, such as didacticism, denotation, argument- and proof-based methods of falsification, and rules of diachronic rhythm; German Idealism, with its concern to synthesize the various sub-branches of knowledge through a totalizing meta-narrative that understood both this knowledge and itself as moments in the becoming of Spirit; the early modern defence of the possibility of consensus among transacting citizens; and recent technocratic proposals for abandoning the old ideals of liberal democratic humanism in favour of effectiveness and efficiency – *performativité* – as the sole criterion of legitimacy.

In each case, Lyotard emphasizes the heteromorphous and wholly conventional nature of language games, thereby raising doubts about their 'imperialist' claims to be absolute. Lyotard's interrogations do not necessarily lead (as Benhabib claims[45]) to a self-contradictory privileging of one language game – a mathematically guided natural science which emphasizes discontinuity and self-destabilization – over other possibly incommensurate language games. Lyotard is not caught in a performative contradiction. He covers himself against this danger by rehabilitating the logic of occasion as it is found, say, within the writings of the Greek sophists. The curious feature of this logic is its claim to give the lie to the logic of the one universal truth, by supposing that the latter is only a particular case of the logic of the particular, of the special case, of the unique occasion. This procedure is not self-contradictory since, in contrast to the Cretan Epimenides, who truthfully declared that all Cretans were liars, the logic of particularity upon which Lyotard relies is presented as neither a more universal logic nor a 'truer truth'. Lyotard's interrogations *consistently* depend upon the logic of particularism, and consequently they contribute decisively, or so I would argue, to a revised theory of the ideological functions of language games – and in a way that satisfies the second and third objections to the classical Marxian theory of ideology.

Under pressure from the type of enquiry defended by Lyotard, ideology can no longer be understood, nor its riddles explained and criticized, within the classical Marxian schema. Lyotard's interrogations suggest, contrary to Marx, that ideology is not a form of posthumous misrepresentation of a prior reality of class-divided material life processes, which function (as Marx thought) as both the pre-linguistic, Archimedean point 'outside' and 'below' language games and as the point of truth that contradicts and exposes the 'false' dissimulations of ideology. Language games cannot be conceived as simply a 'level' or 'dimension' of any social formation: they are coextensive with social and political life as such. It follows that ideology is not simply (in the most vulgar Marxian sense) a veil-like substance draped over the surface of 'reality'. Ideology operates *within* language games, and it is therefore a constitutive feature of the social and political domains it inhabits. That means also that ideology knows no particular home, and that it can wander into the most surprising locales. Lyotard's theses remind us that the concept of ideology should not be tied exclusively to class-based power relations. Ideology is not only a bourgeois phenomenon (as Marx supposed). It may be generated and sustained by intellectuals, churches, social movements, political parties, armed forces and other power groups within civil society and the state.

Furthermore, Lyotard's emphasis on language as a medium of social and political life suggests that there can be no 'end of ideology' in the sense of a future society finely tuned to a 'reality' freed from the rules and effects of language games. Finally, his emphasis on the heteromorphous and wholly conventional character of language games implies a more humble, but still critical conception of ideology, one that abandons the search for foundations and totalizing truth and instead embraces the logic of particularity and context-dependent polytheism. From this revised, post-Marxian standpoint, ideology would be understood as a *grand récit*, as a particular type of (potentially) hegemonic language game which functions, not always successfully, to mask the conditions of its own engendering as well as stifle the pluralism of language games within the established socio-political order of which it is an aspect. In other words, the concept of ideology would apply to any and all language games which endeavour to represent and/or secure themselves as a general or universal interest, as unquestionable and therefore freed from the contingencies of the present.[46]

Ideological language games are those which demand their *general* adoption and, therefore, the exclusion and/or repression (the 'terrorizing', as Lyotard would say) of every other *particular* language game. So understood, the criticism of ideology would abandon the arrogance of the classical Marxian theory of ideology, namely, its attempt to devalue the false universality of an opponent's language game by presenting its own language game as empirically true and ethically justified, hence unassailable. To criticize ideology in this revised way – in conformity with the logic of occasion – would also avoid the familiar self-contradiction of relativism, in which the very propositions asserting such relativism are ipso facto invalidated. The criticism of ideology (by social groups and movements, political parties, intellectuals and others) would not presume itself to be a privileged language game, standing high above the rough and tumble of social and political life. In giving the lie to particular language games posing as universal, it would include itself as only a particular case of this logic of the particular, as a specific language game which tolerates other language games just so long as they remain humble and self-limiting, and hence particular. To criticize ideology in this revised way would be to emphasize that there is an inverse, but nevertheless intimate relationship between ideology and democracy: to tolerate ideology is to stifle and potentially undermine the very plurality of language games upon which both the critique of ideology and democracy itself thrive.

Democracy and Ideology

Here I admit to drastically extending and 'politicizing' a line of thought which is merely hinted at in most defences of cognitive and ethical relativism, including Lyotard's. In general, relativists seem deeply reticent about developing the social and political connotations of their relativism. Its social and political credentials – its implications for the existing distribution and legitimacy of power crystallized in state and non-state institutions – remain wholly ambiguous. Relativism is said to involve challenging master narratives with the discourse of the excluded; becoming more sensitive to difference; emphasizing discontinuity, incompleteness and paradoxes – and yet phrases such as these remain amorphous and pre-political.[47] More troubling still are those solipsistic, deeply cynical aspects of relativism which propose that we are at last entering an age devoid of grand narratives, a period of post-ideological austerity, it seems, in which individuals can only laugh cynically down their noses or smile happily into their own beards at every belief taught them.[48] This supposition is preposterous. It imagines, falsely, that ideologies are everywhere dead and, again falsely, that all individuals and groups presently living, say, in both halves of Europe already enjoy the full civil and political liberties necessary for defending themselves against present and future ideologies. It imagines, again falsely, that the path of relativism leads necessarily to a life without qualities (Musil) – to a hovering existence defined by the subjunctive mood. It further imagines, by means of a lapse into a curious and misleading form of romantic expressivism, that an age devoid of ideologies would witness the withering away of power and conflict, as if the array of specifically modern democratic mechanisms for limiting serious conflicts as well as concentrations of power could be superseded, like water wheels, handicrafts and other historical curiosities, by a fully transparent and harmonious social order.

Relativists argue persuasively that language games are intelligible and interpretable only in terms of their own or other language games' rules and that, lacking a privileged language game, there is no alternative but to recognize the *difference* among language games, the potential infinity of rules defining them. This is well and good. But if this relativist conclusion is to have any social and political credibility, if it is to avoid sliding into an uncritical deference to contemporary patterns of inequality and unfreedom (thereby succumbing to the dangerous charms of Wittgenstein's maxim that philosophy should only take note of language games, leaving everything in its place), and if it is to recognize the institutional division between civil society and the state as a fundamental modern achievement, then it must engage in a further questioning of its own tacitly presupposed conditions of possibility. In my view, there is potentially an intimate connection between cognitive and ethical relativism and the line of argument in favour of democratization defended throughout these essays. How can this be?

To begin with, the relativist thesis that language games may be incommensurable, and that they are intelligible and interpretable only in terms of their difference from, or similarity to, other language games, implies an opposition to all claims and contexts which thwart or deny this thesis. A self-consistent relativism, that is to say, is compelled to devote itself to the philosophical, social and political project of questioning and disarticulating all essentialist or absolutist truth claims, or what I have called ideologies. Relativism therefore cannot rest content with pre-political assertions about the need for tolerating the incommensurable, supporting our culture 'conversationally' through the telling of stories,[49] or, in Lyotard's version, 'marvelling at the diversity of discursive species, just as we do at the diversity of plant and animal species'.[50] And relativism certainly cannot cling naively to the complacent view (with which it is often stereotyped by its critics) that 'every belief about every matter is as good as every other'. Relativism rather implies the need for democracy, for institutional arrangements and procedures which guarantee that protagonists of similar or different forms of language games can openly and continuously articulate their respective forms of life.

Relativism further implies, no doubt, the need for *political* mechanisms (of conflict resolution and compromise) which limit and reduce the serious antagonisms that frequently issue from struggles among incompatible forms of life. Relativism does not imply anarchism, for active and strong political institutions are a necessary condition of democratization. Citizens living together under democratic conditions are obliged to submit themselves to a political authority, without which they would fall into confusion and disorder (and, it is important to add, into the peculiarly modern type of yearning for existential security through grand ideologies that is produced by the unique experience of temporal and institutional discontinuity unleashed by modern states and civil societies).[51]

If relativism implies the need for state mechanisms of conflict mediation, it also suggests the need for mechanisms capable of preventing the build-up of dangerous monopolies of state power. An active and powerful legislative assembly subject to periodic elections, combined with the rule of law and an independent judiciary, for instance, minimize the risk of despotism by ensuring that political power frequently changes hands and adopts different courses of action, thus preventing them from becoming excessively centralized and all-embracing. These kinds of political checks upon state power must be reinforced by the growth and development of *civil* associations which lie beyond the immediate control of state institutions. A pluralist and self-organizing civil society is an implied condition of relativism. Civil associations consist of combinations of citizens preoccupied (as Tocqueville observed) with 'small affairs'. Civil associations no doubt enable citizens to negotiate wider undertakings of concern to the whole social and political system. But they do more than this: they also nurture and powerfully deepen the local and particular freedoms so necessary for resisting the growth of ideologies, actively expressing particular interests and securing complex freedom and equality among individuals and groups.

This line of argument, which is so near and yet so far from much literature on relativism, suggests that the separation of civil society from the state, as well as the democratization of each – a socialist civil society guarded by a democratic state – are implied counterfactual conditions of relativism. To defend relativism requires a social and political stance which is thoroughly modern. It implies the need for establishing or strengthening a democratic state and a civil society consisting of a plurality of public spheres, within which individuals and groups can openly express their solidarity with (or opposition to) others' ideals. Understood in this new way, the concept of democratization would abandon the futile search (evident in Habermas's communication theory) for definite truths of human existence. It would teach us to live without an assumed 'historical agent of emancipation', as it would discard, once and for all, the indefensible ideological concepts – Order, History, Progress, Humanity, Nature, Individualism, Socialism, Nation, Sovereignty of the People – upon which the early modern advocates of democracy based their claims for greater equality and freedom. Understood in this novel way, the idea of democratization could also meet the objection that it is an essentially contested (and therefore contradictory and deluded) concept, not just in the limited sense that it is debatable, but in the stronger sense that the differing interpretations of democracy each have genuine merits, such that a definitive resolution of the muddled substantive debate about what democracy means is impossible.[52] The view of democracy defended here acknowledges its essentially contested quality. But it draws from this the conclusion that an ongoing public consideration of the principles and procedures of democracy – and not their outright abandonment – is an implied condition of the possibility of its contestability, and that this consideration in practice requires a pluralist civil society guarded by an open and accountable state: paradoxically, it understands that what is viewed as 'democratic' at any given time and place can be maintained and/or contested as such only through *these* democratic procedures.

The view of democracy outlined here could also no longer stand accused of being a substantive ideological 'ought', an Eleventh Commandment, a type of heteronomous principle or grand narrative that seeks to foist itself upon social and political actors in the name of some universal interest. As Hans Kelsen first hinted, sociopolitical democracy is an implied, counterfactual condition of relativism, and not a type of normative (or as Kant would have said, imperative) language game.* This means, however, that democracy cannot be interpreted as merely one language game among others, as if particular groups struggling to defend or realize their particular language games could decide self-consistently to conform to democratic arrangements for a time, only later to abandon them. On the contrary, their rejection of democracy would constitute a lapse into ideology – it would evidently contradict the particularity of their own language games. They would be forced to portray themselves to themselves and to others as bearers of a universal language game, thereby covering up the wholly conventional social and political processes of conflict and solidarity through which all particular language games are practically established, maintained and altered.

---

* Hans Kelsen, *Vom Wesen und Wert der Demokratie* (1929), Tübingen 1981, pp. 98-104. This implication often remains implicit in recent democratic theory. A case in point is Chantal Mouffe and Ernesto Laclau, *Hegemony and Socialist Strategy. Towards a Radical Democratic Politics*, London 1985, chapter 4. They explicitly reject the distinction between civil society and the state, on the ground that it is based on a priori reasoning. They further insist that there is no possibility of establishing a general theory of social and political life around topographic categories such as civil society and the state – which 'freeze' the meaning of social relations, absolutizing them into hard and fast differences, which are in fact wholly conventional outcomes of struggles to define and redefine the social ad infinitum. Laclau and Mouffe go on to speak of the need for radical democracy – whose logic is subversive of all relations of subordination protected by a priori representations. They recognize that radical democracy in this sense produces not only diversification. It also courts the twin dangers of disorder and social implosion. Faced with this implication, they argue for the importance of 'nodal points' around which the social fabric can be constituted and stabilized. Radical democracy requires taming and 'managing' through hegemonic strategies: 'the multiplication of antagonisms and the construction of a plurality of spaces within which they can affirm themselves and develop ... requires ... the ... hegemonic articulation between them' (p. 192). Laclau and Mouffe do not specify the institutional mechanisms of hegemonic articulation. This leaves their interpretation of democracy wide open to traditional Left appropriations (a possibility encouraged by authoritarian phrases such as 'management of the positivity of the social' and references to the 'politically virgin masses'). It remains unclear from their vague account who is to be 'articulated', for what purpose, by whom, and with which means. This difficulty is of their own making. They fail to see that their defence of 'stable openness' or self-limiting democracy counterfactually implies – at a minimum – the same procedural framework to which they are hostile: a pluralist civil society secured through accountable state institutions.

From this perspective, finally, democratization could no longer be seen as synonymous with the withering away of social division and political conflict. In democratic societies, as Tocqueville recognized, the foundations of social and political order are permanently unstable.[53] Having severely weakened the power of norms whose legitimacy depends upon either transcendental standards (such as God) or a naturally given order of things (such as cultural tradition), modern democratic societies – even if their democratic mechanisms are poorly developed – begin to sense the need to summon up their sociopolitical identity from within themselves. Processes of democratization (among other factors such as capitalism and the nation state) bring about an end to naturalistic definitions of the means and ends of life. Pomp, mystery and power become ever more separated. Actors within modern democratic systems begin to sense the destruction of the old reference points of ultimate certainty. They learn that they are not in possession of any ultimates (based on knowledge, conviction or faith), and that they are continually, and forever, forced to define for themselves the ways in which they wish to live. Trotsky's remark that those people desiring a quiet life had done badly to be born into the twentieth century in fact applies to the whole of the modern epoch. Modern democratic societies tend to be historical societies par excellence. It becomes evident to their members that theirs is a society marked by social and political indeterminacy. They sense that the so-called ultimate social and political means and ends do not correspond to an immutable and 'real' origin or essence, and that their techniques and goals are therefore always subject to debate, conflict and resistance and, hence, to temporal and spatial variation.

This is why institutions and decisions within fully democratic systems would never be accepted fully, as if controversies concerning power, justice, or law could somehow be resolved once and for all through the adoption of a universal metalanguage. Fully democratic systems could never become a perfect commonwealth. They would recognize the necessity of relying always on judgement, for they would know of their ignorance, which is to say (cf. the Socratic attitude) that they would know that they do not or cannot know or control everything. Fully democratic systems would adopt a certain reserve towards the world. They could not flatter themselves on assumptions about their capacity to grasp the whole directly, for they would always consist of risky and often ambiguous action and self-invention in all quarters of life. To defend democracy in this sense is to reject every ideology which seeks to stifle this indeterminacy by demanding the general adoption of particular forms of life that are clothed in a broad repertoire of old and new metaphors: every woman needs a man, as the herd needs the shepherd, the ship's crew a captain, the proletariat the party, and the nation a Moral Majority or Saviour; mankind is the master and possessor of nature; scientific evidence is the most rational criterion of knowledge; capitalism is the chief guarantor of liberty; the end justifies the means; doctors know best; whites are superior to blacks; and so on. These (and other) ideologies are the enemy of democracy, for they each contain a fanatical core. Fortified by *their* Truth, they each seek to break loose from contingency, and to crash into the world, throttling everything which crosses their path.

To defend democracy against these and other ideologies is to welcome indeterminacy, controversy and uncertainty. It is to fight in the open, and with 'generous anger' (Orwell), against every arrogant orthodoxy which contends for the souls of citizens within civil society and the state. It is to be prepared for the emergence of the unexpected, and for the possibility of creating the new. It is to recognize the need for *continuing* the modern process of democratization which remains incomplete, highly vulnerable, and today threatened by a world heaving with an assortment of old and new anti-democratic trends.

Notes

1. The best study of the *idéologues* is Brian William Head, *Ideology and Social Science, Destutt de Tracy and French Liberalism*, Dordrecht 1985. According to Head (p. 22), the term *civisme* (like its opposite, *incivisme*) was coined during the early years of the Revolution to denote appropriate sentiments for the citizen who cheerfully performs his duties ... Under the Jacobin regime the need to demonstrate one's *civisme* was increasingly identified with support for current policies, and became part of an inquisitorial procedure of popular committees.' See also C. Welch, *Liberty and Utility: The French Idéologues and the Transformation of Liberalism*, Guildford 1984; G. Gusdorf, *La conscience révolutionnaire: les idéologues*, Paris 1978; and Emmet Kennedy, *A Philosophe in the Age of Revolution, Destutt de Tracy and the Origins of 'Ideology'*, Philadelphia 1978. On the late eighteenth century idea of civilization, see Helmut Kuzmics, 'The Civilizing Process', in *Civil Society and the State*; Lucien Febvre, *'Civilisation*: Evolution of a Word and a Group of Ideas', in his *A New Kind of History*, edited Peter Burke, London 1973, pp. 219-57.

2. György Màrkus, 'Concepts of Ideology in Marx', in John Keane ed., *Ideology/Power*, special double issue of *Canadian Journal of Political and Social Theory/Revue canadienne de théorie politique et sociale*, Hiver/Printemps 1983, pp. 84-103.

3. Karl Marx and Frederick Engels, 'Manifesto of the Communist Party', *Selected Works*, vol. 1, Moscow 1970, p. 123.

242

4. Daniel Bell, *The End of Ideology*, New York 1962, pp. 402-3; cf. Chaim Waxman, ed., *The End of Ideology Debate*, New York 1968.

5. See especially his contribution to Václav Havel et al., *The Power of the Powerless. Citizens Against the State in Central-Eastern Europe*, edited John Keane, London 1985, and my interview, 'Doing without Utopias – An Interview with Václav Havel', *The Times Literary Supplement*, 23 January 1987, pp. 81-3.

6. *The Power of the Powerless*, p. 31.

7. Alvin W. Gouldner, *The Dialectic of Ideology and Technology. The Origins, Grammar, and Future of Ideology*, New York 1976, pp. 54-5.

8. Theodor W. Adorno, 'Ideology', in The Frankfurt Institute for Social Research, *Aspects of Sociology*, London 1974, p. 202. Adorno's thesis is critically examined in my *Public Life and Late Capitalism*, Cambridge and New York 1984, chapter 3.

9. See especially Jürgen Habermas, 'Technology and Science as "Ideology"', in *Toward a Rational Society*, London 1971, pp. 81-122.

10. Jürgen Habermas, *Legitimation Crisis*, Boston 1973, p. 23.

11. Jürgen Habermas, *Strukturwandel der Öffentlichkeit. Untersuchungen zu einer Kategorie der bürgerlichen Gesellschaft*, Neuwied and Berlin 1962, p. 111; cf. ibid, p. 278. In this early formulation, Habermas is close to Theodor Adorno ('Beitrag zur Ideologienlehre', *Kölner Zeitschrift für Soziologie*, vol. 6, 1953-4, p. 366), for whom ideology is an objective and necessarily illusory form of consciousness, marked by the 'coalescence of the true and the false'.

12. Jürgen Habermas, *Kultur und Kritik. Verstreute Aufsätze*, Frankfurt am Main 1973, p. 73; cf. 'Technology and Science as "Ideology"', p. 111.

13. See Jürgen Habermas, *Communication and the Evolution of Society*, Boston 1979, pp. 96-7; *Knowledge and Human Interests*, London 1972; *Theorie des kommunikativen Handelns*, vol. 1, Frankfurt am Main 1981, pp. 367-452; and my criticisms of this approach in *Public Life and Late Capitalism*, chapter 5.

14. Karl Marx, 'Preface to a Contribution to the Critique of Political Economy', in *Selected Works*, vol. 1, Moscow 1970, p. 504; cf. 'The German Ideology', *Writings of the Young Marx on Philosophy and Society*, Garden City, N.Y., 1967, pp. 408-9, where Marx and Engels write that the premises of historical materialism are not arbitrary, but 'actual premises' which can be substantiated 'in a purely empirical way'.

15. See the discussion of Marx's 'latent positivism' in Albrecht Wellmer, *Critical Theory of Society*, New York 1971, chapter 2; Leszek Kolakowski, *Positivist Philosophy: From Hume to the Vienna Circle*, Harmondsworth 1972, chapter 3; and Jürgen Habermas, *Knowledge and Human Interests*, chapters 2-3.

16. See *Public Life and Late Capitalism*, chapters 4, 6; and Paul Feyerabend, 'How to Defend Society Against Science', in Ian Hacking, ed., *Scientific Revolutions*, Oxford 1983, pp. 156-67.

17. Zygmunt Bauman, 'Ideology and the Weltanschauung of the Intellectuals', in John Keane, ed., *Ideology/Power*, pp. 104-17.

18. Karl Mannheim, *Ideology and Utopia. An Introduction to the Society of Knowledge*, London 1960, pp. 248-9.

19. György Márkus, 'Concepts of Ideology in Marx', in John Keane, ed., *Ideology/Power*, pp. 84-103.

20. Antonio Gramsci, *Selections from the Prison Notebooks*, edited Quintin Hoare and Geoffrey Nowell Smith, New York 1971, pp. 376-7: 'historically organic ideologies, those, that is, which are necessary to a given structure ... have a validity which is "psychological"; they "organize" human masses, and create the terrain on which men move, acquire consciousness of their position, struggle, etc.'

21. Louis Althusser, 'Ideology and ideological state apparatuses (notes

towards an investigation)', in *Lenin and Philosophy and Other Essays*, London 1971, pp. 121-73.

22. Karl Marx, *Theories of Surplus Value*, vol. 3, Moscow 1971, p. 536. Commenting on this myth (appropriated from Luther's version), Marx notes: 'An excellent picture, it fits the capitalist in general, who pretends that what he has taken from others and brought into his den emanates from him, and by causing it to go backwards he gives it the semblance of having come from his den.'

23. See Karl Marx, *Capital*, Moscow 1971, vol. 3, passim.

24. 'The German Ideology', in *Writings of the Young Marx on Philosophy and Society*, pp. 413-14.

25. Ibid, p. 472.

26. Karl Marx, *Selected Writings*, edited David McLellan, Oxford 1977, p. 64.

27. Ibid, p. 64.

28. See, for example, Marshall Sahlins, *Culture and Practical Reason*, Chicago 1976, especially chapter 3. A parallel criticism is developed by Althusser, who considers ideology not as the dissimulation of an underlying 'reality', but as an indispensable condition of subjects' living their social and political relations *as if* they were subjects. See Louis Althusser, *For Marx*, London 1977, p. 232: 'Human societies secrete ideology as the very element and atmosphere indispensable to their historical respiration and life. Only an ideological world outlook could have imagined societies without ideology and accepted the utopian idea of a world in which ideology (not just one of its historical forms) would disappear ... Historical materialism cannot conceive that even a communist society could ever do without ideology.'

29. *Grundrisse*, translated Martin Nicolaus, Harmondsworth 1973, p. 111.

30. *Theories of Surplus Value*, vol. 1, p. 285.

31. David McLellan, *Ideology*, Milton Keynes 1986, pp. 18-19; Bhiku Parekh, *Marx's Theory of Ideology*, London 1983, pp. 219ff.

32. See Milan Šimečka, 'A World With Utopias or Without Them?' in P. Alexander and R. Gill, eds., *Utopias*, London 1984, pp. 169-77; Leszek Kolakowski, 'Ideology in Eastern Europe', in Milorad M. Drachkovitch, ed., *East Central Europe: Yesterday, Today, Tomorrow*, Stanford 1982, pp. 43-53; and 'Doing Without Utopias – An Interview with Václav Havel', *The Times Literary Supplement*, 23, 1987, pp. 81-3.

33. Leszek Kolakowski, 'Ideology in Eastern Europe', p. 51; cf. the similar remarks of Alexander Zinoviev, *The Reality of Communism*, London 1985, pp. 281-312.

34. Václav Belohradský, 'In Search of Central Europe', *The Salisbury Review*, 1, Autumn 1982, p. 33. The nationalist dangers implicit in this position are well criticized in Jan Jozef Lipski, 'Two Fatherlands – Two Patriotisms', *Survey*, vol. 26, 4, Autumn 1982, pp. 159-75; and in the study of Russian nationalism by Alexander Yanov, *The Russian Challenge*, Oxford 1987.

35. See Michel Pêcheux and Françoise Gadet, 'La langue introuvable', in John Keane, ed., *Ideology/Power*, pp. 24-31; Anthony Giddens, 'Four Theses on Ideology', in ibid, pp. 18-21; and N. Abercrombie et al., *The Dominant Ideology Thesis*, London 1980.

36. These points are elaborated in Charles Perrow, *Normal Accidents. Living with High-Risk Technologies*, New York 1984; Larry Hirschhorn, *Beyond Mechanization: Work and Technology in a Post-Industrial Age*, London 1984; and Mike Cooley, *Architect or Bee? The Human/Technology Relationship*, Slough 1983.

37. According to Jürgen Habermas, the Marxian attempt to 'find the new world through criticism of the old' could draw upon extant traditions of moral-practical reason (classical political economy, modern natural law, German Ideal-

ism, utopian socialism). In late capitalist systems, these old ideologies have retired hurt; official consciousness tends to become cynical, with the consequence that democratic theory is forced to make an ontological turn by elucidating the guiding rules and political norms inherent within communicative action. See *Knowledge and Human Interests*, especially pp. 301-17; *Communication and the Evolution of Society*, Boston 1979, pp. 96-7; and my *Public Life and Late Capitalism*, chapter 5.

38. See the final chapter of Hans Barth, *Wahrheit und Ideologie* (1945), Erlen-bach-Zurich and Stuttgart 1961.

39. John B. Thompson, *Critical Hermeneutics. A Study in the Thought of Paul Ricoeur and Jürgen Habermas*, Cambridge 1981, and *Studies in the Theory of Ideology*, Cambridge 1984.

40. *Studies in the Theory of Ideology*, p. 12.

41. Jürgen Habermas, *Communication and the Evolution of Society*, pp. 4, 35-41, 208, note 1, 209-10, note 2, and *Theorie des kommunikativen Handelns*, Frankfurt am Main 1981, chapter 3; cf. my criticisms of the pre-political character of the theory of communication in *Public Life and Late Capitalism*, essay 6.

42. Jean-François Lyotard, *La Condition postmoderne: Rapport sur le savoir*, Paris 1979. All translations from this edition are my own.

43. Ibid, pp. 20-23.

44. Ibid, pp. 24-9.

45. Seyla Benhabib, 'Epistemologies of Postmodernism: A Rejoinder to Jean-François Lyotard', *New German Critique*, 33, 1984, p. 120.

46. Cf. the pertinent remark of Claude Lefort, *Les Formes de l'histoire. Essais d'anthropologie politique*, Paris 1978, p. 296: 'ideology is the chaining together of representations which perform the function of restoring the dimension of society "without history" within the very heart of historical society'; cf. Hannah Arendt, *The Origins of Totalitarianism*, New York and London 1973, p. 469: 'Ideologies pretend to know the mysteries of the whole historical process – the secrets of the past, the intricacies of the present, the uncertainties of the future – because of the logic inherent in their ideas.'

47. An example is Hal Foster, ed., *The Anti-Aesthetic: Essays on Postmodern Culture*, London 1983.

48. Examples of this attitude are evident in Lyotard, *La Condition postmoderne*, pp. 8, 63-8. On the ideology of cynicism, see Peter Sloterdijk, *Kritik der synischen Vernunft*, 2 vols, Frankfurt am Main 1983.

49. This view is presently associated with Richard Rorty's *Philosophy and the Mirror of Nature*, Oxford 1980. Aside from its failure to deal with the type of non-foundational, counterfactual reasoning sketched in this essay, the conversational model fails to acknowledge the dangers of totalitarian language games, to which (as Claude Lefort has pointed out in his *L'Invention démocratique* (Paris 1982)) modern societies are prone constantly because of their self-revolutionizing, self-questioning character. More recently ('Habermas and Lyotard on Postmodernity', *Praxis International*, 4, 1984, p. 34), Rorty has argued for the reliance upon a poten-tially anti-democratic instruction ('let the narratives which hold our culture together do their stuff'), as if the fact of existence of certain narratives automatically implied their sacred right to an undisturbed future existence.

50. Lyotard, *La condition postmoderne*, p. 47.

51. Cf. Reinhart Koselleck's important discussion of concepts of movement in modern times in *Futures Past: on the Semantics of Historical Time*, London 1985, and especially p. 288: 'The lesser the experience, the greater the expectation: this is a formula for the temporal structure of the modern'.

52. On this problem, see Russell L. Hanson, *The Democratic Imagination in America: Conversations with Our Past*, Princeton, New Jersey 1985. David Held's fine

review of the variety of interpretations of democracy, from classical Athens to late modern times (*Models of Democracy*, Cambridge 1987), proposes a view of democratization similar to mine, without however addressing the serious (potentially anti-democratic) objection that it merely adds to the confusion caused by the plurality of meanings of democracy.

53. See my 'Despotism and Democracy. The Origins and Development of the Distinction between Civil Society and the State, 1750-1850', in John Keane, ed., *Civil Society and the State*.

Index

Democracy and Civil Society